Science Studies

Science Studies

An Advanced Introduction

David J. Hess

NEW YORK UNIVERSITY PRESS

New York and London

NEW YORK UNIVERSITY PRESS
New York and London

Library of Congress Cataloging-in-Publication Data
Hess, David J.
Science studies : an advanced introduction / David J. Hess.
p.   cm.
Includes bibliographical references and index.
ISBN 0-8147-3563-0 (clothbound).—ISBN 0-8147-3564-9
(paperbound)
1. Science—Philosophy.   2. Science—Social aspects.
3. Technology—Social aspects.   I. Title.
Q175.H428   1997
501—dc21   97-4782
                CIP

New York University Press books are printed on acid-free paper,
and their binding materials are chosen for strength and durability.

Manufactured in the United States of America

10 9 8 7 6 5 4 3 2 1

Contents

Acknowledgments

I would like to thank Steve Fuller, Ed Hackett, Lowell Hargens, Brian Martin, Sal Restivo, and students at Rensselaer and the Universidade Federal Fluminense for comments on various parts of earlier drafts of the book, and Eric Zinner for his editorial help in shaping the final version of the text.

1

Introduction

Science has become an integral part of many issues of public concern—medical, informational, and environmental, to name a few. Scientific experts frequently square off on the evening news. At work, professional discourses have become increasingly technical, and at home we face an ocean of competing claims about topics such as carcinogens in our food or the technical features of competing appliances.

Science studies provides a conceptual tool kit for thinking about technical expertise in more sophisticated ways. Science studies tracks the history of disciplines, the dynamics of science as a social institution, and the philosophical basis for scientific knowledge. It teaches, for example, that there are ways of developing sound criteria for evaluating opposing theories and interpretations, but also that there are ways of finding the agendas sometimes hidden behind a rhetoric of objectivity. In the process, science studies makes it easier for laypeople to question the authority of experts and their claims. It teaches how to look for biases, and it holds out a vision of greater public participation in technical policy issues.

In short, science studies provides a forum where people who are concerned with the place of science and technology in a democratic society can discuss complicated technical issues. Because of that role, science studies is not always a popular field. In the mid-1990s the "science wars"—a wave of attacks on some prominent figures in science studies—became particularly intense. These attacks tended to single out a few feminists and radical constructivists, subject them to distorting readings, then dismiss the entire field as a hotbed of postmodern irrationalism. Although I am not in agreement with the radical relativism that characterizes a corner of the science studies community, I am more disturbed by the attackers' dismissive caricatures and distortions of a huge volume of theory and research. I have experienced science studies as a vibrant intellectual field that is bubbling with novel research and ideas. This book presents some of that exciting work.

The issues surrounding science, technology, and society are of increasing interest in our technological society not only to the public in general but also to scientists and other researchers. Scientists have come to recognize the political nature of the institutions of science, and their research problems have become increasingly tied to public and private agendas outside their disciplines. Likewise, as humanists and social scientists encounter technological issues with increasing frequency, they also find themselves drawn into the interdisciplinary field. However, as newcomers from all disciplines enter the field, they sometimes end up reinventing the wheel because they do not have a background in its principal concepts and theories.

There is widespread need, then, for a concise overview of the key concepts of the interdisciplinary field as a whole, one that points the way to the more specific literatures of the philosophy, sociology, anthropology, history, cultural studies, and feminist studies of science and technology. This book introduces many of the key concepts and provides one map of a wide range of the terrain. In the process, the debates that have received media attention as the "science wars" are set in their proper context as only one of the issues that are part of an ongoing dialogue within the field. When outside critics dismiss the field for its relativism, they are actually riding on debates internal to the field, and not particularly new or interesting ones at that.

The book had its origin as a teaching text for graduate students and advanced undergraduates. Students who were new to the field—including many graduate students who were established professionally in other fields, such as engineering—complained of confusion when they first confronted the interdisciplinary Babel of science studies. They found my focus on some of the interdisciplinary misunderstandings helpful, and they used the text to provide a menu of what to study in more detail.

The field can be very confusing for newcomers, as I remember well from my own relatively recent entrance in the mid-1980s. Even the name of the field is not uniform. Some people preferred to use their disciplinary designations and call themselves, for example, philosophers of science. Others preferred the initials HPS (history and philosophy of science) to describe a position known as philosophical historicism, which was considered quite distinct from the more social science–oriented studies of science, technology, and society. Sociologists who studied scientific knowledge at first tended to refer to the field as "science studies" in contrast to the more institutionally oriented sociology of science. As they became more interested in technology, they began to add a "T" for technology: STS.

However, even the acronym "STS" is controversial. There has been a debate over whether it should mean science, technology, and society studies or simply science and technology studies. The first definition reflects a time when social studies of science and technology were more separate from the history and philosophy of science and technology. By the late 1980s there had been so much interdisciplinary dialogue among social scientists, historians, and philosophers—not to mention natural scientists and more recent arrivals from anthropology, cultural studies, and feminist studies—that there has been an increasing tendency to use the term STS to mean "science and technology studies." I am among those who think of STS as an interdisciplinary conversation among a wide range of "constituent disciplines," rather than merely the social studies of science, technology, and society. However, to those who came to the field with a background in science activism, dropping the term "society" signaled the lamentable professionalization of the field and a waning concern with social justice issues. Furthermore, to those who speak languages in which "studies" begins with an "e" or some other letter *(études, estudios),* the switch was a reminder of Anglophone hegemony in the field. Many continue to use the term "science studies" as a more identifiable phrase or a designation for a subset of STS that is parallel to technology studies. I've used "science studies" for the title of this book because it has come to be used colloquially as a broad and inclusive name for the field.

Notwithstanding the growth of interdisciplinarity, the disciplinary divisions remain strong, and they underlie the organization of this book. Chapters 2, 3, and 4 are therefore organized as introductions to the philosophy of science, the sociology of science, and the sociology of scientific knowledge. These fields still constitute the major sources of specialist terminology and theorizing. The title of chapter 5, "Critical and Cultural Studies of Science and Technology," is suggestive of my view of where the field is moving. This chapter introduces theoretical concepts from a number of overlapping fields: anthropology, critical social theory, cultural studies, feminist studies, critical technology studies, and the cultural history of science.

The interdisciplinary field embraces a vast literature, and I cannot claim to be fluent in all areas or to cover it all in this short introduction. Rather, I have selected concepts with an eye toward interdisciplinary dialogue and with a sense of their salience in transdisciplinary theorizing. There are introductions available for some of the constituent disciplines, and a guide to the introductory literature is included at the end of the book. But *Science Studies* provides the first overview of the field that is not restricted to one of the constituent disciplines. In addition, I cover important developments during recent years, such as philosophical naturalism and realism, actor-network theory, the anthropology of science and technology, and cultural/feminist studies. Other introductory books also tend to miss the cross-disciplinary misunderstandings. In contrast, I explore in more detail the interdisciplinary cross-talk, and I occasionally suggest solutions.

Consistent with contemporary science studies theories, I do not claim to draw a neutral or value-free map of the interdisciplinary territory. However, I do claim to approach the project with a modicum of fairness and a spirit of interdisciplinarity, and I do provide the reader with the courtesy of presenting my best understanding of the positions of others before I give my own position. Even so, there will be some areas that are not covered. The book has an American focus and, as the title suggests, it focuses more on science issues than technology issues. The book also sticks to the major concepts of the interdisciplinary nexus of history, philosophy, and the social and cultural studies of science. Consequently, other fields such as the psychology and rhetoric of science, which up to now have made relatively marginal contributions to the main lines of the interdisciplinary discussion, receive relatively short coverage. Policy discussions occur in almost all the journals and across the disciplines, and policy implications are flagged throughout the book. My own approach to policy issues is provided in the conclusion.

The field can be acrimonious, perhaps because science and technology are so fundamental to the people involved. Imagine a religious studies conference in which theologians and practicing clergy from a range of religions, as well as historians and social scientists, came together to discuss their ideas, and one can get a sense of why "science wars" tend to flare up. My hope is that a better understanding of the various constituent disciplines may help the reader avoid some of the interdisciplinary misunderstandings. Many students and scholars tend to dismiss everything about an author or a subfield because they disagree with one or two points. I try to encourage instead what some of my more open-minded colleagues call a charitable reading: examining the other text or discipline for what it has to offer one's own projects. Certainly, I have found a wide range of concepts and disciplines useful for developing what I believe is a more coherent framework for my own special areas of empirical research interest.

My hope, then, is to realize the transdisciplinary promise of an ongoing conversation among philosophers, sociologists, anthropologists, political scientists, historians, and others, including natural scientists. Each field, even each theorist and each empirical study, has a unique contribution to make, if read with the proper spirit. Sometimes I disagree with the excesses and more grandiose claims, but my vision is always focused on finding those moments of transdisciplinary insight that occur when we put on someone else's lenses, if only for a moment. By moving from the discipline-bound blinders of a sociology, history, philosophy, or anthropology of science to a transdisciplinary field, science studies is able to provide a valuable set of conceptual tools for public discussions of the role of science and technology in a democratic society.

2

The Philosophy of Science
An Interdisciplinary Perspective

The Philosophy of Science in an Interdisciplinary Context

Although STS or science studies is becoming an increasingly interdisciplinary conversation, there is still a gulf of understanding among the different constituent disciplines, especially between the philosophical and social studies wings. I use the term "social studies" to include historians, cultural studies researchers, and social scientists. Following the American usage, I use "social scientist" to refer to sociologists, cultural anthropologists, political scientists and policy analysts, economists, management and administration scientists, and some other researchers such as geographers. (In other countries the term "social scientist" has a much more restricted usage, generally referring to anthropologists, sociologists, and political scientists.) In contrast, the term "humanities" refers to fields such as history, literature and cultural studies, rhetoric, philosophy, and perhaps some of the more humanistically minded cultural anthropologists and sociologists. Sometimes "human sciences" is used as an umbrella term for the social sciences and humanities. Although the humanities/social science divide has been the subject of controversy within some disciplines, in the STS field the most significant disciplinary division has been between those who have some allegiance to traditional Anglo-Saxon and German philosophy of science and those who have a more social or cultural orientation. The term "philosophy" is generally adequate to cover the first group (even though there is a continental philosophical tradition that is more influential in technology studies), but some other term is necessary to cover the second group of socially oriented social scientists and humanists. In the Anglophone world, "social studies" is probably the best term to designate descriptive, empirical research that includes the work of social scientists as well as humanities scholars in history, cultural studies, and other humanities fields. In the humanities, "cultural studies" is sometimes used as an umbrella term, but the term would exclude several of the social sciences. Thus, I will use "social studies" as a generic but imperfect term to cover social scientists and those humanists who are concerned with social aspects of the world they study.

This chapter begins the survey of key concepts in science studies by reviewing the philosophy of science through an interdisciplinary lens. Introductions by professionally trained philosophers can accomplish a much more detailed and inclusive level of discussion than will be achieved here.[1] This chapter complements those introductions by focusing on two aspects of the philosophy of science in the general interdisciplinary setting: misunderstandings and possibilities in the sometimes acrimonious dialogue between philosophers and social studies researchers, and the application of the philosophy of science to the problem of designating good criteria for choice among major theories or research programs. Following Steve Fuller (1988), I will seek a middle ground in the dialogue between philosophers and social studies researchers by beginning with the distinction between prescriptive and descriptive approaches to science and technology. Although some philosophies of science (such as evolutionary epistemology) are descriptive, for the most part it is helpful to see the central problem of the philosophy of science as making clarifications that could help scientists decide how they *should* go about improving the ways they think about and do science. Fuller has probably developed the prescriptive role of the philosophy of science more clearly than any other philosopher, and he has introduced the term "social epistemology" for one type of prescriptive use of the philosophy of science. In his words, the fundamental question of social epistemology is,

> How should the pursuit of knowledge be organized, given that under normal
> circumstances knowledge is pursued by many human beings, each working
> on a more or less well-defined body of knowledge and each equipped with
> roughly the same imperfect cognitive capacities, albeit with varying degrees
> of access to one another's activities? (1988: 3)

Although social epistemology brings the philosophy of science into the realm of prescriptive work for science in society, I will also interpret the traditional philosophy of science as prescriptive in a more narrow sense: its contribution to understanding how to make better scientific theories and explanations. Fuller's work is a good starting point because it clearly locates the division of labor between philosophy and social studies in the distinction between prescription and description, or normative versus empirical

8 | *The Philosophy of Science*

approaches (xi). Although philosophers certainly describe science and technology, and social studies researchers often engage in discussions of policy and activism that can be explicitly prescriptive, Fuller's distinction is useful as a way of moving toward a productive dialogue between philosophical and social studies outlooks on science and technology. In other words, philosophy may be helpful to social scientists and humanists when they are in the prescriptive mode, and likewise the research of social and cultural studies may be helpful to philosophers when they are making descriptive claims about science and technology.

This review of some concepts in the philosophy of science will focus on one type of prescriptive question: what grounds *should* scientists use to justify their choices among major theories or research programs? To answer this question, as in other philosophical problem areas, philosophers pursue a dialogue of arguments and counterarguments. Although the dialogue may never result in a final consensus, the back-and-forth procedure makes it possible to progress by finding the shortcomings in previous solutions and providing alternatives that answer those shortcomings. This review will cover the following major positions: positivism, conventionalism, falsificationism, historicism, naturalism/realism, constructivism/relativism, and feminism.

Positivism

In the philosophy of science "positivism" is shorthand for logical positivism or logical empiricism, terms that are not exactly identical but will be treated so here for the sake of simplicity. In STS circles the term "positivism" is usually associated with the philosophical positions that emerged around the Vienna Circle. However, for social scientists the word "positivism" may also refer to the thought of Auguste Comte, a nineteenth-century French social theorist. Comte believed in the unity of sciences and supported an evolutionary theory of scientific progress that led to a positive stage that happened to match his nineteenth-century understandings of science. In this sense the term "positive" might be glossed as "I'm positive I'm right because my position is founded on science." In the humanities and cultural studies, another use of the word sometimes appears. "Positivist" can be a pejorative label for (1) someone perceived to have a simplistic and uncritical view of science, and/or (2) someone who wishes, in a very simplistic way, to base social science or humanities methods on an ideal version of those in the natural sciences. In polemical debates, the label "positivist" is usually opposed to "postmodernist," although in debates where these labels get hurled back and forth there is usually little substance.

Returning now to philosophical positivism, the Vienna Circle was a group of philosophers whose work flourished during the interwar period. Many were trained in physics and influenced by British formal philosophy in the tradition of Bertrand Russell. Because some were Jews and some were leftists, their social position set the stage for the fragmentation of the circle when the Nazis came to power. Most of the circle's members moved to Britain or the United States, where they had an important impact on the Anglo-American philosophy of science. Members of the Vienna Circle included Moritz Schlick, Ernst Mach, Otto Neurath, and Rudolf Carnap; A. J. Ayer, Herbert Feigl, Kurt Gödel, and Hans Reichenbach were among those associated with the circle. Karl Popper maintained close ties with some of the members of the circle, but he was not considered a true positivist.

Perhaps the key concept associated with the positivist philosophy of science, at least in its early versions, was the verifiability principle, which held that statements are meaningful if verifiable. (A weaker version of this principle held that statements are meaningful if confirmable to some degree.) Although some statements could be verified by logic or by definition, the more important means of verification was experience. For example, the sentence "Crows are fifteen" is meaningless because the sentence cannot be confirmed as either true or false in the sense that the sentence "Crows are black" can be.[2] Although the verifiability principle lost importance with the passage of time, the empiricist interpretation of meaning continued to underlie the sharp distinction that positivists often drew between theoretical terms and observational terms. Theoretical terms such as energy in physics can therefore be interpreted as meaningless in the strict sense because they are not observable directly or even relatively directly through measuring devices.

The interpretation of meaning as reference contrasts sharply with the semiotic understanding of meaning that is common in the humanities and some social sciences. This is one of the first major opportunities for cross-disciplinary misunderstandings. For example, under Ferdinand de Saussure's definition of value, the meaning of a statement derives from its relative position in various codes of semantic difference.[3] Thus, the meaning of the sentence "The coyote is laughing" is understood through a series of con-trasts. These include the contrast between the coyote and other animals (it is not a raven, a swan, or a crow); the contrast between laughing and other activities (it is not remaining black, turning white, or flying into a wall); the grammatical juxtaposition of coyote and laughing in a sentence com-pared with other possibilities; and the semantic mapping of associations of "coyote" and "laughing" (for example, the coyote clan may harbor a tricksterish shaman whose attributes are like those of the coyote totem). This view of meaning has been enormously influential in contemporary linguistics, cultural anthropology, history, and literary/cultural studies through the various intellectual currents known as structuralism, poststruct-uralism, and deconstruction.

Thus, one view of meaning associates a word with the thing to which it refers, whereas another view opens up a world of interpretations. In con-trast with the positivists' project to formulate a universal, formal language, semiotic approaches to meaning interpose languages and cultures as a necessary point of reference. Although the differences between the positiv-ist and semiotic views of meaning are profound, the two can nonetheless be made compatible. In effect, they are two ways of looking at the same linguistic fact: reference and semiotic value. This is the first of the clarifica-tions that I wish to make regarding the "duck-rabbit" (or crow-coyote) nature of philosophy and social/cultural studies. As is the case with the gestalt diagram that switches back and forth between a duck and a rabbit, it is not necessary to choose between the two views of meaning. Rather, it is better to understand how each is bound up in a different set of questions and issues.

One misleading way to interpret this difference is to compare positivist and semiotic views of meaning with what are sometimes called correspon-dence and coherence views of truth. As a rough first approximation, a correspondence view of truth holds that statements are true when they refer to things that exist, whereas a coherence view holds that statements are true if they can be situated logically within a coherent body of knowl-edge. It would be a great misunderstanding to argue that the positional theory of meaning associated with de Saussure implies that those social science and humanities fields that use Saussurean and post-Saussurean theo-ries of meaning will assume a coherence theory of truth. Because social scientists such as linguists are making theories of linguistic observations, philosophically they may hold either a correspondence or a coherence view of truth. Thus, a semiotic view of meaning and a coherence view of truth should not be confused, even if there may be some cases of specific theorists for whom they coincide.

Consistent with the view of meaning that was anchored in observation, positivists distinguished sharply between theory and observation. Carnap, for example, distinguished simple, local observations from general empirical laws that remained grounded in observational language, and in turn he distinguished empirical laws from theoretical laws or theories, which were not grounded in observational language (1995: 27). The gap between theoretical terms (e.g., thermal energy) and observational terms (e.g., a temperature measurement) posed a problem of translation. Positivists attempted to resolve the problem by proposing what were variously called correspondence rules, rules of operationalization, bridge laws, or a dictionary. These rules or definitions made it possible to translate across categories.

Consistent with the sharp distinction between theoretical and observational terms is the doctrine of instrumentalism, the view that theories are computational devices for predicting or explaining observable phenomena. Note that in the social sciences instrumentalism may refer to a type of analysis that interprets the motivations for action in terms of gain or turf protection, usually by using economic or military metaphors. In philosophy, instrumentalism contrasts with ontological realism, which holds that theoretical terms capture something of the deeper structures of reality. Some positivists were suspicious of the metaphysical (and therefore meaningless) nature of realist claims for theoretical terms. In this sense, one can argue that positivists who endorsed instrumentalism were not realists. In his later work even Carnap seemed to recognize the power of the realist argument that theoretical terms tended to become observational terms over time, but he preferred to reframe the debate with the question, "Shall we prefer a language of physics (and of science in general) that contains theoretical terms, or a language without such terms?" (1995: 256).

With the vocabulary now established, it is possible to turn to the problems of justification, induction, and theory choice. Hans Reichenbach (1938) made popular the central distinction between the context of discovery and that of justification.[4] As Ian Hacking explains, philosophers are more concerned with the latter issue. In order to justify a theory or law, one asks,

Is it reasonable, supported by the evidence, confirmed by experiment, corroborated by stringent testing? These are questions about justification or soundness. Philosophers care about justification, logic, reason, soundness, [and] methodology. (1983: 6)

In a similar vein, Karl Popper (1959: 110) used the metaphor of a court-room to describe the philosophical understanding of justification. Scientific knowledge is like the verdict of a jury, whereas philosophical justification is like the judgment of a judge. A verdict simply exists, whereas a justification or judgment can be correctly or erroneously related to a general set of principles.

Philosophers of this persuasion therefore viewed the context of discovery—how scientists arrive at a theory or law—as the realm of history, psychology, or sociology. They were quite willing to admit a role for social factors in science, as long as these factors were relegated to the context of discovery. From this perspective, philosophers see their task as the study of the rational aspects of science, whereas social studies are relegated to the arational aspects of science (Laudan 1977). However, this view is very difficult to maintain because social action is also rational, and rationality is socially conditioned. It is possible to develop historical and sociological descriptions of rational processes such as methodology or logic, and this characterization of the division of labor between social studies and philosophy is bound to fail. The misunderstandings are eliminated when the key disciplinary division is seen as descriptive versus prescriptive work.

Ronald Giere understands this fundamental point. He notes that for Carnap, and presumably many other philosophers in the positivist tradition, philosophy is "the study of how, a priori, an ideally logical scientist *should* think" (1988: 24). This is an important point, because some philosophers seem to think they are describing historical cases when in fact they are reconstructing idealized scientists to derive prescriptive accounts. Giere adds, "For logical empiricism, then, the gap between the psychology or sociology of science and the philosophy of science is like the gap between 'is' and 'ought.' It is logically unbridgeable" (24). The fallacy of positivism was not to make a distinction between is and ought, but to view philosophical prescription as founded in rational processes that were somehow outside society and culture.

The choice of the word "justification" points to one complex of values that underlay the positivist program. The concept of "justification" in Western science and philosophy might be compared with its sibling in Western religion. The Calvinist wing of the Protestant Reformation argued for justification by faith alone in contrast with justification by good works. Justification in this context meant the basis upon which one would be deemed a good Christian and therefore able to pass muster when confronted with the gatekeepers of heaven. Prior to the Reformation, the pope sometimes remitted penalties for sins, including those that would be paid for in purgatory, and he sometimes granted these favors in exchange for monetary contributions to the church. The doctrine of justification by good works was therefore extended to financial contributions to the church, and in effect rich people were buying a stairway to heaven. In arguing for justification by faith alone (which in turn sanctioned good works), Protestants such as Martin Luther were attempting to rationalize the justification process.

In a similar way, positivists wanted to rationalize the justification process in science. To do so, they attempted to anchor justification in logical rules that were derived from a process of reasoning akin to mathematics: justification by reason or logic alone. Like theologians, they viewed their logical systems as located outside the influence of human history or culture. Although this position may strike readers today as philosophically theological and anthropologically naive, let us for the moment follow out their arguments before considering the counterarguments and alternative positions.

One central problem in the philosophical justification of scientific knowledge was the problem of induction, that is, how to derive general empirical laws from observations. As Carnap asked, "What justifies us in going from the direct observation of facts to a law that expresses certain regularities of nature?" (1995: 19). In deductive logic, conclusions follow with certainty from premises as long as the proper logical rules are followed. For example, if all swans are white and if this bird is a swan, then this bird is white. (Another example of deductive logic is the style of mathematical proof that many people had to learn in high school.) However, the certainty of deductive conclusions did not apply to inductive logic, that is, deductively invalid inferences from experimental data to empirical laws. Carnap defended the idea that it was possible to work out an inductive logic for the confirmation or justification of empirical laws. Although he rejected the view that this logic could be simplified to the point of an inductive machine, he believed that it was "in many cases possible to determine, by mechanical procedures, the logical probability, or degree of confirmation," of a hypothesis based on a set of observations (1995: 34). Thus, he could determine the logical probability, or degree of confirmation, of a prediction or even a set of laws on the basis of observations.

A much larger justification problem emerges when two scientists induce two different theories. What criteria should one use to choose between two well-formulated theories? This is perhaps the most interesting question in the philosophy of science. If philosophers can help sort out this question, they can contribute to making theory choice work better in both the natural and social sciences. Clearly, a first answer to the question is that one should prefer the theory that corresponds better to the empirical laws or observations. Find out which theory fits all the observations better, either by examining the set of observations already available or by performing a crucial experiment that will allow a choice between the two theories. In practice, this approach often works in science, and little else is needed from philosophy.

However, the situation is not always so simple. In some cases the two theories are evidentially indistinguishable; in other words, they can explain the same set of facts. In this case the theory that can predict and explain new laws or observations is clearly preferable. However, there is also a stronger form of evidential indistinguishability, which occurs when "two theories lead in all cases to exactly the same predictions" (Carnap 1995: 151). Some realists argue that positivists bite the bullet when they face this kind of evidential indistinguishability. The choice between two theories that meet the stronger form of evidential indistinguishability is metaphysical and therefore not part of science.

However, in this circumstance Carnap admitted simplicity as a criterion of choice. In his case study of the choice between Euclidean and non-Euclidean geometry, he even distinguished between two types of simplicity. Non-Euclidean geometry was more complicated but it greatly simplified the system of physical laws, and Einstein and his followers opted for the systemic form of simplicity rather than the computational form (Carnap 1995: 162–64). The simplicity criterion has a long history dating back at least to William of Ockham and is known as Occam's (Ockam's, Ockham's) Razor or the rule of parsimony. This principle states that entities should not be multiplied beyond necessity. Carnap therefore updates a very old criterion for theory choice and clarifies which type of simplicity is better. The problem appears to be solved.

Interlude: The Unity of Science Thesis

The unity of science thesis provides one line of continuity between nineteenth-century positivism and twentieth-century logical positivism. Nineteenth-century positivists John Stuart Mill and Auguste Comte built grand schemes of the relations among the sciences in which the hierarchy of scientific disciplines also corresponded to a hierarchy of phenomena. As then, unifying schemes for the sciences today usually involve a defense of reductionism. For example, the biological level can be reduced ultimately to biochemistry and physics, and mental states can be reduced to neural states.

Fuller notes that there were significant variants in the unity of science thesis, even during the 1920s and 1930s when the thesis was strongest.[5] In Europe, the unity of science thesis emphasized the mathematical unity of the sciences, and mathematics or the mathematical side of physics was seen as the model science. Fuller argues that in Germany, where chemistry and physics were associated with the losing World War I effort, positivists tended to distance themselves from those fields. In contrast, in the United States, where technology was associated with the war victory, theorists such as John Dewey linked science and technology.

As a philosophical proposition, the unity of science thesis holds that theories across different scientific disciplines should not be contradictory, even when the different levels of science and observations are not reducible or not yet reducible. Thus, it should be possible to use different theories conjointly to predict new observations. At the level of methods and justification criteria, the unity of science thesis would hold that a philosophy of science as it is understood in one discipline could be transported to other disciplines. In other words, philosophies of science based on physics could be generalized to other scientific disciplines.

Probably the greatest weakness in this position comes when the philosophy of science is generalized from the natural sciences to the human sciences. The tendency for philosophers of science to use physics as their model has been another source of cross-disciplinary misunderstandings with social scientists and humanists. Some humanities scholars have defended a radical difference between the natural and human sciences in terms of a methodological difference of explanation versus interpretive understanding. Thus, in the more humanistic social sciences and in many of the humanities, the preferred method is some type of hermeneutics or interpretation rather than explanation. However, others have held (and I would agree) that interpretive understanding is merely a type of explanation. Thus, it is possible to maintain a unitarian view in terms of this methodological issue, even if one does not accept other types of unity such as a reductionism of the social/symbolic to the neurological/biological (a project about which I am very skeptical). Still, the emphasis on predictive explanation in physics seems impossible for much of the phenomena studied by the social sciences. Many social phenomena are far too complicated to be predictable, at least at the present time. Consequently, as social scientists read philosophies of science that draw their arguments from physics or even other natural sciences, they immediately see the failure of some of the arguments to transport to their own field and they become skeptical of the entire enterprise. The counterargument of some philosophers that the social sciences are merely undeveloped or inferior sciences only makes matters worse by underscoring the social scientists' and humanists' perception that philosophers of science do not understand their endeavors.

Another dimension of the natural/human science divide is the cultural meaning attributed to the difference. The difference between the human sciences and the natural sciences is a reproduction, internal to the field of science, of the division between science and cultural domains that are understood as not science, such as the arts and to some extent (via the tradition of biblical hermeneutics) religion. This difference of viewpoints is often so dramatic that C. P. Snow's old formulation of "two cultures" continues to be relevant (1959). Feminist science studies analysts have shown how the classic divide between the natural sciences and the humanities, and the associated but not identical divide between hard and soft sciences, are laden with highly gendered imagery (Keller 1985: 33, 77; Bleier 1986: 6). These divisions are recursive; in other words, gendered divisions often occur not only in formulations of the difference between science and nonscience or between the sciences and the humanities (with the social sciences mediating the divide), but across disciplinary divisions in the sciences (e.g., physics versus, for example, biology) or even across divisions within disciplines (e.g., molecular biology versus ecology, or experimental versus clinical psychology). Thus, feminist theory points not only to one type of disunity of the sciences but also to the masculinist biases that may be built into some formulas of the grounds for the unity of science, particularly the claim of reductionism.

A related division is the distinction between idiographic and nomothetic science. Idiographic science is the study of historical particulars, as in the natural history of a geological or ecological region, or a historical, textual, or ethnographic study in the humanities/social sciences. Nomothetic science is characterized by the search for general laws. This division occurs both in the natural sciences (biology versus natural history) and in the social sciences and humanities (sociology versus history). Even within some disciplines different phases are considered idiographic and nomothetic. Thus, within anthropology ethnography (the description of a people) is idiographic, whereas ethnology and cultural/social anthropology seek general patterns. The different goals, methods, and histories of the various idiographic and nomothetic disciplines suggest another basis for questioning the unity of science thesis.

Another way in which the social sciences complicate the question of the unity of science is through the use of the disunity of science as a useful research tool in social studies of science. For example, as Sheila Jasanoff (1990) has shown, the standards for judging acceptability in regulatory science and research science vary greatly. In the former, legal versus statistical tests of sufficiency play a relatively greater role. In the next chapter I will cover some other examples of the disunity of the sciences in empirical social science research. Robert Merton (1973), for example, distinguished between codified sciences, or those vertically built on previous findings, and noncodified sciences, in which new research horizontally adds new empirical material but does not necessarily build in a linear way on previous research. This distinction is similar to the nomothetic/idiographic distinction but not quite identical to it. He found the distinction useful in formulating some empirical patterns on age effects and cumulative advantage processes. Furthermore, a number of measures show stable differences across the range of sciences. Those measures include some of the findings of the institutional sociology of science to be discussed in the next chapter, such as differences across disciplines in acceptance rates for journal submissions and the proportion of publications in articles and books.

Thus, social science research suggests ways in which the unity of science thesis is limited, and in this respect it has philosophical implications. Many philosophers today are equally skeptical about such abilities to generalize across fields. As Paul Durbin has noted, "Now philosophy of science is itself a multiply diversified field . . . and each of the sciences, with endlessly multiplying subspecialties of all sorts, goes its own way in total defiance of any unity of science model" (1988: 334). It would still be possible to defend the thesis on one or several dimensions while recognizing a disunity of science on other dimensions. Likewise, it would still be possible to formulate a prescriptive position that views the unity of science as a goal to be achieved. However, the empirical research on the ways in which the sciences are not unified can contribute to assessing how realistic and desirable it would be to invest time in formulating such projects.

Conventionalism

Conventionalism is historically the first major alternative to the positivist philosophy of science. Although conventionalism is usually identified with Pierre Duhem, it may be more accurate to view Jules Henri Poincaré as the originator of this position (Gillies 1993: 67, 90). Conventionalism holds that scientific laws (such as those of Newtonian mechanics) and mathematical axioms (such as those of Euclidean geometry) are neither experimental inferences nor a priori knowledge but instead are disguised definitions or conventions. Two specific theses associated with conventionalism are underdetermination and theory-ladenness.

The underdetermination thesis of Duhem and W. V. Quine holds that a theory can be maintained in the face of contradictory observations provided that an adjustment is made to the auxiliary hypotheses derived from the theory.[6] In this sense theories are underdetermined by evidence. Thus, a core theory can be protected from refutation if after-the-fact changes are made in auxiliary hypotheses. An auxiliary or ad hoc hypothesis is a modification in a theory made in the face of a refuting instance in order to cover that refuting instance but no further problem.[7] An example is epicycles, little circles within the planetary orbits, which were used in early models of the solar system to account for observations of planets that violated the ideal of perfect circular motion.

Related to the underdetermination thesis is the thesis of the theory-ladenness of observations, which was defended by Duhem and later by Paul Feyerabend, Thomas Kuhn, and Norwood Hansen. Although it is now generally accepted that theories shape, constrain, or color observations, in most cases the conditioned nature of observations is not considered to be strong enough to prevent theory choice based on observations obtained in research protocols designed to evaluate or test competing theories.

Regarding conventionalism, two limitations should be kept in mind. First, underdetermination and theory-ladenness are not necessarily as damaging as they first appear. In practice it may be possible to design experiments in which auxiliary hypotheses are more highly confirmed by existing evidence than the theory to be tested (Laudan 1990: 42 ff.). Second, acceptance of the conventionalist account does not necessarily imply that it is impossible to maintain general prescriptive criteria for theory choice. One could follow Duhem and accept conventionalism as argued, but make theory choice subject to correspondence at a general level and coherence for specific theories. Thus, Duhem argued that a confirmation criterion could be maintained for a body of theories as a whole that must approximate the totality of empirical laws or generalizations. For specific theories, theory choice criteria should include internal consistency and consistency with other theories (Duhem 1982: 220). Furthermore, Duhem did allow for a degree of disconfirmation to settle a dispute between empirically equivalent theories. In a description of theory change that sounds similar to Kuhnian paradigm shifts, he wrote, "We may find it childish and unreasonable for the [scientist] to maintain obstinately at any cost, at the price of continual repairs and many tangled-up stays, the worm-eaten columns of a building tottering in every part, when by razing these columns it would be possible to construct a simple, elegant, and solid system" (1982: 217). Of course, the classic example is the heliocentric view of the solar system that assumes simple elliptical orbits instead of the whistles and bells of epicycles. In this comment, Duhem also seems to be adding simplicity and elegance as prescriptive theory choice criteria to his more general criterion of consistency. Note that the simplicity criterion was also endorsed by Carnap, so one sees that on this issue the two positions of positivism and conventionalism are not as contradictory as they may first appear.

Falsificationism and the Demarcation Problem

Popper is known for having developed a critique of positivism that avoided conventionalism. Often considered a positivist, he was not a member of the Vienna Circle and held views at odds with leading figures such as Carnap. Ian Hacking provides a succinct formulation of their differences:

> Carnap thought that *meanings* and a theory of *language* matter to the philosophy of science. Popper despised them as scholastic. Carnap favored *verification* to distinguish science from nonscience. Popper urged *falsification*. Carnap tried to explicate good reason in terms of a theory of *confirmation;* Popper held that rationality consists in *method*. Carnap thought that knowledge has *foundations;* Popper urged that there are no foundations and that all our knowledge is *fallible*. Carnap believed in *induction;* Popper held that there is no logic except *deduction*. (1983: 4–5)

On the last point Popper (1963) resurrected David Hume's argument against inductive inference. In other words, just because all swans observed up until time *t* are white, there are no logical grounds for concluding that the next observation will not be a black swan. Hume argued that inductive logic led to an infinite regress: I do not know whether one additional observation will confirm or disconfirm the law, so I make an additional observation. However, I am still in the same position, so I make an additional observation, and so on. I am caught in an infinite regress. (As will be discussed, this argument reappears in the sociological literature as an analysis of the experimenter's regress.)

The view that scientists induce theories or laws from observations was, according to Popper, a myth. Instead, they jump to conclusions, conjecture a hypothesis, and then try to refute it through observations. Thus, they do not proceed by confirming theories or laws, but only by failing to falsify them and therefore becoming increasingly convinced of their correctness. In principle any theory or law is defeasible, and Popper therefore also defended fallibilism, the view that no beliefs are immune from error.

Note that Popper criticized the positivist view of induction by using what appears to be a descriptive argument: scientists do not in fact extract theories or laws from observations. However, he does not have any credible research from the historical record or from social science surveys to back up the argument. Thus, one way of defending positivism against Popper would be to draw on empirical research to argue that scientists do in fact reason in a probabilistic manner similar to the inductive logic proposed by Carnap. In turn, a Popperian might counterargue that recourse to the historical record or empirical social science studies would be largely irrelevant. Even if scientists do in fact reason this way, they *should* reason as a Popperian scientist does by starting first with a theory or a law and then attempting to refute it. This example is one case of the slippages between description and prescription that sometimes occur in philosophical arguments.

Although Popper rejected the positivist view of induction, in other ways he remained very similar to the positivists. For example, his account of science was still a rational one and therefore he was still engaged in a project of justification in a general sense. He had merely switched the problem from how to induce good hypotheses to how to refute bad ones. Yet the problem of evaluating theories or laws still required justification, and this justification was anchored in empirical practices akin to those of the positivists. Popper still believed that testing was the key to accepting or rejecting a hypothesis (1963). In this sense he was squarely aligned with the positivists, and consequently his falsificationism position has sometimes been called an extreme form of verificationism. One way of expressing this continuity is in terms of the "hypothetico-deductive method." A positivist interpretation was that if a hypothesis is true and if a confirming observation is true, then the hypothesis is confirmed to some degree. Popper tweaks this method by arguing that if a hypothesis is true and if a confirming observation is false, then the hypothesis is not confirmed.

Popper originally developed his falsificationist argument as a solution to the demarcation problem, or how to distinguish science from nonscience. From the viewpoint of positivists (or at least some positivists), a claim that was in principle verifiable (or at least subject to testing and some confirmation) could be considered meaningful and scientific. A pseudoscientific statement was therefore in principle not capable of confirmation. Concerned with what he saw as the pseudoscientific successes of Marxism and psychoanalysis, Popper formulated falsifiability as a better demarcation criterion.

Popper's formulation of falsificationism as a valid demarcation criterion is not the only possibility. Thomas Gieryn (1994) argues that Robert Merton's formula of a set of universalistic norms represents another attempt to resolve the demarcation problem, as does Thomas Kuhn's criterion that sciences have a paradigm. Mario Bunge supplied eight negative criteria that served as indicators of nonscience (1982). Larry Laudan (1983) argues that the demarcation criteria of philosophers such as Aristotle, Carnap, and Popper were developed to rule out specific cases (such as psychoanalysis and Marxism for Popper), but the criteria all would allow other cases of nonscience to pass as science. He argues instead that a more honest approach would be to develop specific arguments against specific inadequacies of apparent pseudosciences rather than to develop universal criteria for which exceptions are likely to be found (cf. Fuller 1988: ch. 7). Subsequently, Charles Taylor (1996) surveyed a wide range of STS approaches to the demarcation problem and argued that they could be incorporated into a broader rhetorical framework.

The demarcation problem may seem to be an obscure philosophical issue, but it has direct policy implications in a number of areas. One example is the legal problem of determining criteria for acceptable expert testimony. In the United States a long-standing criterion was based on the 1923 *Frye* ruling, which defined the scientific by a criterion of general acceptance in the field in which the claim is made. In philosophical terms, this amounts to a grounds for theory choice based on a consistency criterion. In the context of legal disputes, there is a high danger of conservative bias in research fields that are not very autonomous and instead are more clearly structured by corporate, professional, or other interests (as in, say, research on environmental carcinogens or pharmaceuticals). Rule 702 of the Federal Rules of Evidence, issued during the 1970s, allowed greater leeway in expert testimony by basing acceptable expertise on knowledge, skill, training, or experience. However, this rule resulted in what some considered to be the problem of junk science. A 1993 Supreme Court ruling *(Daubert v. Merrell Dow Pharmaceuticals, Inc.)* developed four guide-posts, which included the *Frye* criterion but also added testability, peer review and publication, and a declared (and presumably) low error rate.[8] One can see how the courts have struggled with the very difficult problem of demarcation. As attorney Richard Jaffe (1996) has pointed out, the implications are enormous, given the fact that the *Frye* and *Daubert* criteria may work against plaintiffs who rely on the expertise of fields such as environmental medicine.

Popper also provided prescriptive criteria for theory choice. He agreed with a criterion of simplicity, and he used the theory of gravity as the example: "The new theory should proceed from some *simple, new, and powerful, unifying idea* about some connection or relation (such as gravita-tional attraction) between hitherto unconnected things (such as planets and apples) or facts (such as inertial and gravitational mass) or new 'theoretical entities' (such as field and particles)" (1963: 241). Note that this criterion also includes accuracy; in other words, it takes for granted the argument that the theory will explain a set of facts or the same set of facts as a rival theory. Second, the new theory must be independently testable, that is, in addition to explaining accepted evidence in a better way, it must have some new and testable consequences. Third, in addition to passing attempted refutations, it must make successful, new predictions of new effects. Thus, in developing his criteria for theory choice, Popper pushed the falsifica-tionist position to an extreme by narrowing falsification to successful, new predictions. The criteria may have worked for the examples from physics that he was thinking about, but they are problematic for other sciences, especially the social sciences and other sciences that work with phenomena too complicated to be predicted.

Historicism

One major criticism of Popperian falsification, which philosophers such as Imre Lakatos recognized, came from Thomas Kuhn. In *The Structure of Scientific Revolutions,* Kuhn argued that scientists often continue to work under a theory or set of theories even when faced with anomalies or refuting instances. However, Kuhn's work had a much more important place in the philosophy of science than merely providing an argument against falsificationism. His work contributed greatly to what philosophers of science call historicism, the period and style that responded to positivism/Popperism and antedated naturalism, roughly from the 1960s to the 1980s. This tendency in philosophy—epitomized in the work of Kuhn, Paul Feyerabend, Stephen Toulmin, and to some extent Imre Lakatos— rejected the lack of concern among positivists, Popperians, and conventionalists with the historical record and instead advocated a greater role for historical facts in philosophical argumentation. The emergence of historicism also brought about what anthropologists call the "peace in the feud" between Popper and the positivists. Hacking argues that in contrast to Kuhn—at least in *The Structure of Scientific Revolutions*—Carnap and Popper held many similar views: observation can be sharply distinguished from theory, knowledge growth is cumulative, science has a deductive structure, terminology is or ought to be precise, there is a unity to science, and a distinction can be maintained between the context of discovery and that of justification (Hacking 1983: 4–5).

Kuhn's *Structure of Scientific Revolutions* had a substantial impact on both the philosophy and social studies of science, but after the 1970s the impact was increasingly that of a foil against which other positions and theories were articulated. In the sociology of scientific knowledge, the various positions developed during and after the 1970s rapidly replaced Kuhnian analysis, as did naturalistic and realistic approaches in philosophy. Furthermore, as the alternatives were formulated, the novelty of Kuhn's work also came into question. Many of Kuhn's sociological ideas had antecedents in the 1930s studies of Ludwik Fleck (1979) on thought styles and collectives (a social unit in science such as a discipline, network, or community), and Kuhn's philosophical arguments also had predecessors in the conventionalist tradition within the philosophy of science. The final verdict is that as a sociologist Kuhn has been shown to be more or less Mertonian, and as a philosopher he has been read increasingly "*pace* [Dudley] Shapere, less [as] a revolt against positivism than a continuation of it."[9]

By the 1990s the importance of *The Structure of Scientific Revolutions* within STS was generally seen as historical rather than contemporary, and many regarded the historical influence as a conservative one in the sense that it continued rather than challenged fundamental theories in social studies and philosophy. However, outside STS circles Kuhn's work continued to have a life of its own as scientists, popular writers, and others continued to talk about his revolutionary ideas about revolutions. Certainly, there is still a place for good philosophical and sociological accounts of scientific revolutions, and Kuhn's work deserves some credit for providing a spur to theorization of the topic. Scientific revolutions, controversies, and normal science have sometimes been referred to as the three phases of scientific research. Controversies will be covered in the chapter on the sociology of scientific knowledge, and if one wishes to build a more thoroughly sociological account of scientific revolutions, then the controversy literature is probably the best starting point.

The other phase of scientific research was what Kuhn characterized as normal science or puzzle solving, that is, the incremental additions of observations and minor theoretical innovations. Under these conditions, knowledge claims are not likely to be controversial and replication is likely to be less salient. Puzzle solving does not involve attempts to refute a theory, and the bulk of scientific work involves puzzle solving. Thus—and here is one philosophical implication—the bulk of scientific work does not follow the Popperian model of falsificationism.

Kuhn's theory attributes scientific revolutions to a paradigm crisis, which is occasioned by the accumulation of anomalies that leads to the formulation of a new paradigm. The concept of a "paradigm" shifted the discussion on falsification and confirmation from a single theory to something more encompassing. In *The Structure of Scientific Revolutions,* the term "paradigm" suffered from ambiguity, and as many as twenty-two different uses have been isolated. The multiple uses of the term, Kuhn's insistence on its linkage to communities, and the learned nature of paradigms all suggest parallels with the rubric nature of the term "culture" for anthropologists, and therefore in some ways it seems that Kuhn was trying to reinvent anthropologists' culture concept. In subsequent work Kuhn specified more concretely the meanings he attributed to the paradigm concept (1977: ch. 12). He underscored its connection to a scientific community, which he thought of in terms of specialties or disciplines but defined as having multiple levels. Thus, the most general meaning of paradigm was "disciplinary matrix," the interconnected elements associated with a discipline. The list of elements shifts from the 1970 postscript in *The Structure* to the version published in 1977 in *The Essential Tension,* which describes three main components or elements to the disciplinary matrix: (1) symbolic generalizations, or formal parts of the paradigm; (2) models, which provide the group with "preferred analogies" or an ontology, as in the idea that an electrical circuit may be "regarded as a steady-state hydrodynamic system"; and (3) exemplars, or shared examples, usually concrete problems that a theory has solved and that serve as guides for new research. For several reasons—the fuzziness of the concept; the tendency for science studies researchers to think more in terms of networks, schools, fields, and arenas than research communities; and the existence of other, more generally accepted terms that do much of the same work (culture, episteme, research program, research tradition, and theory or global theory)—the term "paradigm" seems to have had more success outside science studies circles than inside them.

The other crucial term is "anomaly," an observation that raises doubts about a theory, although it is not necessarily logically inconsistent with the theory. Thus, the idea of an anomaly puts Kuhn somewhere between Popperian refutation and conventionalism. Although Kuhn does not endorse the algorithmic nature of falsification through refuting instances, he still leaves a place for the role of negative instances, particularly through their accumulation over time and the difficulty of producing and maintaining an increasing and increasingly complicated network of auxiliary theories.[10] Furthermore, a new paradigm does not merely subsume the empirical evidence of the previous one. A paradigm shift or large theoretical change is not necessarily unequivocally progressive; the part of the old knowledge base that is lost has been referred to as "Kuhn loss" (Fuller 1988: 223). As Hacking (1983: 67) points out, Kuhn's description of theory change is considerably different from the idea of theory subsumption (as defended by Ernest Nagel and others), in which a successor theory or paradigm explains the new phenomena and makes the same accurate predictions of the previous one.

The concept of Kuhn loss is important for an understanding of the incommensurability thesis, which is associated mostly with Kuhn, although Feyerabend also defended it and the thesis has antecedents in the work of Carnap. Originally the thesis held that the advocates of different paradigms live in such different worlds that their theories are mutually unintelligible, but over the years the thesis has shifted to the problems of translatability across theories (Earman 1993: 17; Kuhn 1989: 10; 1993). Another reconstruction of the thesis is that the earlier theory is not encompassed by the later one and cannot be derived from the later one. This is clearly not always the case, as in Newtonian mechanics and twentieth-century physics, and philosophers have consequently refined the thesis.[11] In social studies of controversies, the incommensurability thesis has not proven very useful because opponents may be able to sidestep translation and move to direct rehearsal of procedures and protocols. This argument has become more important as social scientists have studied science as practice rather than merely as theory making (Pickering 1992). Furthermore, opponents often are quite adept at understanding the terms of the opposing side (MacKenzie and Barnes 1979: 200).

One implication of incommensurability among grand theories or paradigms is that change may be more like a conversion process than a change of minds led by argument and evidence. As a result, Kuhn followed Max Planck (1949) when he argued that paradigm change is often associated with a shift of generations, in which an older paradigm becomes extinct as an older generation dies off. However, Kuhn also denied criticisms that he had reduced the problem of theory choice to "mob psychology." Instead, he defended a loose set of more or less universalistic criteria for theory choice, thus heading off criticisms that his theory of paradigm change reduced theory choice to epistemological relativism. Kuhn listed the major criteria for theory choice as the following:

> First, a theory should be accurate: within its domain, that is, consequences deducible from a theory should be in demonstrated agreement with the results of existing experiments and observations. Second, a theory should be consistent, not only internally or with itself, but also with other currently accepted theories applicable to related aspects of nature. Third, it should have broad scope: in particular, a theory's consequences should extend far beyond the particular observations, laws, or subtheories it was initially designed to explain. Fourth, and closely related, it should be simple, bringing order to phenomena that in its absence would be individually isolated and, as a set, confused. Fifth—a somewhat less standard item, but one of special importance to actual scientific decisions—a theory should be fruitful of new research findings: it should, that is, disclose new phenomena or previously unnoted relationships among those already known. (Kuhn 1977: 321–22)

Because Kuhn referred to his theory choice criteria as values, he evidently believed that he was describing a set of values that indeed guided scientists in action. His criteria therefore apparently doubled as a description of, on the one hand, what he thought (without doing any empirical research) scientists actually held as values that guide theory choice and, on the other hand, a prescription of what he thought should guide theory choice. Subsequent empirical research by social scientists has questioned the Kuhnian argument that scientists' action is in fact guided by these or other lists of universalistic values, such as the complementary list of institutional values known as Mertonian norms. However, when interpreted as prescriptive criteria, Kuhn's "values" no longer suffer from the problem of lack of empirical evidence.

Thus, I suggest viewing Kuhn's values as prescriptive theory choice criteria. From this perspective, Kuhn synthesizes theory choice criteria as articulated by Carnap, Duhem, Popper, and other philosophers. Note that the accuracy criterion could be reconciled with some type of verificationism or falsificationism. Scope and fruitfulness are similar, and they could be interpreted as corollaries of the accuracy criterion when applied to future predictions. The consistency criterion is similar to the theory choice criterion favored by conventionalists like Duhem, and simplicity was also advocated by Carnap, Duhem, and Popper. In fact, because simplicity must be judged against a background of other theories, it is closely related to consistency. In short, Kuhn's main contribution to the theory choice issue is to articulate and synthesize previous discussions. I would add that scope, fruitfulness, and accuracy are closely related as one group, and simplicity and consistency are closely related as a second group. Do other philosophical traditions help expand this list in new directions?

Post-Kuhnian Theories of Progress

Imre Lakatos accepted Kuhn's argument that theories coexist within an ocean of anomalies and therefore are not easily rejected even in the face of potentially refuting instances. However, unlike Kuhn he proposed a methodology of scientific research programs that developed what he called a sophisticated falsificationism. Lakatos argued that the "basic unit of appraisal must be not an isolated theory or conjunction of theories but rather a 'research program'" (1978: 110). An example is Newtonian science, which at its core consisted of a conjunction of theories or conjectures: the three laws of mechanics and the law of gravitation (4). These constitute what Lakatos calls the hard core or negative heuristic of a research program; they are the sacred space that must be protected at all cost from anomalies or refuting instances. The hard core of the research program is defended by a "protective belt of auxiliary hypotheses" that digest anomalies (48). The positive heuristic "consists of a partially articulated set of suggestions or hints on how to change, develop the 'refutable variants' of the research program, how to modify, sophisticate, the 'refutable' protective belt" (50). As descriptions of the theoretical structure of some sciences, the concepts of a hard core with its negative heuristic and a protective belt with its positive heuristic seem to correspond well to some cases.

However, as for Lakatos's prescriptive criteria for choosing among research programs, when the smoke clears there is not much new. Lakatos wrote, "All the research programs I admire have one characteristic in common. They all predict novel facts, facts which had been either undreamt of, or have indeed been contradicted by previous or rival programs" (5). Lakatos designated as "progressive" those research programs that are generating successful, surprising predictions, in contrast with "degenerative" programs. In progressive programs there is a series of theories, each of which is better than the previous one. "Better" is defined as meeting three criteria: the new theory has excess empirical content over the previous one, that is, it predicts novel facts; the new theory explains the success of the previous theory, that is, it subsumes the previous theory; and at least some of the new theory's excess content is corroborated (32).

One problem with Lakatos's proposal is that the requirement of subsumption means that his criteria would not apply to cases where there is Kuhn loss, and consequently the real-world applicability of his second criterion is limited. Furthermore, his use of successful, surprising predictions as the criterion for choice among theories (or research programs) is not very new and restricts the applicability of the criteria to sciences that provide predictive explanations. One might recall that Carnap and Popper (as well as Kuhn) used new predictions as a basic criterion for theory choice, so at best the Lakatosian criterion is a clarification of what the other philosophers had suggested. Moreover, Lakatos does not provide for the strong form of evidential indistinguishability, as described by Carnap, in which two theories (or research programs) made similar predictions. Here, one would have to return to other sorts of criteria, such as simplicity or consistency.

Lakatos also contributed to the muddle of the interdisciplinary dialogue when he used Marxism as his exemplar of a degenerative research program (1978: 6–7). He compared the failed predictions and post hoc explanations of Marxism with the successful, surprising predictions of Newtonian mechanics. The comparison was motivated more by his historical location in Cold War politics, but it assumes a version of the unity of science thesis that is highly questionable. It is unlikely that he could find any social theory or social science research program that provided successful, surprising predictions similar to those of Newtonian mechanics, simply because social phenomena are considerably more complex. He suggests as much when at another point he refers to the social sciences as "underdeveloped" (9). One of the reasons social scientists lose patience with philosophers of science is that we are constantly told that we are in some sense deficient scientists— we lack a paradigm, predictive ability, quantitative exactness, and so on— instead of being seen as divergent or different scientists.

Larry Laudan developed a slightly different approach to Lakatos's analysis of research programs and progress in science. He proposed the concept of a "research tradition" to replace the Kuhnian paradigm or Lakatosian research program:

1. Every research tradition has a number of specific theories which exemplify and partially constitute it; some of these theories will be contemporaneous, others will be temporal successors of earlier ones.
2. Every research tradition exhibits certain *metaphysical* and *methodological* commitments which, as an ensemble, individuate the research tradition and distinguish it from others.
3. Each research tradition (unlike a specific theory) goes through a number of different, detailed (and often mutually contradictory) formulations and generally has a long history extending through a significant period of time. (By contrast, theories are frequently short-lived.) (Laudan 1977: 78–79) [12]

The concept of a research tradition, as defined here, loses some of the conventionalist wisdom that Lakatos retained in his definition of a research program as having a negative and positive heuristic. However, like the Kuhnian paradigm Laudan's definition of the research tradition has the benefit of pointing to extratheoretical commitments, that is, something closer to what I call a research culture. This change represents an improvement on the formal emphasis of Lakatos's research program. He also is more willing to allow for internal contradictions and a sense of historical evolution.

What does Laudan contribute to the problem of theory choice? He defined progress as increasing problem-solving ability. Problems are understood as either empirical, such as resolving an anomaly, or conceptual, such as when a theory is either internally inconsistent or inconsistent with another accepted theory (1977: 49). Thus, the first criterion amounts to a type of empirical subsumption, and the second returns us to a version of consistency and simplicity criteria. A supporter of Kuhn would say that to the extent that Lakatos and Laudan have added anything new to his list of accuracy, consistency, scope, simplicity, and fruitfulness, they have clarified and extended the list rather than overturned it. [13]

The term "progress" or "progressive" as used by Lakatos and Laudan provides another possibility for interdisciplinary misunderstandings. For example, consider one social scientist's approach to the problem, Derek de Solla Price's "scientific doomsday" thesis (1965). Price argued that world science had been expanding since its inception at an exponential growth rate, so much so that it was doubling every ten to fifteen years. Because that growth rate could not be sustained, Price predicted a scientific dooms- day, and his prediction seems to have become a reality in the cost-cutting years of the 1990s. (Sometimes social scientists do make successful, even somewhat surprising, predictions.) Although it is still possible to define some kind of "progress" in an era of cost cutting and accountability to pragmatic interests, it is useful to inject this social science finding into the philosophical debate to destabilize the concept of progress. Why should one be content with such a narrow definition of progress as appears in Lakatos's and Laudan's formulas? Can one also set up criteria for the progress of science at the institutional level, such as the minimal mainte- nance of wages and resources at cost-of-living levels, or the increased amount of diversity and equity in the institutional organization of scientific and technical production? These definitions might even be linked to prog- ress in the sense of content, such as the argument that an increasingly diverse institutional organization of science tends to lead to the weeding out of some of the most egregious instances of gender, race, and other biases (Haraway 1989). I therefore interpret Lakatos's and Laudan's descrip- tions of scientific progress—replacing one theory with a better one—as very narrow. Social studies therefore can contribute to a more general philosophical analysis of the idea of "progress" in science.

Naturalism and Realism

Laudan's work was influenced by American pragmatism, as is evident in his definition of progress through the concept of problem solving. In philoso- phy pragmatism has sometimes been referred to as the Chicago school of philosophy, and it is useful to pause with this term because it is another example of variation across disciplinary cultures. In philosophy the term "Chicago school" usually refers to the period when John Dewey was at the University of Chicago. The term probably was born in 1903 when William James hailed Dewey's *Studies in Logical Theory* as the birth of the Chicago school of pragmatist philosophy (although later Carnap came to Chicago, thus bringing positivism to pragmatism). The Chicago school in philosophy can be distinguished from Chicago schools in the social sciences, which influenced North American STS in a different way and will be described later. Leading early pragmatist philosophers were Dewey, James, George Herbert Mead, and Charles Sanders Peirce. For pragmatists, knowledge is derived from experience and work (including scientific experimentation), and truth is determined through practical results such as prediction and control or desired psychological/social consequences. Like positivists, pragmatists were critical of metaphysical speculation, but like contemporary naturalists pragmatists tended to rely on scientifically generated natural facts as a ground or touchstone for philosophical argumentation. Pragmatism is therefore a contributing current to naturalism in the contemporary philosophy of science.[14]

Naturalism is, according to one prominent American naturalist philosopher, the view "that all human activities can be understood as entirely natural phenomena, as are the activities of chemicals or animals" (Giere 1988: 8). Often naturalism is described as the third phase in the philosophy of science after the early debates among positivism, Popperism, and conventionalism and the second wave of historicism. Some naturalist philosophers consider the American pragmatists (such as Dewey, Peirce, and James) to be closer intellectual ancestors than the leaders of the major traditions within the philosophy of science. However, there are also clear lines of influence from the earlier schools of the philosophy of science. Like historicism, naturalism tends to move away from argumentation grounded on formal, a priori reasoning that was characteristic of the positivists, and instead it interjects accepted empirical facts into philosophical argumentation. However, unlike historicism naturalism tends to rely more on the natural facts of cognitive and/or evolutionary processes as a reliable model for distinguishing truth from belief. Naturalists also are usually more deeply involved in the discipline-specific philosophies of science such as the philosophy of biology or cognitive science, in contrast with the emphasis on physics in earlier generations of philosophy. Their deep involvement in specific disciplines tends to make the philosophy of science more continuous with theoretical debates within scientific disciplines. Consequently, justification is often formulated not against an imaginary skeptic but instead against a goal of producing approximately true knowledge about the world.

Perhaps the most influential type of naturalistic approach in the contemporary philosophy of science is evolutionary epistemology, that is, any theory that explains human and animal cognition with evolutionary theory. Werner Callebut (1993: 286) argues that it is important to distinguish two different programs: (1) biological evolutionary epistemology (also known as bioepistemology or EEM, for evolutionary epistemology mechanisms), which is the natural science of the evolutionary basis of animal cognitive and perceptual systems; and (2) an evolutionary account of science or EET, evolutionary epistemology of theories (following Bradie 1986). Daryl Chubin and Sal Restivo (1983) called the latter the "mild program" in STS. Leaders in the development of an evolutionary approach to science have been Donald Campbell, David Hull, and Popper. Hull's contribution to evolutionary theory includes the delineation and/or elucidation of the following: a replicator, "an entity that passes on its structure largely intact in successive replications"; an interactor, "an entity that interacts as a cohesive whole with its environment in such a way that this interaction *causes* replication to be differential"; selection, "a process in which the differential extinction and proliferation of interactors *cause* the differential perpetuation of the relevant replicators"; and lineage, "an entity that persists indefinitely through time either in the same or an altered state as a result of replication" (1988: 408–9). Hull argues that his distinction between inter-actors and replicators is an advance on Campbell's term "vehicle," which does not entail the distinction and is therefore likely to create conceptual confusion (Hull 1988: 414; Campbell 1979).

These terms apply to biological as well as conceptual, scientific, and cultural evolution, and thus they have relevance for social sciences such as cultural anthropology. However, in general cultural anthropologists and sociologists today tend not to be interested in evolutionary approaches to social phenomena. These approaches have a checkered history in the nine-teenth century, when they were often used to order societies in a way that legitimated the "white man's burden" of colonialism. In the twentieth century, evolutionary approaches were linked to functionalism, as in Talcott Parsons's social theory, which is now discredited for reasons that will be explained. The different meanings and histories of evolutionary theory in philosophy and the social sciences therefore provide another opportunity for cross-disciplinary misunderstandings.

Usually naturalists such as evolutionary epistemologists are also realists, a term that also provides enormous opportunities for misunderstanding. Several realists are also Marxists, and in Britain the term "critical realist" usually is a code word for a Marxist. Hacking distinguishes three types of realism:

1. ontological, in which scientific theories are either true or false "in virtue of how the world is" (opposed to instrumentalism);
2. causal, in which "the theoretical terms of the theory denote theoretical entities which are causally responsible for the observable phenomena";
3. epistemological, in which "we can have a warranted belief in theories or in entities (at least in principle)" (Hacking 1983: 28).

The first type of realism is usually connected with some theory of scientific progress, such that theories and/or methods describe the real world beyond observations increasingly better over time, or theoretical terms that seem to be merely instrumental acquire ontological status over time.[15]

The second definition of realism involves the philosophy of explanation. Generally, two major approaches are distinguished: inferential and causal. The inferential approach treats explanation as either an inductive or deductive argument in a tradition developed by Carl Hempel (1965; Hempel and Oppenheim 1948). To summarize, if the set of premises (explanans) is true, and the conclusions (explanandum) are logically related to the explanans, then the conclusions are true or probably true. Under the covering law model, the conclusions are subsumed under a general law or laws and some antecedent conditions. The first type of explanation is called nomological-deductive, and explanations are understood as predictions of events made after the events occur (retrodiction) and based on universal laws (nomological). When at least one of the laws is of a statistical nature, the type of explanation is deductive-statistical rather than deductive-nomological. However, some would argue that the conclusions (explanandum) may also be derived inductively; hence, the third type of inferential explanation: inductive-statistical. In all cases explanation is seen as a kind of description. Hence, this understanding of explanation is consistent with the view that one sometimes hears from scientists, namely, that science provides only highly general descriptions of the world but not explanations.

Because the covering law model is subject to countercases, some philosophers have defended the causal approach, a version of which appears as Hacking's second type of realism. From this perspective, explanations consist not of an argument that shows that the phenomenon was to be expected but of a statement of causes that shows how the phenomenon was brought about. A classical starting point in discussions of causality is Humean causation, which as reconstructed by twentieth-century philosophers is as follows: given two events E_1 and E_2, E_1 causes E_2 if (1) E_1 happened before E2, (2) it is possible to deduce E2 by knowing E1 occurred, a set of laws of nature, and statements of mutual conditions; and (3) it is not possible to deduce E2 from E1 by knowing only the set of laws of nature and statements of mutual conditions. This description more or less describes the understanding of causality implicit in medical research that follows Koch's postulates.[16] Hacking's description of a causal form of realism, which applies to theoretical terms, is an example of another type of causal explanation.

The third type of realism involves an opposition to epistemological relativism. Philosophers have occasionally charged some social scientists who work in the constructivist tradition with epistemological relativism. These debates often involve a great deal of cross-talk and therefore warrant some clarification. Before proceeding to that issue, one might ask whether realism contributes to the basic problem discussed in this chapter: providing better grounds for theory choice. Probably the unique contribution of the realist would be a criterion that, assuming evidential indistinguishability, preference should be given to the theory that uses terms that are more realistic. In other words, preference would be given to a theory with more observational terms or theoretical terms that could be transformed someday into observational terms. Likewise, preference would be given to a research program for which theoretical terms showed some tendency toward conversion into observational terms over time, and to a program that gave increasingly better technological benefits. For example, viruses were theoretical terms that have, over time and with better technology, become observational terms. Other than this criterion, realism probably would not add much to the discussions of theory choice criteria.

Constructivism and Relativism

Although philosophers are usually very precise at using terms, there seems to be a great deal of confusion regarding constructivism and relativism. Both labels are sometimes applied to the work of historicists such as Kuhn as well as some social scientists. It is helpful to distinguish the various meanings of both constructivism and relativism.

In the social studies of science and technology, the term "social constructivism" is often used as a general label for studies that examine how social variables shape the pattern of choices about what research gets done, how it is done, how choices among theories are made in controversies, and the extent to which observations, laws, theories, and other knowledge claims become accepted in wider scientific communities. Philosophers tend to use the term "constructivism" somewhat differently to refer to the idea that scientists do not discover the world but impose a structure on it or in some sense "make" the world. In its extreme version, constructivism amounts to more than an instrumentalist account of theories; it refers to a social idealism in which there is no material reality that constrains or structures sensory observations. Furthermore, regarding the problem of theory choice, this extreme version would hold that the world does not in any serious way constrain theory choice; in this sense the world is made or constructed rather than discovered. Some philosophers argue that the constructivism of social studies of science necessarily implies social idealism and epistemological relativism, but I suggest that there is no necessary connection between the two. There may be some social scientists who would accept the philosophical position of social idealism and epistemological relativism, and if they exist I would suggest calling their philosophical position "radical constructivism." Certainly some sociologists of scientific knowledge have made statements that suggest they accept radical constructivism or they did at one point.

An alternative to radical constructivism is the position that scientific theories are realistic maps or explanations of a real world and at the same time vehicles that encode culture-bound linguistic categories and cultural values (what I call cultural constructivism), and/or are shaped by social interests and other social variables (what I call social constructivism). I think of this hybrid philosophical position as moderate constructivism, although similar positions have been articulated under the banners of constructive realism or realistic constructivism. Many researchers in the social studies of science would probably accept some version of moderate constructivism. They believe that scientific theories and observations are constrained by a real, material world, but not completely so. Social variables and cultural values also play a shaping role. The mix of the material and social/cultural varies greatly across discipline and phase of research.

I would suggest adding yet a third philosophical position: conservative constructivism, which would hold that social interests and cultural values shape scientific theories only by instilling bias. Eventually that bias can be removed, thereby producing a utopian state in which science is objective or freed from infusion with cultural values and categories. A moderate constructivist would not see the referential and sociocultural aspects of scientific representations in such a zero-sum manner. Cultural values are not weeds to be picked from the garden of science to make room for flowers; rather, they are the soil upon which the flowers grow. In other words, scientific theories participate in their general epistemic, national, temporal, gender, and other cultures, thereby encoding values even as they simultaneously represent nature.

Let us take, for example, Marx's famous pronouncement about Darwin's evolutionary theory, that it encodes quite nicely the nineteenth-century bourgeois order of competitive capitalism as projected onto nature. A radical constructivist might argue that evolutionary theory, as well as the observations Darwin made, were a projection of nineteenth-century capitalism onto a natural world that was more or less a tabula rasa. We continue to believe in evolutionary theory today because we continue to live in a capitalist society that is permeated by the same metaphors and cultural structures as in Darwin's day. From this viewpoint, there would be no way to choose between evolutionary theory and creation science, except through power and persuasion or consistency with a surrounding cultural ethos and worldview.

A conservative constructivist would maintain that any cultural biases in evolutionary theory that entered into Darwin's model have been successively eliminated by subsequent versions of the theory. Even if Darwin did project some of his society onto nature and did produce a distorted map of nature, subsequent developments of evolutionary theory (and observations) have progressively weeded out those distortions. Like a progressive research program, evolutionary theory has improved over the years. Therefore, evolutionary theory is asymptotically approaching a pure, transparent representation of nature.

A moderate constructivist would argue that Darwinian evolutionary theory both projected Darwinian society onto nature and provided a relatively accurate map of a selected aspect of the natural world. Subsequent developments in evolutionary theory represented more accurate maps, pace the conservative constructivist, but those developments did not entail escaping from culture. Instead, subsequent changes correspond in part to general cultural shifts in science and society. For example, as evolutionary theory developed in the twentieth century toward equilibrium models and later nonlinear models, these changes drew on general metaphors and structures that were appearing as part of the general cultural shifts from the nineteenth century through modernism to postmodernism. It is thus possible to think about scientific theories as both realistically and socially constructed, much as in duck-rabbit Gestalt drawings in which two interpretations are simultaneously consistent with the material. In a similar but not quite identical formulation, Fuller argues that " 'the social' and 'the cognitive' are not separate parts of the scientific enterprise; rather, they are two relatively autonomous discourses that are available for analyzing any part of science" (1993a: 57). Thus, I would prefer to think of the sociocultural and referential aspects of scientific theories as two dimensions of the same phenomenon rather than two alternative approaches to it. Some version of this view is supported by philosophers such as Giere under the terms "perspectival realism" or "constructive realism" and Fuller under the term "realistic constructivism," as well as by some social scientists.[17]

To argue that scientific theories or models are representations may require some unpacking because the term "representations" shifts across disciplines.[18] For realist philosophers such as Giere, representations imply the idea that scientific theories represent or map reality. In history and cultural studies, Durkheim's "collective representations" are the shared ideas and beliefs of a community or other social unit, as in religious cosmologies. Given the multivocality of the word "representation," it may be uniquely situated for the hybrid world of moderate (realistic) constructivism. In other words, scientific representations are both referential—maps or models of the world—and sociocultural—encodings of values, general cultural categories, interests, and so forth.

Now that I have outlined the moderate constructivist position, let us play devil's advocate and accuse it of question-begging. What causes scientists to choose among theories: the fact that they accurately represent the world or that they represent social interests or cultural values and categories? From a prescriptive viewpoint, there may not be much disagreement: the former should inform good theory choice. At a descriptive level, however, the situation is more complicated. One might answer the question by saying both, that theory choice is overdetermined. Or, as I would advocate, one might refuse to answer the question in the universalizing terms in which it is posed and instead answer it on a case-by-case basis. By adopting these two strategies—separating the prescriptive from the descriptive question and reformulating the universal grounds of the question—the problem of relativism can be avoided.

Relativism is for philosophers a word similar to positivism for social scientists and humanists: it is better to accuse someone else of having it. To make the word useful, I like to distinguish four types. In social sciences such as anthropology, cultural relativism refers to a research stance and method that begins with the understandings of a community, actor, or some other social unit. In other words, social action is interpreted relative to the cultural meanings attributed to it by the actors involved. However, cultural interpretation or social science analysis does not end with local meanings; in turn those meanings are explained by general theories available in the social sciences. The recourse to theories and explanation usually puts cultural relativism in opposition to epistemological relativism.

Epistemological relativism is the position that (1) evidence and other universalistic criteria (such as consistency) do not play a crucial role in theory choice, which instead is largely conditioned by contingent or particularistic social factors; and (2) attempts to articulate prescriptive theory choice criteria are useless because scientists will not follow them. Although some social constructivists may support this position, many social scientists believe that although theory choice is heterogeneous, evidence still plays a crucial role in many if not most controversies. Thus, the first assumption is violated, and therefore attempts to articulate prescriptive theory choice criteria still are worthwhile.

Metaphysical (ontological) relativism is the position that theories and theoretical language do not necessarily capture anything of the deep structure of reality behind observations. Both positivists (as instrumentalists) and radical constructivists would therefore tend to be relativists in this sense, as opposed to realists and realistic/moderate constructivists. Because the realist position can add something to the theory choice debate that the relativist position cannot, on this issue realism seems warranted.

Finally, moral relativism is the position that there should be no universally upheld values, such as United Nations–sanctioned lists of human rights. Generally, anthropologists and others who employ cultural relativism as a method today support a political and moral stance of tolerance of and aid to marginalized groups; thus, in their minds cultural relativism is linked to opposition to moral relativism. People who attempt to argue that cultural relativism and moral relativism are identical, or that cultural relativism leads to moral relativism, simply are confusing the issues. Usually, the opposite is the case.

Note that accepting one type of relativism does not necessarily imply accepting another, although cultural and moral relativism are often opposed, and epistemological and ontological relativism are often linked. Furthermore, my four types of relativism are not the only ways of thinking about the topic. For example, Karin Knorr-Cetina and Michael Mulkay distinguish epistemic relativism, which asserts "that knowledge is rooted in a particular time and culture," from judgmental relativism, which holds "that all forms of knowledge are 'equally valid,' and that we cannot compare different forms of knowledge and discriminate among them" (1983: 5). In my terms, this is a distinction between moderate constructivism and epistemological relativism. Harry Collins also endorses relativism (probably my second and third types) in his empirical program of relativism (1983, 1985). Fuller (1993a: 66–69) distinguishes between realism/antirealism and relativism/objectivism. The former involves the question, "Are there legitimate grounds for criticism in science aside from those having to do with judgments of empirical adequacy?" and the latter revolves around the question, "Are there legitimate grounds for criticism in science aside from those having to do with judgments of expert authority?" Laudan (1990) provides a humorous parody of relativism, in which the relativist serves as a philosophically uninformed Simplicio/skeptic character in dialogue with a more intelligent positivist and realist, and an even more intelligent pragmatist. Unfortunately, the parody leaves the impression that social scientists are stupid and incapable of finding a philosophically coherent position for themselves, and as a result it only fans the flames of the cross-talk rather than attempting to find a way of moving beyond it. To be clear, I support only cultural relativism in the narrow sense defined here of methodology in cultural anthropology.

Social Studies and the Problem of Theory Choice

It is now possible to return to the problem of justifying theory choice and to consider how social studies of science can contribute to this problem in a helpful way that avoids the trap of epistemological relativism. Social scientists have often invoked underdetermination and theory-ladenness as philosophical license for a descriptive account that shows how particularistic values or social interests shape theory choice (e.g., Knorr-Cetina and Mulkay 1983: 3). However, the conventionalist arguments are largely irrelevant, not because conventionalists such as Duhem provide other prescriptive grounds for theory choice, but because prescriptive arguments are distinct from descriptive accounts. How scientists should choose theories is largely irrelevant to the empirical problem of describing how they in fact do choose theories. However, is the reverse also the case?

Descriptive accounts of scientists in practice suggest that they often do not follow the universalistic, prescriptive criteria suggested by the philosophy of science, even a loose family of criteria such as those articulated by Kuhn. To understand these accounts, it is useful to distinguish between private or covert criteria for theory choice (those that individuals keep to themselves or share only among networks of allies) and public criteria, which often emerge to legitimate positions in controversies. Often public criteria (as they appear in publications, memoirs, or public disputes) correspond to one of the philosophical ideals for theory choice, whereas private or covert criteria do not. Thus, it is important to follow scientists in action—in the laboratory and behind the scenes. Empirical studies of this sort have shown that in addition to universalistic values—such as accuracy, consistency, and simplicity—scientists evaluate theories and observations by reference to particularistic or personalistic criteria. In the social sciences a universalistic value orientation refers to the situation whereby actors use the same value system consistently across social situations. In the case of theory choice, this would mean applying the values of accuracy, consistency, scope, and so on. In contrast, particularism means that social actors shift their value system depending on the social situation (such as one set of values for friends and family, or for one's own social group, and other sets for other groups).

Philosophers who have thought carefully about the social studies of science recognize the limitations of universalistic values for descriptive accounts of scientists' action, because scientists turn out to be much more particularistic than they may admit in public. Helen Longino is one example of a philosopher who recognizes the limitations of universalistic values in descriptive accounts when she discusses the problematic nature of the distinction between constitutive and contextual values. She defines the former as internal to the sciences and "the source of rules determining what constitutes acceptable scientific practices," whereas contextual values "belong to the social and cultural environment in which science is done" (1990: 4). For our purposes here her distinction between constitutive and contextual values can be translated (more or less) as examples of the social scientist's distinction between universalistic and particularistic values. Longino argues that the traditional claim of value-freedom in science amounts to an argument that the two types of values are distinct and independent from one another. In general, the older view that good science is value-free or governed wholly by constitutive/universalistic values, whereas bad science is infiltrated or corrupted by contextual values, now seems naive to many researchers. Longino argues that the traditional distinction between the two types of values cannot be maintained. Instead, there has been a shift toward thinking about the two types of values as coexisting in the processes of science production.

What exactly is meant by particularistic values? As they apply to the problem of evaluation of research and theory choice, they would include the following somewhat overlapping categories:

1. Favoritism: The person who is proposing a scientific claim or theory is a friend (or an enemy), or allied with networks of friends or enemies, or I owe them a favor (or vengeance).
2. Social prejudice: The person is a member of *x* social category external to science, which I either like or dislike. In other words, in the ideal world of science, the person has a "functionally irrelevant status" such as gender, race, ethnicity, religion, nationality, sexuality, and so forth. (Cole 1992: 162).
3. Cognitive cronyism or cognitive particularism: The person is writing outside my area of expertise or outside my research network, so I am inclined to give them less than a fair hearing because I am unfamiliar with their research framework or the network in which they move.[19]
4. Personal gain: I should support or block the person in order to help (or prevent damage to) my career, funding, or reputation, or that of my friends and allies.
5. Reputation: The person occupies what I perceive as *x* position in the social hierarchy of science, according to criteria such as educational credentials, institutional location, fame, awards, and journal prestige.

These and other particularistic criteria for theory choice are part of science. Reputation is complicated because if the reward and gatekeeping systems in science are universalistic and fair, then indices of reputation are not necessarily particularistic. However, most of the empirical research suggests that the reward and gatekeeping systems are not completely universalistic and fair. In a perfect world one would evaluate a scientist with minimum credentials by ignoring indices of reputation such as their institutional location. Because this does not occur in practice, reputation can be classified as at least somewhat particularistic.

These particularistic values can be hard to document because when scientists make public or retrospective statements about their theory choices, they tend to pave over the particularistic criteria with universalistic criteria that correspond more closely to philosophers' "rational" criteria such as Kuhnian values. In other words, they may justify or rationalize their decisions. However, particularistic criteria are more than dirty laundry that tends to remain hidden; they also play an important functional role in science as preliminary screening devices. For example, even though criteria such as reputation may be dismissed as at least potentially ad hominem and particularistic, they are widely used and relatively effective preliminary screening guides. Can we therefore say that particularistic criteria should be included in a list of prescriptive criteria for theory choice? Not necessarily: to make that leap would not only confuse description and prescription but also commit the naturalistic fallacy (things are this way; therefore, they should be this way). Statements about what is the case can be relevant to an attempt to formulate prescriptive rules, but only because they allow one to argue that certain prescriptive options seem unrealistic given our present descriptive accounts of the way things are.

Instead, consider two productive philosophical implications of social science research that suggests that particularistic values, especially cognitive particularism, do play a nontrivial role in the evaluation of research programs, theories, and empirical claims. One argument is that the mixing of particularistic and universalistic criteria in actual science seems not to have harmed science. Stephen Cole takes this position even further by suggesting that a particularistic system may have benefits such as allowing researchers to spend less time writing proposals and providing conditions for more creative work (1992: 203). He argues that cognitive particularism may be ubiquitous and a functional requirement for high productivity in science. Therefore, one of the implications of social science research for a prescriptive philosophy of science is that it might be worthwhile to sort through particularistic criteria to determine whether any of them should be included in a prescriptive list of theory choice criteria, and if so under what circumstances.

A related argument is that even apparently universalistic criteria for theory choice may vary across disciplines and over time. For example, an empirically derived list of universalistic criteria used for evaluating a good theory in late twentieth-century anthropology would not overlap completely (or necessarily at all) with a similar list used for physicists' theory choices in the late nineteenth century. One implication for philosophical projects is that prescriptive criteria might be more useful if pegged to the temporal and disciplinary context of knowledge making and perhaps also to the stage of knowledge production and consumption (laboratory work, paper writing, assessing written fact claims, taking sides in a controversy, and so on). Of course, this argument assumes a widespread disunity of science.

Clearly, the insight of good descriptive accounts from history and the social sciences does not necessarily imply a radical relativism in which anything goes. Rather, these empirical findings can only complicate the prospects of prescription. Conversely, philosophers are right to challenge some of the descriptive accounts in the social studies of knowledge that may have underestimated scientists' use of universalistic criteria, even in controversies.[20] Yet, it seems precipitous to reassert blindly the overwhelming importance of universalistic criteria based on a few counterexamples. If philosophers want to challenge descriptive accounts, they must go and do the research (as in Giere 1988) and suffer evaluation according to the standards of the social studies discipline in which they are working empirically. In general, I would not advocate making a broad statement about whether universalistic or particularistic criteria operate more powerfully throughout the sciences. Rather, I suspect that particularistic criteria operate more powerfully the closer the case is to applied science, economic and political interests, gender- and race-related issues, the research front, and controversies. It seems better to leave the relative role of universalistic and particularistic criteria open to empirical analysis that allows for considerable variation.

In sorting out the problem of the relative role of the two types of values, I prefer the distinction of particularistic versus universalistic over that of cognitive/rational versus social/cultural. These other distinctions are imprecise ways of referring to the extent to which personalistic or particularistic criteria enter into decision-making processes that are supposed to be governed by universalistic criteria. To think of this problem in terms of the cognitive versus social or the rational versus cultural invites confusion. To begin, the opposition between the cognitive or rational on one side and the social or cultural on the other is tenuous. Styles of reasoning cannot be wholly reduced to psychobiological processes of cognition; therefore the pattern of rationality is subject to variation across time and culture. For example, Fuller problematizes the concept of rationality by delineating three major types in Western history: Greek telos, in which reason is inherent in the world; Enlightenment *raison* or *Vernunft,* in which reason is inherent in the world but first has to be released; and modern rationalization, in which reason is not inherent in the world but must be imposed from the outside.[21] Certainly, these three definitions have clear historical and cultural addresses that make a universal claim on the part of one version highly suspect.

Alternatively, if one defines rationality as cognition, it can be considered asocial or acultural only if it refers to universal psychobiological processes that do not vary across cultures. Cognitive processes of this sort exist (such as the ability to acquire language), but there is as yet no widely accepted evidence that these psychobiological cognitive processes are relevant to the problem of the extent to which scientists use particularistic or universalistic criteria in evaluating theories and knowledge claims. Scientists, like everyone else, have access to the same cognitive processes whether they are orienting their action according to particularistic or universalistic values. In other words, it takes reason, cognition, or rationality to make decisions that follow particularistic orientations, just as it does for universalistic orientations. Does this mean that there is no specific type of rationality associated with modern science? Many social scientists would argue that the type of rationality in science is not qualitatively different from that of other specialist occupational groups in advanced capitalist societies. This view seems to be gaining ground among philosophers as well, particularly naturalists who work along cognitive or evolutionary lines. For example, Giere argues for limiting the definition of rationality to the "effective use of appropriate means to achieve desired goals" (1995: 15). My only complaint is that he tends to reduce the adaptation of means in science to the appropriate selection of methods. This may be a good prescription for rationality in science, but descriptively the structure of social action in science involves a wider field of means and ends. Thus, scientists may be acting quite rationally when they employ as means rhetorical strategies, including universalistic ones, for particularistic ends (e.g., using consistency arguments against other theories in order to advance their own careers). Likewise, they could adapt particularistic means and methods to universalistic ends (e.g., diverting funds to do sound research). The assessment of what scientists see as their field of means and ends is an empirical issue, and one that is not easily resolved. I would suggest three guidelines for making this kind of assessment: (1) do not assume that one case study can be generalized to all of science; (2) do not confuse legitimating accounts made in public or in publications with hidden values; and (3) do not accept uncritically claims for universalism in retrospective accounts constructed in memoirs for posterity or in interviews with science studies researchers.

To summarize, the distinction between universalistic versus particularistic value orientations is more clear than categories such as rational (cognitive) versus social. The extent to which universalistic and particularistic values shape scientific decisions is a descriptive problem, and it cannot be resolved by blanket statements designed to cover all cases, disciplines, and time periods. We are still left with the question of whether particularistic criteria should be used as part of prescriptive theory choice criteria. Certainly, Cole has raised an argument in their favor. To answer this problem, we turn to the feminist philosophy of science.

Feminist Epistemologies

Feminists have led the way on the issue of including particularistic criteria in prescriptions for theory choice. One starting point is standpoint epistemologies, which can be viewed as an extension of what I am calling moderate constructivism: they hold that in order to be able "to detect the values and interests that structure scientific institutions, practices, and conceptual schemes," and therefore to move on to better but nevertheless ultimately fallible and culture-bound accounts, one good strategy is to begin research with the perspectives of marginalized groups (Harding 1992: 581; 1986). Of course, in practical terms there are not enough resources to examine the perspectives of all marginalized groups. Even if there were bountiful resources, one would not want to examine the standpoint of every group that has a marginal status. One therefore needs to weigh this particularistic criterion against other ones, such as reputational markers of scientific credentials that would suggest that the arguments of a marginalized group might be of some scientific value. For example, in my research on alternative cancer therapies, I found that there are literally dozens of alternative therapies to consider. One way of using standpoint theory in a limited but coherent way is (1) to select from the field a series of researchers who have relatively good scientific credentials and a published record of empirical research; and (2) within this first category to consider the work of a marginalized network of women researchers (Hess 1997a).

Standpoint epistemologies therefore represent only a starting point in this discussion. "Strong objectivity" represents one way of developing the argument into a more useful program. In Sandra Harding's words, this program would

> specify strategies to detect social assumptions that a) enter research in the identification and conceptualization of scientific problems and the formation of hypotheses about them (the "context of discovery"), b) tend to be shared by observers designated as legitimate ones, and thus are significantly collective, not individual, values and interests, and c) tend to structure the institutions and conceptual schemes of disciplines. These systematic procedures would also be capable of d) distinguishing between those values and interests that block the production of less partial and distorted accounts of nature

and social relations (less "false" ones) and those—such as fairness, honesty, detachment, and, we should add, advancing democracy—that provide resources for it. (1992: 580)

The term "objectivity" here appears to mean the development of representations (theories, models, laws) that capture more of the real or at least the observable, and that project less of the social and cultural, particularly as it appears through biases introduced by unquestioned political or social assumptions (also Porter 1992). In this sense, there is more of the object in the representations, and they can therefore be seen to be more "strongly objective." A related concept is Donna Haraway's situated knowledges, which analyzes theories, theorists, and sciences by giving them a social address or location. "Unmarked knowledges" are those characterized by a presumption of objectivity that usually obfuscates their social embeddedness in white, male, or other dominant cultural perspectives (1991: 111, 188).

The concepts of standpoint epistemologies, strong objectivity, and situated knowledges are valuable starting points for a new prescriptive approach to the problem of theory choice. They are still in the process of being articulated, and they would benefit from more explicit theorization of their limits and of the philosophical claims that they are and are not making. One possible limitation is that standpoint epistemologies may work well only for certain types of sciences. For example, they have already been applied to the social sciences and some areas of the biomedical sciences, where social biases have frequently distorted theorizing and empirical inquiry, but their utility remains to be demonstrated in the exact, physical sciences. They would probably work well in scientific and technical disputes over environmental justice issues. There is little work on the implications of these theories for relatively autonomous fields such as theoretical physics or physical chemistry.

Moreover, standpoint epistemologies and related frameworks need to be embedded in an overall theory of justification if they are to avoid the problem of epistemological relativism. Standpoint epistemologies can be valuable contributions only if they are interpreted to mean that research does not end with the perspectives of marginalized groups. In this sense, a standpoint epistemology amounts to a methodological prescription that is similar to anthropology's cultural relativism: to start with local points of view. Anthropological and standpoint epistemologies are also similar in this respect to Marxist critiques of bourgeois science from a proletarian perspective (Hesse 1994). All three begin their critiques with local or excluded viewpoints, but in the best case their analyses do not stop with those viewpoints. In cultural anthropology this second move is very explicit: analyses still have to be translated into social scientific theory and contested according to the (also contestable) methodological standards of the community of anthropology researchers. Otherwise, the method falls victim to epistemological relativism and becomes incoherent. Stated in these terms, standpoint epistemologies—or better, the more encompassing framework of anthropology's comparative principle of cultural relativism—are one means for achieving new and better scientific theories (something like a stronger form of objectivity, to use Harding's terms). Another means might be simply to work on making scientific communities more diverse socially and wait for the new theories and methods to flow from that diversity. Haraway's studies of primatology (1989) suggest that when women and Asian primatologists entered the field, they led significant reforms that substantially improved the quality of theories, methods, and observations. However, neither cultural comparison nor improved social diversity provides an overall guide to the problem of justification of choices among empirically equivalent theories or research programs.

One coherent formulation of a justification strategy that is friendly to standpoint epistemologies, strong objectivity, and situated knowledges is Helen Longino's six criteria for theory (or research program) choice that she has distilled as implicit in a number of feminist science studies analyses, including those of Harding and Haraway. Longino's criteria are empirical adequacy, novelty, ontological heterogeneity, complexity of relationship, applicability to current human needs, and diffusion of power (1994). Those six criteria are not restricted to gender-based standpoint epistemologies; they could be extended to other dimensions of culture/power exclusion such as class, race, nationality, and sexuality. Thus, they represent a fairly generalized extension and synthesis of feminist contributions to this problem.

First consider the definitions of the criteria. By novelty Longino is thinking of Harding's and Haraway's call for knowledges situated in the standpoints of women and other categories historically excluded from the conversation of science. By ontological heterogeneity Longino refers to (1) a concern with diversity in the object of study, as in Barbara McClintock's attention to the diversity of the kernels of a corn cob (Keller 1985) or women primatologists' attention to diversity within and among primate groups (Haraway 1989); and (2) the rejection of theories of inferiority, that is, theories that see difference as substandard, a deviation, or a failure. By complexity of relationship Longino refers to the rejection of "single-factor causal models for models that incorporate dynamic interaction" (479). Applicability to current human needs implies "improving the material conditions of human life or alleviating some of its misery," and diffusion of power refers to research choices that favor programs that are less limiting in terms of access and participation (479).

Longino's justification criteria can be compared to Kuhn's values of accuracy, simplicity, fruitfulness, consistency, and scope. As in the case of Kuhn, the six criteria are subject to interpretation; Longino also sees them as fallible and therefore subject to revision. I interpret the Longino criteria as complementing rather than displacing a list such as Kuhn's. There is some overlap, as in the call for accuracy and empirical adequacy, which after all remains the key to resolving many differences of opinion in science. Without it, science would simply be politics by the same means. However, in other cases the two lists appear to be in conflict, such as novelty versus consistency and simplicity versus complexity. Comparison of the strengths and weaknesses of the two lists warrants further work.

To begin a discussion of a synthesis, consider the case of Brazilian Spiritism, a religious-philosophical movement whose members insist that it is scientifically grounded (Hess 1991b). Spiritists claim empirical adequacy or accuracy for their observations of phenomena such as poltergeists, hauntings, materializations, apparitions, and correspondences in messages from the same spirit across different mediums. As with any theoretical claim, one could certainly contest the empirical adequacy or accuracy of Spiritists' observational base, but for the sake of the argument let us go on. Two alternative and (let us assume for the sake of argument) evidentially indistinguishable theories could be a skeptical psychology of deception or dissociation and a parapsychology of extrasensory perception and psychokinesis.

Let us consider Kuhn's criteria first. The Spiritist theory is simple; we do not require a maze of psychological processes or a complex unconscious with extrasensory powers. Instead, things are exactly as they seem. Sometimes a *cigano* (gypsy spirit) is just a *cigano*. The theory is fruitful, at least to Spiritists, for they have developed new and different forms of mediumship, from the old Victorian types of psychography (automatic writing) and materialization to the new, Brazilian forms of mediumistic painting and spirit surgery. It seems to be progressive. The theory has a wide scope, and in Brazil I found that the Spiritists applied it to many problems of everyday psychology. For example, spirit intervention can explain good luck and bad luck, disease, mental illness, the ups and downs of love, and any number of issues of great importance in everyday life, including the Weberian problems of ultimate meaning. Finally, the theory is internally consistent; it is encoded in six volumes that lay down the fundamental principles, the negative heuristic. It only fails on the external consistency criterion.

Now let us consider Longino's criteria. The Spiritist theory is novel, or at least it could claim to be novel with respect to the current assumptions of materialism and mechanism that a mainstream psychological theory of deception and dissociation would rely on. To borrow a phrase Harding used to describe an argument of Haraway's, one might claim that the Spiritist theory shows "enthusiastic violation of the founding taboos of Western humanism," at least of secular humanism (1986: 193). The theory is also elaborated in a Third World culture, and women often provide leadership roles in Spiritist centers, so from the standpoint of standpoints it looks like a good candidate to provide a point of comparison for seeking out unrecognized biases in the accepted scientific wisdom. In fact, Spiritists bemoan the materialistic bias of orthodox science, even the "orthodox parapsychology" of the First World. The spirit world is ontologically heterogeneous; there are many types of spirits. There is even some interesting gender-bending in the world of mediums and spirit guides; for example, some of the well-known male mediums are gay. One might argue that the Spiritist theory is weak on the second aspect of ontological heterogeneity criterion, because it describes a hierarchical world in which difference is measured against a standard. However, the form of hierarchy is modern and meritocratic; all spirits are presumed to be equal in terms of their human value and their opportunity to achieve high levels of spiritual development. Thus, the theory would seem to pass the ontological heterogeneity requirement.

On the complexity criterion, the Spiritist theory could be given a pass because it cannot be reduced to single-factor causal models. Spiritists could also argue that their theory does well on the criterion of applicability to current human needs. Millions of Brazilians go to Spiritist centers to receive Spiritist healing treatments. Furthermore, Spiritists see their work and that of the spirits as one of educating, evangelizing, and uplifting their fellow Brazilians, and therefore transforming their country into a successful, developed land. Finally, in terms of diffusion of power, Spiritist mediumship/science does not require access to expensive resources.

Nevertheless, I suspect that most feminist scientists and science studies researchers would probably reject Spiritism out of hand as an alternative research program, theory, or successor science to modern psychology. The "theory" could even be demarcated off the playing field by claiming that it was not a science at all. On one criterion, however, Spiritist science would not pass muster: consistency in the sense of consistency with the rest of science. Spiritist "science" (and I am using the label here only for the sake of argument) is not a peninsula attached to the mainland of science but an island unto itself. Yet, consistency is the very problem that standpoint epistemologies seek to redress. Recall the revisions of the *Frye* ruling and the conservative bias implicit in the consistency criterion. Feyerabend (1978: 35) went even further and argued that a consistency criterion is unreasonable because it preserves the older theory. Certainly from a feminist perspective one is likely to be suspicious of the consistency criterion as a license for androcentrism and other undesirable values.

Kuhn and Longino both make clear that their lists are not complete and are not intended to be so. They merely provide a loose set of guideposts that can aid in the problem of evaluation of the grand theories of science. I have used this admittedly hol(e)y example merely to make the larger point that judgment is necessary even when clearly articulated criteria are available, and even when the criteria involve purportedly better or more equitable values than Kuhn's synthesis. I suspect that no list of lists will be complete, even if the spirits of Campbell, Carnap, Duhem, Kuhn, Popper, Lakatos, and others have continued their dialogues in the metaphysical world and would be willing to communicate their results to us via a Brazilian medium.

Elsewhere I develop and apply a synthesis that brings together the various proposals for prescriptive theory choice criteria that have been considered in this chapter (Hess 1997a). This evaluation draws on four groups of criteria: what I call the positivist, conventionalist, pragmatist, and feminist/antiracist groups. I argue that the best evaluation of a scientific research program (or a major theory)—which is altogether a different matter from the evaluation of a specific scientific observation or generalization—needs to include considerations of accuracy, consistency, social utility, and lower social bias than the alternative. My synthesis of the Kuhn, Longino, and other criteria for theory choice would solve the spirit world problem but still allow some place for the considerations raised by Longino and other feminists.

My synthesis of theory choice criteria implies that each of the philosophical traditions discussed here has its contribution to make, and that no simple formal algorithm can ever be developed for the evaluation of a theory. Like Longino and Kuhn, I would still put accuracy, evidence, or empirical adequacy at the top of the list. There seems to be little disagreement among anyone—natural scientists, social scientists, or philosophers—on this point. Still, the other criteria are useful, particularly in cases of evidential indistinguishability. One can successfully use general guideposts that begin with Kuhn's list but amend it by consideration of subsequent philosophical traditions, particularly pragmatism and feminism, as discussed in this chapter. It is also possible that the list of evaluation criteria may need to be revised as it is applied to different disciplines. My list was developed for a particularly politicized field of medical research, where considerations of social utility and social bias were important. In some of the more autonomous and formalized fields, these criteria may be less important, less evident, or less easy to operationalize as part of an evaluation of a theory. Like all philosophical discussions, this one is by no means closed, and it is part of an ongoing dialogue in which the strengths and weaknesses of alternatives are clarified.

3

The Institutional Sociology of Science

Social scientists who redeveloped the sociology of scientific knowledge (SSK) in the 1970s and 1980s did so in opposition to two other, more established fields: the philosophy of science and the "sociology of science" (or, perhaps more accurately, the institutional sociology of science). From the perspective of the SSK researchers, the institutional sociology of science failed because it did not analyze "content" sociologically. In other words, the traditional sociology of science did not examine how social factors shape or permeate relatively technical questions such as design choices, methodologies, theories, the interpretation of observations, and decisions about what to observe in the first place. Therefore, the sociologists of scientific knowledge tend to view as passé or undertheorized any analyses that focus on institutional aspects of science. This dismissive stance is unfortunate. The institutional sociology of science deserves to be recognized as a dynamic field of its own, and the research of this field needs to be incorporated into any complete, transdisciplinary study of science and technology. At the same time, the interdisciplinary field of science studies may help prod the institutional sociology of science to ask new and different research questions.

There are several reasons why the sociology of scientific knowledge (SSK), as it was formulated in the 1970s and early 1980s, failed to interest and influence significantly the institutional sociology of science.[1] Whereas SSK was largely British and European, the latter was a largely American endeavor. This alone would not have prevented a productive dialogue, but the groups published in different journals. The institutional sociology of science developed from the sociology of occupations, and from this perspective science was seen as another occupation. Sociologists in this tradition tended to view with suspicion the argument that a good sociology of science required an understanding of the content of science, just as, for example, one might argue that an adequate sociology of religion required a deep understanding of religious experience or theology, or a sociology of medicine required a practitioner's level of medical knowledge. In contrast, SSK developed largely in dialogue with the philosophy of science, for which the question of the content of science—especially claims of the unique status of scientific knowledge—was central.

Another factor that accounted for the lack of communication between the SSK researchers and the institutional sociologists of science was that in the United States the sociologists of science were probably more concerned with their internal divisions. One group—the Columbia "school" of Robert Merton, Harriet Zuckerman, Jonathan Cole, and Stephen Cole—had a favorable view of science as a relatively just institution that worked well. Another group—a Wisconsin-Berkeley-Cornell network that included Paul Allison, Randall Collins, Warren Hagstrom, Lowell Hargens, and their students—produced more critical studies of science as an institution with significant gender and race inequalities.[2] The two networks shared a concern with the study of stratification and status attainment issues, and both tended to use the quantitative methods for which the empirical tradition of American sociology is known. However, the differences between them were significant enough that the SSK criticisms were less salient.

Perhaps a more important reason for the lack of dialogue between the American sociologists and the SSK networks was that some of the theoretical arguments raised in the early SSK studies of the 1970s had already been rejected by the American sociologists. For example, the SSK critique of the normative nature of science was already old hat by the 1970s, and the SSK application of interest theory in the late 1970s—as well as the criticisms that followed in the SSK community—had already appeared in American sociology circles in other forms, such as C. Wright Mills's use of interest theory (1959) and criticisms of his work.[3]

Although the analysis of scientific norms had been superseded in the American sociology of science circles by the late 1950s, and in the SSK circles by the early to mid-1970s, it is still a useful starting point for a review of the institutional sociology of science. The distinction between universalism and particularism has continued to provide one theoretical reference point for the stratification studies that characterized the institutional sociology of science from the 1960s to the present.

Furthermore, discussions of norms and values provide a common ground for the range of STS disciplines from philosophy and sociology to anthropology and history. Therefore, a historical appreciation of Merton's contribution provides a helpful background to contemporary discussions, including prescriptive discussions of how science should be organized as an institution.

Norms, Boundary-Work, and Autonomy

The adjective "Mertonian," after the American sociologist Robert Merton, is often used as a general term for what I am calling the "institutional" sociology of science. However, the term "Mertonian" is inadequate because a number of the theoretical assumptions of Merton's original program are no longer accepted, and the sociology of science was more complicated than either Merton or the affiliated Columbia school. To understand Merton's early assumptions about norms and values, it is helpful to back up and examine the historical place of functionalism in social science theory.

Merton was one of the leaders in the development of American functionalist sociology. His teachers at Harvard included Talcott Parsons, who is probably the most influential theoretician of functionalism.[4] In anthropology the corresponding functionalist school was led by Bronislaw Malinowski (1944) and Alfred Radcliffe-Brown (1952), and the versions of functionalism defended by Radcliffe-Brown and Parsons are sometimes called structural-functionalism. Throughout the social sciences in the United States functionalism was widely accepted during the middle decades of the twentieth century. Theoretical roots can be traced to Émile Durkheim's work on solidarity, Max Weber's studies of legitimacy and religion, the nineteenth-century utilitarian philosophers, and in some cases early twentieth-century psychologists and economists. In sociology Parsons's version of functionalism dominated the field for a while (Mullins 1973b). Through his students Parsons influenced work not only in sociology but also in anthropology, even in postfunctionalist forms such as interpretive or symbolic anthropology. For example, Clifford Geertz's influential essay "Deep Play: Notes on the Balinese Cockfight" develops an interpretive analysis of ritual that is organized along the lines of Parsonian functional systems (Geertz 1973).

Parsonian functionalism was explicitly linked to evolutionary theory. Like some other functionalist accounts of society, the task was to explain the problem of order and survival, in other words, what it takes for a society to keep from falling apart, to reproduce itself, and to satisfy the basic requirements of adaptation to the environment of the natural world and of other societies. Parsons's general theory of action was based on four basic functional requirements: pattern maintenance, integration of units, goal-attainment, and adaptation. In human systems, these four functions correspond respectively to the cultural system, the social system, the personality system, and the organism. The functions are organized recursively; thus, within the social system the four functions correspond to the maintenance of institutionalized cultural patterns (as in schools and churches), the societal community (as in kinship and social structure), the polity, and the economy. In turn, the subsystems can be broken down according to the same functions (Parsons 1966).

Merton was not a grand theorist like Parsons; he is known instead for having defended theories of the middle range that were more relevant to empirical research problems. Late in life he also abandoned the label of functionalist analysis in favor of what he called "structural" analysis (Crothers 1987: ch. 4). However, the background on functionalist theory helps in understanding one of Merton's major contributions to the sociology of science: his description of what have come to be known as "Mertonian norms." This description rests on a functionalist account of norms and values in society, and it also entails a modernist vision of science as a self-regulating social system. Although many social theorists do not distinguish between norms and values, Parsons did: values connect the social and cultural systems, whereas norms are primarily social. As Parsons wrote, norms "have regulatory significance for social processes and relationships but do not embody 'principles' which are applicable beyond social organization, or often even a particular social system" (1966: 18). In the essay "The Normative Structure of Science," originally published in 1942 as "Science and Technology in a Democratic Order," Merton describes the ethos of science as a complex of norms and values, with institutional values legitimating norms that are expressed as prescriptions, proscriptions, preferences, and permissions (1973: 268–69). He then distinguishes technical norms—adequate and reliable empirical evidence, logical consistency, and systematic and valid prediction (something like Kuhnian values for theory choice)—from "institutional imperatives." The word "imperatives" seems unnecessarily confusing here; probably he could have used the word "norms" without any loss of meaning. Merton envisioned a complementarity between technical and institutional norms, and this complementarity accounts in part for what Sal Restivo (1994b) has described as the friendly relationship between Merton and Thomas Kuhn.

More generally, Merton's complementarity allowed philosophers to pursue their debates as a separate endeavor from the sociological analysis of functional social norms in science as an institution. These "Mertonian norms" include the following: (1) universalism: truth claims should be subjected to preestablished, impersonal justification criteria that exclude consideration of particularistic criteria such as a scientist's race, nationality, or religion; (2) communism: the findings of science constitute a common heritage to be shared with the whole community, with recognition and esteem the sole property right of scientists; (3) disinterestedness: scientists must subject their work to the rigorous scrutiny of fellow experts and they are ultimately accountable to their peers rather than to lay clientele; and (4) organized skepticism: scientists should engage in the "detached scrutiny of beliefs in terms of empirical and logical criteria" that is free from infection by outside institutions such as religion (Merton 1973: ch. 13). Other norms have been added, such as individualism, and Merton's original formulation has been clarified, but for the present purposes these four basic norms are sufficient (Barber 1952; Zuckerman 1977).

Subsequent research failed to confirm the existence of Mertonian norms, or even their coexistence with a balancing set of counternorms.[5] Although the standard citations in the critique of norms are from the 1970s, the movement away from the analysis of norms began at least as early as 1957, when Merton published his presidential address in the *American Sociological Review* on priorities in scientific discovery. The analysis of norms remained part of his framework, but the address marked a transition toward a concern with the study of the reward system, which in the 1960s became directed toward the analysis of status attainment and stratification.[6] According to Joseph Ben-David (1978: 200), a key publication that marked the transition was Warren Hagstrom's book *The Scientific Community* (1965), which emphasized competition for recognition among scientists in which norms of independence and individualism were more salient than the list of norms Merton outlined. Although Merton continued to write on norms after his 1957 paper, by the early 1960s he had moved away from his original formulation. Instead, he developed the concept of sociological or social ambivalence to describe the situation of contradictory demands that people in general, including scientists, face as a result of conflicts among values, statuses, and roles (Merton 1976).

Support for the existence of generalized norms, not only in scientific cultures but in all cultures, also declined among anthropologists. Led by feminist and postcolonial anthropologists, by the 1980s cultural anthropologists were moving increasingly toward a view of culture as contested rather than integrated and shared. From this perspective any attempt to articulate a shared set of norms or values across a culture seemed increasingly to represent a misinterpretation. Previous outlines of a society's norms and values seemed instead to look more like descriptions of the norms and values of men and the dominant groups.

For decades the consensus among social scientists has been that, as descriptions of the norms that actually guide scientists' action, Merton's norms do not exist in any pervasive form. Particularistic norms and values of all sort play an important part in the de facto evaluation process in science. For example, studies by J. Scott Long, Robert McGinness, and Paul Allison documented that even though predoctoral research productivity is a good predictor of later career productivity, departments pay more attention to where candidates come from and who recommends them (Long et al. 1979; McGinness et al. 1982). It is possible to salvage Merton's delineation of the norms of science, but only as a prescription of how scientists should behave ideally. As an alternative, Mertonian norms might be reinterpreted as a description of the legitimating ideology of science—in Michael Mulkay's terms (1976), the occupational ideology—to which scientists may turn as a rhetorical resource in cases of controversy or boundary-work. In other words, Merton confused the ideology and the practice.

The question of norms and values is related to theories about the autonomy of science. Merton's discussion of norms implied that in democratic countries science is and should be a relatively autonomous institution. In other words, it is and should be free from direct control by the state, the church, private capital, or other interested parties and patrons. As for other topics in science and technology studies, it is helpful to distinguish descriptive and prescriptive claims.

As a description, the argument for the autonomy of science as an institution is based on the understanding of modernity as a process of differentiation. As societies modernize, the various institutional domains (church, state, science, the legal-juridical system, the professions, etc.) achieve bounded but somewhat autonomous authority over limited areas of social life. As a description of science, it is more or less accurate to say that many disciplines of "pure" (as opposed to applied) science became more or less institutionally autonomous in Western democracies, particularly after the nineteenth century. However, the institutional autonomy of science is by no means guaranteed, and scientists have had to defend actively this position. Thomas Gieryn, a student of Merton, developed the idea of "boundary-work" to describe the ways in which scientists establish and police their boundaries and thereby defend their autonomy (1983). He charted out four types of boundary-work: monopolization, as in seventeenth-century natural philosopher Robert Boyle's claim for unique cultural authority for his experimental method; expansion, when insiders "push out the frontiers of their cultural authority into spaces claimed by others"; expulsion, when insiders "expel not real members from their midst"; and protection, when scientists attempt to prevent outside invasion of their resources and privileges (1994: 429–34). I have added to the theory of boundary-work by examining the recursive and graduated divisions across a demilitarized zone between science and nonscience, and I have shown how debates over what is and is not science can be partially shaped by and in turn shape general cultural values (1993).

From a prescriptive perspective, Merton viewed autonomy as a good worth defending in a liberal democracy. He viewed the strong universalism of science as a "dominant guiding principle" of democracy (1973: 273). Likewise, the organized skepticism of science helped provide society with a system of sociocultural checks and balances, by which scientific knowledge could "invalidate particular dogmas of church, economy, or state" (278). Merton wrote at a time when the countercases of Nazi and Soviet science were vivid parts of the contemporary cultural landscape. He was concerned that direct state interference in science could produce distorted and inaccurate accounts of the natural world. By the 1980s and 1990s, the threat to autonomy appeared to come more from private capital and the increasingly permeable boundary between universities and industries such as biotechnology and information technology. In this context, state intervention may actually play a democratic role by providing a mechanism for the public to be involved in setting broad research agendas that reflect general values rather than specific industrial interests. Merton's concern with autonomy therefore remains an important issue today, but it needs to be recast.[7] It is likely that the lasting legacy of the Mertonian analysis of norms will be the often implicit prescriptive aspect of his analysis: the question of what social norms ideally should guide scientists and the question of how different levels of scientific autonomy should be linked to the preservation and strengthening of a democratic society.

Stratification Studies I: Cumulative Advantage Theory

In the 1960s studies of stratification and status attainment in science came to occupy an increasingly prominent place in the institutional sociology of science. Access to new statistical tools and computer analyses helped attract new researchers and propel the field into a growth phase. The term "stratification" will be used here to mean all status differences in the scientific community. Although Pierre Bourdieu (1975) argued that the concept of class should be part of the theory of stratification in science, class has been relatively unimportant in the institutional sociology of science in the United States. Instead, sociologists of science have focused more on questions of status.

Probably the most influential theory in stratification studies is cumulative (sometimes accumulative) advantage theory. The theory holds that early career success tends to allow scientists to accrue recognition and resources that, in an increasing returns pattern mediated by higher productivity, lead to even greater recognition and access to resources. Cumulative advantage and role performance (scientific productivity) constitute the two major determinants of receipt of scientific recognition (Cole 1992: 165). Cumulative advantage theory is important because it provides an instance of apparently nonuniversalistic processes in science as an institution. Stephen Cole summarizes the issue at stake:

> As pointed out in J. R. Cole and S. Cole (1973: 235), because in a completely universalistic reward system quality of role performance should be the sole criterion upon which scientists are rewarded, the operation of accumulative advantage represents a departure from the ideal. Whether such an ideal is "bad" for science depends on the answer to the most important question generated from the study of accumulative advantage: Is this process an outcome of the unequal distribution of talent, which tends to cluster at the prestigious centers, or is "talent" a result of the unequal distribution of resources and facilities (J. R. Cole and S. Cole 1973: 75)? (Cole 1992: 165)

Before examining this issue, it may be helpful to flesh out cumulative advantage theory. It is often equated with the Matthew effect, but the latter is a special case of cumulative advantage theory. Merton coined the term from the biblical passage Matthew 13:12: "For unto every one that hath shall be given, and he shall have abundance: but from him that hath not shall be taken away even that which he hath." As Merton applied the concept to science, "The Matthew effect consists of accruing greater increments of recognition for particular scientific contributions to scientists of considerable reputation and the withholding of such recognition from scientists who have not yet made their mark" (1973: 446). Although this definition focuses on recognition, Merton recognized that resources also tend to flow uphill to the scientists in highly ranked centers (457). Merton further developed the concept by drawing on Zuckerman's research to argue that the Matthew effect appears principally in cases of collaboration and independent multiple discoveries (Merton 1973, 1988). He noted that a corollary of the Matthew effect is that when a highly ranked scientist makes a scientific contribution, it is more likely to be noticed than that of a lesser-ranked scientist (1973: 447).

Related to the Matthew effect is another term that sometimes appears in the literature, the "halo effect" (Crane 1967). This term describes the advantage conferred on a scientist by virtue of having a superior institutional location. Diana Crane (1965) showed that there is a relationship between current academic affiliation and recognition. Her analysis suggested that location in a prestigious department affords new opportunities for visibility and contact that in turn lead to increased recognition.

Margaret Rossiter (1993) comments that the Matthew effect is well named because the Christian disciple did not actually write the gospel for which he is given credit. She argues that Merton's analysis misses the key question of gender in science. She named the parallel but inverse "Matilda effect" after the largely forgotten nineteenth-century writer and editor Matilda Gage. Gage was an American feminist and Bible critic who played an important role in the women's suffrage movement. She also wrote *Woman as Inventor* (1882), in which she argued that the inventor of the cotton gin was a woman. The Matilda effect refers to the tendency in the history of science for women to be ignored or denied credit in their time, and subsequently dropped from historical accounts of recognition. A now notorious example is the case of Rosalind Franklin, whose contribution to the Nobel Prize-winning research on the structure of DNA was ignored and "then further minimized in the survivors' distorted autobiographical account of 'their' discovery" (Rossiter 1993: 329). Consistent with cumulative advantage theory, although in a negative direction, the Matilda effect also points to structural and fairness problems not recognized in the Matthew effect version of the theory. Both effects bolster my argument in the previous chapter for classifying reputation as a particularistic evaluation criterion, an argument supported by some sociologists of science (e.g., McGinness et al. 1982).

Consistent with the Matilda effect, there is a substantial body of research on cumulative disadvantage effects for women in science. In a review essay Mary Fox argues that research on gender and attainment in science grew rapidly after several landmark studies in the mid-1970s.[8] Some of the researchers suggested that gender inequalities were not the product of ascriptive processes or particularistic norms. In other words, women occupy less prestigious positions because they are less productive (Cole 1987). However, the consensus moved in the direction of Barbara Reskin's work, which questioned the extent to which universalistic processes governed status attainment for women scientists (Reskin 1978a, 1978b). In a study of the postdoctoral experience of 450 chemists, Reskin found that in contrast to men "the female chemists accumulated no advantage with respect to postdoctoral experience" (1976: 609). J. Scott Long and Robert McGinness (1985) documented that the mentor plays a key role in initiating the cumulative advantage process, often through collaboration with the student. Long (1990) showed that the mentors of women scientists tend to be less prestigious, less productive, and more often women (three separate variables) than those of male scientists. Similar processes of cumulative disadvantage in science were suggested by studies of race and career success (Pearson 1978).

The research on women, productivity, and status attainment is related to the general finding that the publication productivity of scientists at higher-status institutions is greater, even when one controls for age. This returns us to Cole's basic question. One explanation of the productivity-status correlation is that higher status confers more recognition and resources that lead to higher productivity, but an alternative explanation is that scientists with higher status achieved those positions because they were more productive. Attempts to test the two explanations empirically suggest that institutional location is the cause, rather than the effect, of productivity. Long, Allison, and McGinness (1979) showed that when the prestige of the mentor and the doctoral department are controlled, preemployment productivity has no effect on the prestige of the first job. Even for subsequent moves to new university jobs, Allison and Long (1987) showed that the prestige of the doctoral department and prestige of the prior job continue to play an important role in job attainment. However, publication productivity during the previous six years does have some impact on job attainment, and publication quality (operationalized as quantity of citations that a person receives) does have some impact on attaining raises with the move.

Once employment has been obtained, productivity levels tend to correspond to those of the local environment. Thus, if scientists want to maintain high productivity, they need to be in a major research university or some other environment where there is a norm of high productivity.[9] To the extent that particularistic norms channel women and underrepresented ethnic groups into lower-status positions, cumulative disadvantage processes tend to work against those groups via social position effects on productivity.

Another way in which social position affects productivity is through preferred treatment in the peer review process. In at least some disciplines, scientists with higher social position or status have a better chance of having their publications accepted (Merton 1973: 489; cf. Crane 1967). One well-known study began with a sample of twelve articles by researchers in prestigious American psychology departments. Each article had been published in one of twelve prestigious journals. New names and institutions were added, and the articles were resubmitted to the same twelve journals. Only three of the thirty-eight reviewers and editors detected the articles as resubmissions. Eight of the nine remaining articles were rejected, usually for "serious methodological flaws." The pattern applies to a behavioral science, and a physicist responding to the article claimed that the pattern would not hold for the discipline of physics (Peters and Ceci 1982). However, the study suggests another powerful mechanism whereby those who occupy a disadvantaged social position may have trouble getting out of it.

By definition, cumulative advantage/disadvantage increases with time; therefore, successful senior scientists will tend to reap greater rewards and recognition. Some have also argued that cumulative advantage dynamics also vary across disciplines. This has led to a combination view that cumulative advantage dynamics involve an age-discipline interaction. However, the evidence has not been entirely positive for this auxiliary hypothesis of cumulative advantage theory (Oromaner 1977).

Cumulative advantage/disadvantage dynamics probably also vary across the phases of disciplinary or subfield development. Henry Menard's model (1971) suggests that in fast-growing and relatively young fields ambitious younger scholars may be able to rise more quickly to positions of prominence, whereas in older and more established fields such recognition is likely to be delayed. Lowell Hargens and Diana Felmlee have extended the model as follows:

A higher field growth rate increases seniority-specific citation rates for individual scientists, and it also increases the degree of inequality in the citation rates for the field as a whole. The citation of recent rather than older work reduces such inequality by discounting the older contributions of senior members of a field. (1984: 685)

In other words, there are at least two interacting processes. One is a high growth rate for a field of research, which benefits younger scholars who are among the founders of the field. The other is a low obsolescence rate for the literature. This can be measured by Price's Index, the percentage of references during the preceding five-year period (Price 1963). In general, the index is high in the sciences, because they have a higher rate of obsolescence, than in the social sciences. Thus, at an individual level young researchers will benefit most if they are among the founders of a rapidly growing field with a literature that has a relatively low rate of obsolescence, as in a new social science field. At a structural level, the same factors that benefit a young scholar who is among the founders of a field will contribute to increased inequality in the citation rates for the field as a whole.

By combining the Menard model with research by Reskin and others on negative cumulative advantage dynamics for women, it becomes evident that some social groups may be doubly disadvantaged when they miss out on opportunities to become founders of rapidly growing fields. However, as Rossiter (1987) has argued, rapidly growing fields with a shortage of highly qualified people may be places where women will have a better chance for toleration, employment, and even recognition. There is some empirical evidence to support this hypothesis, but Rossiter also recognizes the limitations of the evidence: "Other factors, such as the vast predominance of men, rigid entrance barriers, availability of government employment, or other peculiarities, prevent the model—which assumes that sexual discrimination is a function of crowding—from working more accurately in all fields" (1987: 40).

In summary, the dynamics of cumulative disadvantage help make sense out of troubling figures such as the relatively stable disparities between women and men in salary and rank, even when controls are included for many possible shaping variables (Fox 1994). Research on status attainment and related issues provides a basis for assessing policy issues such as affirmative action and personnel management. Clearly, cumulative disadvantage dynamics magnify the effects of sexism, racism, and other particularistic values in the institution of science, just as the same dynamics magnify the effects of affirmative action programs. As affirmative action programs have become increasingly unpopular with the electorate, the research suggests alternative ways of improving equality by modifying institutional mechanisms that magnify cumulative disadvantage.

The research also has implications for the general discussions of content. To the extent that particularistic norms govern career attainment and recognition in science, and these norms tend to disfavor women and members of underrepresented ethnic groups, the ability of women and other excluded social groups to play a role in reforming social biases in the content of scientific disciplines will be limited. If women and ethnic minorities are challenging the negative heuristics of a research program and are not protected by powerful mentors, then they are likely to experience very strong Matilda effects. Thus, the research on social position effects and cumulative advantage/disadvantage theory suggests powerful conservative forces in science.

Stratification Studies II: Evaluation

A key mechanism in the maintenance of stratification in science is evaluation. The term "gatekeeper" usually refers to journal editors, following Crane (1967), but Merton and Zuckerman (see Merton 1973) argue that this definition is too restrictive. They suggest instead that gatekeeping would be better understood as a general evaluation process: "continuing or intermittent assessment of the performance of scientists at every stage of their career, from the phase of youthful novice to that of ancient veteran and providing or denying access to opportunities" (Merton 1973: 522). In this interpretation, gatekeeping involves three main functions: evaluating aspirants to new positions, determining the allocation of facilities and rewards, and evaluating publications. Clearly, if young scientists are respected by their mentors, and if the mentors belong to a powerful network and a prestigious department, the young scientists are more likely to benefit from the largess of the gatekeepers (Long and McGinness 1985). There is also evidence to suggest that particularism in scientific gatekeeping extends from network loyalties to clear cases of social prejudice or evaluation by criteria based on "functionally irrelevant" statuses such as race and gender. For example, in one study psychology department chairpersons were asked to rank ten resumes in which male and female names were randomly assigned, and most chairpersons ranked the male as the associate and the female as the assistant professor (Fidell 1975).

However, gatekeeping also works through less overtly particularistic mechanisms. The previous chapter introduced the concept of cognitive cronyism, that is, a form of bias that involves similarities of intellectual style or assumptions rather than merely network affiliation, institutional location, or social discrimination. This form of gatekeeping is more complex because gatekeepers may think of their assessments as objective and universalistic, whereas those who are rejected may see the assessments as the biased products of the views held by hegemonic networks.

Most research on acceptance rate differentials has examined variation across disciplines. The general consensus is that there are consistently higher rejection rates in the social science journals. In Zuckerman and Merton's words, "The more humanistically oriented the journal, the higher the rate of rejecting manuscripts for publication; the more experimentally and observationally oriented, with an emphasis on rigor of observation and analysis, the lower the rate of rejection" (Merton 1973: 472). There is less consensus on why there is an acceptance rate differential across disciplines. One theory holds that articles in the humanities and social sciences tend to be discursive and therefore take up more space. Using longitudinal data, Hargens (1988b) challenged the space shortage explanation and developed instead a model that attributed the lower rejection rates in the natural sciences to their higher level of consensus. Cole, Simon, and Cole (1988) argue that at the research front all fields have equivalently low levels of consensus, and therefore other variables would explain better the variation in acceptance rates across disciplines. These other variables include field-specific publication norms, variation in the diffuseness of journal structures across fields, and differences in training practices (also Cole 1992). Hargens's reply provides a number of reasons why these arguments are not convincing, and he concludes, "Perhaps a future study should examine the probability that a published paper will provoke a critical comment as a possible measure of scholarly consensus" (1988a: 160), thus reflexively using the lack of agreement on explanations of the acceptance rate differential as evidence for his consensus-variation hypothesis.

Sociologists have also worked out other aspects of acceptance rate differentials. Zuckerman and Merton suggest that in fields such as physics there may be an age effect in acceptance rate differentials, with a decline in the acceptance rate as age increases (Merton 1973: 489). Race and gender also play a role in acceptance rate differentials, even if one looks beyond overtly particularistic cases of sexism and racism, such as rejection of articles simply because of the sex or race of the writer. The more subtle mechanism works as follows: there is an unequal distribution of social groups in terms of gender, race, and so forth across age, professorial rank, and discipline such that historically excluded groups are more concentrated in the lower-status institutions and ranks, and the humanities and some of the social and biological sciences. Given this unequal distribution of position, acceptance rate differentials will tend to operate negatively for the historically excluded groups because of structural factors even when overtly particularistic criteria are not operating.

An additional dimension to gatekeeping is historical. Rossiter argues that women had entered the workforce and science in increasing numbers during the last decades of the nineteenth century. During the 1880s and 1890s science became increasingly professionalized, and Rossiter suggests that "ejecting women in the name of 'higher standards' was one way to reassert strongly the male dominance over the burgeoning feminine presence" (1982: xvii). In some well-known historical cases successful women have resorted to family finances or developed a "sexless," androgynous persona (Rose 1987: 278; also Abir-Am 1987). These strategies suggest the power of institutional sexism in science. Even today, when the number of women graduate students in some disciplines is roughly equivalent to that of men, women tend not to achieve positions of prestige. In medicine in the United States, 40 percent of the students are women, but women constitute only 20 percent of the physicians, 5 percent of department heads, and 3 percent of medical school deans (Angier 1995). In science and engineering fields, the proportion of women full professors rose only from 4 percent to 7 percent during the fifteen-year period following 1973 (Fox 1994: 212).

Given the success at moving official evaluation functions (such as university admissions) in more egalitarian directions, but the failure to maintain successful starting percentages, attention has turned from formal mechanisms of gatekeeping (admission, journal submissions, and career evaluation) to its informal mechanisms. One example is the role of machista technical cultures that require heroic laboratory schedules, particularly during peak childbearing years (Angier 1995). This leads to the question of marriage, childbearing, and productivity, a topic that overlaps with two fields: cumulative advantage theory and productivity studies.

General Productivity Studies

Although cumulative advantage and status attainment studies often involve productivity measures, the productivity of individual scientists in their career paths can be distinguished from the general productivity of specific types of social units in science, such as age groups, cohorts, sexes, and laboratories. Given the immediate managerial uses for research on general productivity and innovation, these studies tend to be more interdisciplinary than stratification studies.

One prominent area of productivity studies involves age effects. These effects are of increasing concern given the aging structure of the workforce (both scientific and general) in the United States and other developed capitalist nations. Researchers have generally concluded that scientists' major contributions occur in their late thirties and early forties. Contributions probably occur earlier in abstract disciplines such as math and physics and later in empirical ones such as geology and biology. Some findings suggest a second peak at age fifty; others suggest a gradual rise to the early forties and then a decline.

However, as Edward Hackett (1994) warns, the empirical research that underlies these generalizations may suffer from measurement artifacts. For example, productivity has been measured by the midpoint date when Nobel Prize research was performed, rather than when it was published; another option would have been to use a measure of variance to cover the length of research. Furthermore, he notes that the decline after peak productivity tends to be moderate and therefore may not have policy significance. I would add that given the fact that of the 131 scientists who have won the Nobel Prize during the 1970s and 1980s only four have been women, the measurement choice does not speak to the problem of productivity age effects for women in science. Furthermore, Nobel Prize winners may not be representative of the scientific research population as a whole on the issue of an age peak in productivity.

The age effect in productivity is also complicated by several other effects in scientific productivity studies. The cohort effect suggests that the oldest cohort (roughly the oldest generation) shows a decline over age forty, whereas the younger ones merely level off. Furthermore, it is not clear how the age effect in productivity interacts as a whole with the cumulative advantage/disadvantage dynamics.[10]

Another well-known finding is the sex effect for productivity: as indicated above, women tend to publish fewer articles than men. Long's study

(1992) of biochemists showed that men tend to produce more than women during the early stages of their career, but the effect is reversed after the first decade. The overall pattern of lower productivity for women is due to their overrepresentation among nonpublishers and their underrepresentation among the extremely productive. However, the quality of work by women scientists can be interpreted as higher even though the gross number of citations is lower; this is because women receive more citations per article than men.

What explains the sex effect for productivity? One common but probably erroneous explanation is marriage and children. Fox cautions against hasty acceptance of the conventional wisdom that "good scientists are either men with wives or women without husbands and children" (1994: 219). Although there are some well-known cases that fit the image, marriage and presence of children do not correlate directly with publication productivity. In the study of biochemists, Long found that the effect of children on productivity is much greater for predoctoral publication productivity for women than for men; however, the initial negative effect of children on productivity declines for both men and women, and it is gone for both groups by year eleven (1990: 1311). Long also showed that both marriage and children have no direct effect on productivity when their effect on collaboration with the mentor has been controlled (1310). Rather, as variables marriage and children have their effect through collaboration. Reskin (1978b) suggested that the relationship between women graduate students and male advisors tends to be more hierarchical than the parallel male-male relationship. Although Long found that both women and men in his sample collaborate with their mentors at the same rate, the patterns of collaboration are different. For women, marriage doubles the odds of collaboration with a mentor (Long 1990: 1306). Of women scientists' mentors who are male, nearly 90 percent feel that they are limiting the appearance of a nonprofessional, romantic liaison when their women students are married (1307). Having children has the opposite effect from marriage: for women, "each additional child under six decreases the odds of collaborating by a factor of .50" (1306).

In other words, the effect of marriage and children on productivity works mainly through collaboration with the mentor. In turn, collaboration and a number of other differences that are relatively small by quantitative measures—such as less selective baccalaureate institutions and less prestigious doctoral departments—add up to contribute to an overall negative effect on women's achievement and productivity (Long 1990). Through

cumulative disadvantage dynamics, these small initial effects may be enough to explain the overall difference in productivity between men and women.

In addition to age, cohort, and sex, the size of the research group has an effect on productivity.[11] Rikard Stankiewicz (1979) developed a set of four logical hypotheses, extended here to five possible research group size effects: a constant effect, in which productivity remains constant over research group size; a negative effect, in which productivity decreases with size; a positive effect, in which productivity increases with size; a critical-size effect, in which there is a jump in productivity above a certain size; and an optimum-size effect, in which productivity peaks at a certain size. Karin Knorr et al. (1979) found a negative size effect, but Stankiewicz found that productivity increases with size in groups with high cohesiveness and high group-leader research experience. In groups with low cohesiveness, there is a decline in productivity for groups larger than seven scientists, and in groups with low leader experience the relationship between size and productivity is weak. Group age effects (age of research group since it was formed) are strong in groups with low cohesiveness and highly involved leaders.

Subsequent research by J. E. Cohen (1980, 1981) found a constant effect: the marginal productivity of an additional member is constant across laboratory sizes. Cohen (1981: 482–83) argues that the constant effect he found is consistent with the results of Stankiewicz (1979) and other researchers. Hackett's research (1995) has mostly replicated Cohen's finding, although his data suggest a slight increase in per capita productivity as laboratory size increases. Because of the important funding policy implications of the research, the Cohen-Hackett effect may not be the last word on the research group size effect, and continual refinements of the complex and perhaps contradictory results are needed.

Productivity studies have clear implications for all sorts of managerial issues: the debate over lifetime tenure in the academy, incentives for movement into administration, parental leave policies, voluntary separation packages, and so on. For example, if scientists in some fields have their peak years of creativity before midlife, how does this affect the problem of achieving gender equity when these are also the years when childbearing takes place? (In a world in which two-career families are common and men often have a substantial role in child rearing, this question is relevant to the entire scientific workforce, not only women.) Another question involves the cumulative disadvantage theory and the findings of status attainment studies for race and gender. Research in this area suggests that women and

historically excluded ethnic groups would have lower access to large research groups. Can research group size be one area for intervention in making scientific institutions more equitable? To answer this, one would need more research on whether research group size effects vary by gender. It is now known that there is an interaction between an individual age effect and the research group's age (Stankiewicz 1979). Thus, it is possible that research group size effects may interact with gender as well. One sees how complicated the research problems are, but also how applicable the research can be.

The Distribution of Innovation and Productivity

Related to productivity studies is research on the distribution of innovation and productivity. This area includes a number of not very well documented hypotheses as well as some fairly robust empirical laws. For example, the question of simultaneous discovery or invention has received some attention. Under the Kroeber-Merton hypothesis, simultaneity occurs when a common intellectual culture does not correspond to shared social communication.[12] Although frequently mentioned, the Kroeber-Merton hypothesis should probably be put in the less documented category, because simultaneous discoveries also occur in the communication-dense world of biomedical research, where laboratories often compete against each other at breakneck speed.

Of more interest to researchers, probably because the area has policy implications, is the question of who produces greater innovations. The marginality hypothesis of Gieryn and Richard Hirsch (1983, 1984) holds that major contributions tend to come from marginalized scientists, presumably because they have less at stake in existing theories (cf. Simonton 1984). Wiebe Bijker (1987) criticizes the marginality concepts of Gieryn and Hirsch because they are one-dimensional. "For example," Bijker writes, "in one study scientists are considered marginal if they recently migrated from another field, whereas in another study 'marginal' is operationalized as 'being young' " (1987: 174). In a discussion oriented toward technology studies but equally applicable to science studies, Bijker proposes instead the concept of inclusion in a technological frame. A technological frame is similar to a paradigm in that it consists of goals, problem-solving strategies, experimental skills, and theoretical training (174). Thus, the extent to which a researcher is included in a technological frame is multidi-

mensional. Bijker's study of innovation in plastics research suggests that researchers with a low inclusion in the existing frame—that is, those who are not highly committed to it or absorbed in it—and a high inclusion in an alternative frame may tend to be innovators.

Bijker's proposal has some similarities to the older role- and idea-hybrid-ization hypothesis: innovators tend to be scientists who come from other disciplines and draw on ideas from other disciplines (Ben-David 1960). This hypothesis applies well to a number of important innovations in twentieth-century science. For example, physicists and physical ideas played a key role in the origins of molecular biology.

The policy problem is that all of these hypotheses do not provide much insight into deciding which marginal scientists or cross-disciplinary researchers should be supported as potential innovators. Clearly, it would be a waste of limited funds to invest in all marginalized scientists or all discipline-crossers. More research is needed to specify which scientists within these categories tend to be the innovators.

Another area of research relevant to innovation involves the general sentiment that older scientists tend to be rigid and less receptive to novelty. Max Planck (1949) may have first articulated this hypothesis, but it was popularized in Kuhn's theory that paradigms change as the older generation retires or dies off (1970). Empirical research on an age effect in receptivity to novelty is mixed. The first studies suggested that younger scientists tend to cite more recent work than do older scientists, with Nobel laureates excepted (Merton 1973: 514). However, subsequent research suggests that the young and old alike may be more resistant to new ideas, while those in between are less so. Furthermore, so many other variables complicate the picture that it is difficult to determine the effect of age.[13]

Two other hypotheses in this general area are the Ortega and Newton hypotheses. The Ortega hypothesis holds that average or mediocre scientists contribute substantially to the advancement of science. This hypothesis is sometimes contrasted with the Newton hypothesis that great scientists "stand on the shoulders of giants." Of course, the two hypotheses could be reconciled if one defines the advancement of science in two ways: incre-mental (Ortega) and revolutionary (Newton). Some empirical protocols have failed to support the Ortega hypothesis, and these failures have led to calls to reduce the size of science.[14]

Derek de Solla Price, a leading figure in the development of quantitative science studies, suggested another approach to the problem of innovation, a theory of instrumentalities. According to Susan Cozzens, an instrumentality is "a laboratory method for doing something to nature or to the data in hand" (1988: 370). Price argued that developments in this area often brought about major innovations in scientific knowledge and theory (1986: ch. 13). Therefore, from a policy perspective instrumentalities are good candidates for investment. In some universities, faculty may feel the agony of a version of this perspective as it plays out in administrative funding decisions that favor investments in technology over faculty salaries and development.

Price also developed a more robust measure for the distribution of productivity across scientists. Sometimes described as a geometric way of measuring elitism, Price's law is only one of the many patterns discussed in *Little Science, Big Science* (1963). Price's law holds that "half of the scientific papers [in a given research field] are contributed by the square root of the total number of scientific authors" (Allison et al. 1976: 270). In slightly different wording, the "square root of n authors produce half of the papers made by the total of n authors" (Egghe 1987). This figure suggests that in a given research field the bulk of productivity (usually measured by article publications) will tend to be concentrated in a small number of scientists.

Price's law is similar to the older Lotka's law, which holds that the number of authors who produce n papers is inversely proportional to n^2. The law was introduced by Alfred Lotka in 1926 and has gone through subsequent reformulations.[15] The law has also been shown to apply across gender but with a greater skew among women in favor of high producers (Fox 1994).

Bradford's law (or distribution) is to journals what Price's law and Lotka's law are for scientific productivity. This measure represents the pattern of unequal references across journals in a bibliography (Burrell 1991). L. O. Nordstrom defines Bradford's law as follows: "For a search on a specific topic, a large number of the relevant articles will be concentrated in a small number of journal titles" (1990). Bradford's verbal and graphical formulations are mathematically different. The Bradford distribution or law and the Price/Lotka laws have applications in the development of citation indices as well as in library management. For example, the *Science Citation Index* has only one-fifteenth of the source papers but over three-fourths of the cited literature (Price 1986: 257). Likewise, when universities hand out their annual budget cuts, librarians can use Bradford's law to figure out where the cuts will be least painful.

Price's law and Lotka's law are not necessarily in conflict with the Ortega hypothesis. The Ortega hypothesis is about distribution of contribution and Price's law is about the distribution of productivity. However, if contribution is understood as innovation and if innovation is concentrated among the high producers, then Price's law may have similar policy implications to the failures to confirm the Ortega hypothesis. In other words, both may suggest that managers should reduce the size of science and focus investments on the high producers, who one would hope would include some Newtons.

Of course, this strategy raises equity issues in light of the research on cumulative advantage. Furthermore, if the marginality hypothesis turns out to have some basis, then focusing investments on the Newtons or Pricean high producers might only reinforce the status quo and lead to minor innovations. Likewise, if libraries use the Bradford distribution to mitigate cuts, and if high-producing journals are skewed away from women and other historically excluded groups, budget cuts could also further contribute to elitism in science. These are only a few of the questions left unanswered by the current state of research on the distribution of innovation and productivity in science.

Specialty Studies

Another important area of the institutional sociology of science is the study of social units beyond formal organizations such as laboratories, disciplines, departments, and research organizations. In the 1960s the topic began to receive sustained attention when Price extended Boyle's seventeenth-century term "invisible college" to refer to informal groups of scientists who work on similar problems. In Price's words, an invisible college is "a sort of commuting circuit of institutions, research centers, and summer schools giving [scientists] an opportunity to meet piecemeal, so that over an interval of a few years everybody who is anybody has worked with everyone else in the same category" (1963: 85). In the book of the same title, Crane (1972) refers to invisible colleges as "communication networks" and uses "social circle" and "solidarity group" as roughly equivalent terms (also Chubin 1983). The concept of invisible colleges was important for STS research in subsequent decades because it was a forerunner of research on clusters and networks in both the sociology of science and the sociology of scientific knowledge.

From the 1960s to the 1980s an increasing number of "specialty studies" revealed the small-group nature of science, that is, organization via networks or invisible colleges rather than large collectivities of individuals such as disciplines. Based on an analysis of the origins of experimental psychology, Ben-David and Randall Collins (1966) presented a model that drew on role- and idea-hybridization. In their case study, higher-status scientists (physiologists) left their home discipline to colonize a less competitive and lower-status field (philosophy) that had more opportunities. The process of specialty formation involved the three stages of forerunners, founders, and followers.

An alternative, three-phase model of research specialty formation was developed by the Starnberg group. This research group coalesced in Starnberg, West Germany, during the 1970s at the short-lived Max Planck Institute for the Study of the Conditions of Life in the Scientific-Technical World, which was headed by Carl Friedrich von Weizsäcker and Jürgen Habermas.[16] The group is known in the Anglophone literature for having developed a three-stage model of the development of scientific fields that drew on Kuhn's and Lakatos's work. The three phases were an exploratory, pre-theoretical fact-finding phase with no definite theoretical or methodological program; a paradigmatic phase in which a theoretical program comes to organize a field; and a post-paradigmatic phase of normal science. When the third stage of theoretical maturity was achieved, the scientific field was said to have reached finalization. The finalization thesis held "that in the course of its development a science (discipline, or field of knowledge) reaches a state of maturity as a result of which it can be said to have completed its work" (Schäfer 1983: 131). The concept of finalized science was meant to describe an alternative to the traditional category of applied research (Böhme et al. 1976: 308). At this stage, state or private capital could guide scientific development with more success. External interference could also guide the first phase, but the Starnberg group held that such interference was not justified during the second phase, for which they prescribed autonomy (Schäfer 1983: 162).

The Starnberg model had the advantage of making studies of specialty formation relevant to science policy issues, but its heavy reliance on Kuhn resulted in an underanalysis of the role of social relations in specialty formation. Nicholas Mullins (1972, 1973b) probably contributed more to solving this problem than any of the other specialty studies researchers. He found that the Ben-David and Collins model did not apply well to his case studies of molecular biology and subfields in American sociology. Mullins came up with an alternative, four-stage model of paradigm groups or normal science, communication network, cluster, and specialty or discipline. In the case of molecular biology, the first stage involved a loose group of scientists, including physicists, who were interested in studying phage (viruses that kill bacteria) as a way of solving the problem of genetic information transmission (Mullins 1972). At the communication network stage, there was increased connection among the scientists working on the problem and a corresponding decrease in independent persons. At the cluster stage, the scientists became more self-conscious about their patterns of communication, and they tended to spend time together in places such as Cold Spring Harbor. A shared lifestyle among mentors and students— such as the camping trips led by Max Delbrück at California Institute of Technology—helped foster group solidarity. At the specialty stage, the field emerged as a recognized discipline, with meetings, journals, training institutions, and a formal organization. Thus, Mullins delineated the phase of development from the phage group to the subfield of molecular biology.

In a subsequent study David Edge and Michael Mulkay (1976) found that neither the Ben-David/Collins nor the Mullins model worked for their case study of the emergence of radio astronomy. In turn, they developed fifteen dimensions of similarity and difference that drew on their own work on radio astronomy as well as the results of Ben-David and Collins, Mullins, and other specialty studies researchers. The problem of coming up with a simple model to cover a wide variety of cases of specialty formation seems to have been abandoned, although Mullins's work probably has had the most lasting influence. There are many possible reasons for the loss of interest in the question of specialty formation. Among them are the failure to come up with a single model that transported easily to a variety of case studies; the emergence of alternative research questions with the switch in attention to the study of controversies in the Edinburgh and Bath school studies and with the emergence of laboratory studies; and the quantitative solution to the analysis of specialty formation that emerged with cocitation analysis in the 1970s.

Citation Studies and Bibliometrics

Scientometrics is the quantitative study of science, communication in science, and science policy. Founding leadership is attributed to Price and to Maurice Goldsmith of the Science of Science Foundation. The institutional sociology of science is not identical with scientometrics, because the former includes qualitative methods and the latter includes disciplinary orientations other than sociology. For example, the background of Price and some of the other founding figures of scientometrics was in the natural sciences or library/information sciences rather than the social sciences. Scientometrics can also be distinguished from bibliometrics, the measurement of patterns in written communication (Broadus 1987). Bibliometrics is not restricted to scientific communication, and scientometrics is not restricted to bibliometric measures. The more general term "science indicators" is used to describe "measures of changes in aspects of science," generally used for policy making (Elkana et al. 1978: 3).

Many of the studies previously discussed can be considered examples of scientometrics and/or bibliometrics. One area not yet discussed where influential forms of analysis have been developed is citation and cocitation analysis. Citation analysis is the quantitative analysis of research patterns and productivity based on research referenced in publications, usually articles. In the United States Price (1963) together with Eugene Garfield (1955) and the Institute for Scientific Information (ISI) are often given credit as founding figures and locations for the field. An early form of citation analysis was bibliographic coupling, that is, counting the number of references that a given pair of documents have in common. Later, cocitation analysis was developed as an alternative based on authors' citing of two documents in one article. In other words, cocitation is the number of times a given pair of documents is cited together by other documents (Small and Griffith 1974; Griffith et al. 1974). The frequency of cocitation is a measure of association for the number of times two documents are cited together in the same papers. Clusters generated by this type of analysis are believed to reflect research networks or specialties. As a policy tool, cocitation analysis can catalog and chronicle newly emerging subfields and national research strengths. By pointing to emerging strengths and weaknesses, the analysis provides a tool to help decisions about funding.

Citation studies have also delineated an "immediacy effect," the pattern whereby recent publications are cited more frequently than older ones (Price 1986: 164). Like Andy Warhol's fifteen minutes of fame, scientific publications also get a limited time in the spotlight. In Price's terms, "Over the SCI *[Science Citation Index]* literature the rate for recent references is a halving in number with every five years of age of references" (1986: 165). In other words, the immediacy effect can be operationalized as the citation half-life of a paper. The number of citations for most papers declines in a nonlinear way, such that the citations tend to die out at an increasingly rapid rate. Anyone who has published a paper has noticed, perhaps with chagrin, the tendency for it to disappear from the cited literature. Subsequently the concept of an immediacy effect was extended with graphs of citation life cycles that plotted a publication's received citations against time (Cano and Lind 1991). One measure of the immediacy effect (although not limited to it) is the previously defined Price's Index, the percentage of references during the preceding five-year period. This index can measure an individual paper or it can be used on a macro level to evaluate a journal, field, or institution (Price 1986: 166).

The concept of a research front makes sense of the immediacy effect. A research front is contrasted with the general archive, or the older body of references in a field, such as those more than five years old. As new research is added, the research front moves forward and older studies fall into the archive. Price estimates that the research front generally consists of about fifty papers, after which "some sort of packing down production of a review paper or summary seems to be necessary, but perhaps that, too, varies from field to field" (1986: 178). Merton and Zuckerman argue that past contributions are "obliterated" as they are "incorporated" into recent research. This process occurs more clearly in the highly codified fields of the "hard" sciences (Merton 1973: 508). The concept of obliteration by incorporation is parallel to the SSK theory of fact construction, such as the deletion of modalities in the scheme of Bruno Latour and Steve Woolgar (1986).

The immediacy effect—the pattern whereby recent publications are cited more frequently than older ones—varies across disciplines, which have different rates at which the research front is packed down. For example, in physics and the biomedical sciences the citation half-life of a paper is a steeper figure (about every three years), and in some fields it has become steeper over time. An exception to the immediacy effect is that some publications escape obliteration by incorporation and become citation classics. These are very highly cited papers and books that become more highly cited over the years in a positive feedback pattern (Cano and Lind 1991). Often, citation classics are of a methodological nature.

Another complicated finding in the citation studies literature is the multiple authorship effect, that is, the finding that there is an increase in multiple authors over time and that the number of multiple authors is also increasing (Price 1986: 78–79). The increasing need to collaborate emerges from the ever more complex laboratory technologies and the grant structure (123). Price also argues that "part of the social function of collaboration is that it is a method for squeezing papers out of the rather large population of people who have less than a whole paper in them" (128). Fractional productivity is an indicator proposed to solve this complication by assigning

> $1/n$ of a point for the occurrence of [an author's] name among n authors on the byline of a single paper. Thus a man with one paper of which he is the sole author, a second of which he is one of two authors, and a third in which he is one of five, will have a fractional productivity of 1.7 and a full productivity of 3 papers. (127)

Although Price appears to have solved the problem of fractional productivity, adjusted and unadjusted measures for productivity may turn out not to be very different. Furthermore, fractional productivity measures may not capture the productivity elisions of "salami science." In other words, some scientists are skilled at "fractionating data from a single study into several articles," that is, chopping up their research into multiple reports (Chubin 1990: 151). This strategy can falsely inflate estimates of their productivity.[17] In the opposite direction, as Merton notes, outstanding scientists sometimes place a value on publishing a low quantity of high-quality papers (1973: 455). Thus, the gross number of publications is not always the best measure of an individual's productivity; one must also take into account quality, which is usually operationalized as the number of citations per publication.

A number of extensions of or criticisms of citation analysis have emerged. An example of an extension is block-modeling, the scientometric analysis of clusters or networks of research "not on the basis of their choice for one another but in terms of their choices of third parties or persons not in their common block" (Lenoir 1979: 463). In contrast with cocitation analysis, block-modeling "groups individuals together on the basis of the perception of significant others rather than on the basis of mutual awareness" (463). Timothy Lenoir argues that block-modeling can be used together with cocitation analysis to give a more accurate picture of subfield development. Whereas cocitation analysis gives a year-by-year picture, block-modeling treats citation links as a network in a literature over time.

Block-modeling and cocitation analyses are two forms of network analysis as it has been developed in the quantitative tradition of American sociology. Hargens (1978) traces the development of network analysis in the institutional sociology of science to the sociometry tradition that dates back to the 1930s and to the research on invisible colleges and specialty formation in the 1960s. During the 1960s sociologists who attempted to apply sociometric techniques to science met with two technical limitations: the methods could be applied only to groups of fewer than two hundred members and they could not be used to analyze several different sociometric ties simultaneously. Citation and later cocitation analysis provided a solution to these limitations; thus, cocitation analysis may be seen as one outcome of the research tradition on invisible colleges and specialties. Nevertheless, as Hargens cautions, cocitation analyses provide a limited amount of structural information about the authors of the texts, and thus this type of analysis needs to be supplemented with data on other types of ties among the authors (1978: 130).

The concept of a network in this literature should not be confused with that in actor-network theory (described in the next chapter), which nonetheless owes some historical debt to the antecedent research on invisible colleges and specialties. Actor-network theorists have developed a criticism of citation/cocitation analysis by arguing that it embodies the assumptions of the institutional sociology of science because it focuses on social relations and networks as suggested by citation patterns. In contrast, the actor-network theorists developed an alternative analysis that they believe focuses more on the question of the "content" of science rather than its social relations or institutional side. Their proposal is to develop a scientometric analysis of cowords (Callon, Law, and Rip 1986; Rip and Courtial 1984). Cowords are co-occurring key words, usually a description of a document that appears in an abstract, title, or key word listing. Coword analysis is used to describe a network of interactions in science, and therefore it does not privilege human actors in quite the same way that citation analysis may do (Callon, Courtial, and Laville 1991).

From yet another angle, Diana Hicks (1987, 1988) has questioned the utility of citation studies for policy analysis. She argues that overreliance on these studies may lead to policy errors (cf. Franklin 1988). Hicks and Jonathan Potter (1991) have also developed a Foucauldian critique of citation analysis as a mechanism that may lead to self-regulation of scientists. Indeed, I am tempted to posit a "scientometric deautonomizing effect": as the tools of scientometric monitoring of science increase, so does the watchful eye of governmental and local management, and the "degradation of mental labor" (to use Sal Restivo's application of Harry Braverman's phrase) increases as the institutional autonomy of scientists decreases.

Nevertheless, there are also ways to tweak scientometric research toward policy issues other than those concerned with productivity from a managerial and policy perspective. For example, the analysis of cocitation clusters points to new networks, but it also points to those interesting people who are way off in the margins of an *x-y* axis. Can cocitation analysis be used as a tool for exploring better the political economy of citations? Can it be used to locate potential innovators who are marginalized from existing citation networks? Likewise, the phenomenon of packing down a research front warrants unpacking. Who does the packing and who decides what gets obliterated, what gets incorporated, and what papers get spurred toward citation classic status? Thus, in what way do the processes of packing down contribute to the maintenance of powerful and perhaps gendered/raced networks in science? Does the multiple authorship effect operate in ways that permit the Matthews of science to have a greater opportunity to slice their salamis in a way that gives them a greater number of single-authored papers and a higher fractional productivity? These and other questions are examples of the ways in which institutional studies of science promise to continue to provide important insights into the mechanisms of power in science. This research base should serve as a valuable resource for other branches of STS as they formulate descriptions of and prescriptions for science.

4

Social Studies of Knowledge

The Sociology of Scientific Knowledge

The sociology of scientific knowledge (SSK, sometimes also called social studies of knowledge or the new sociology of science) focuses on the content of science. "Content" refers to theories, methods, design choices, and other technical aspects of science and technology, in contrast with institutional or contextual aspects such as those reviewed in the previous chapter. Karin Knorr-Cetina and Michael Mulkay use the term "methodological internalism" to describe the focus on content or the study of how "the 'internal' practices of the scientific enterprise constitute the focus of inquiry" (1983: 6). Their choice of terminology, however, may be confused with the internalism/externalism debate in the history of science, and it has not been widely used.

Sometimes the study of content is described as "opening the black box" (Whitley 1972). In science a black box is any device for which the input and output are specified but the internal mechanisms are not. SSK advocates have accused the institutional sociology of science of leaving the black box of content unopened and examining only the exogenous, institutional aspects of science and technology. Opening the black box and studying the content of science sociologically has been very controversial. From a philosophical perspective, some SSK analyses are philosophically incoherent and mired in epistemological relativism. From a critical science and technology studies perspective, the content of the sociology of scientific knowledge is itself a black box that needs to be examined. For example, in the essay "Upon Opening the Black Box and Finding It Empty" (1993), Langdon Winner argues that the sociology of scientific knowledge failed to explore the political content inside the black box. This issue is taken up better by the feminist and critical wings of STS, which, I argue, open red, pink, purple, brown, and other kinds of boxes. Those studies will be considered in the next chapter.

One way of characterizing the social study of the content of science and technology is with the rubric "constructivism." In a very wide sense, the term can designate any social studies approach that attempts to trace the way in which social interests, values, history, actions, institutions, networks, and so on shape, influence, structure, cause, explain, inform, characterize, or coconstitute the content of science and technology. Note that this very general definition of constructivism does not necessarily imply any of the relativisms discussed in chapter 2. One can analyze the social factors that influence the content of scientific knowledge or technological design and yet also conclude that the constraints of observations or efficacy (the real world) play an equal or greater shaping role in what eventually becomes the consensus.

As I have argued in chapter 2, it is possible to distinguish conservative, moderate, and radical forms of constructivism in the context of philosophical debates over relativism. In the context of social studies of science and technology, however, I will suggest another set of distinguishing terms: social constructivism, heterogeneous constructivism, and cultural constructivism. The terms represent three analytical frameworks for empirical social studies of the relationship between the social world and the content of science and technology. The two axes of constructivism—philosophical and social studies—do not map onto each other in a simple way. Instead one might think of the three types of philosophical constructivism and the three types of social studies constructivism as an x and a y axis, with a variety of combinations possible.

For those who are more attuned to the sociology of scientific knowledge, the term "social constructivism" is sometimes restricted to the laboratory studies and perhaps a few other branches of SSK. This definition implies that some branches of SSK, such as the Edinburgh school interests analyses, are excluded from the term "social constructivism." However, because the Edinburgh school studies attempted to delineate lines of causality from class and professional interests to the content of science understood as sides of a controversy, they were concerned with the social construction of knowledge. I therefore use the term "social constructivism" more broadly to refer to studies that treat the social world as an exogenous, independent variable that shapes or causes some aspects of the content of science and technology. A variety of SSK frameworks therefore would fall under the banner of "social constructivism." Social constructivism, particularly some of the laboratory studies, is sometimes associated with epistemological and ontological relativism. Nevertheless, it would be possible to adopt a social constructivist framework for empirical research and also to accept a philosophical position other than radical constructivism.

Social constructivism defined as such can be distinguished from a more general type of constructivism, what I will call "heterogeneous constructivism," which is usually associated with actor-network theory. This position holds that the content of science and technology is constructed along with the social relations and structures in the wider society. In other words, content and context coconstitute or mutually shape each other in a pattern that is sometimes called a seamless web. Unlike social constructivism, which focuses on the arrow of causality from context to content, this second type of constructivism also examines the opposite direction of causality, whereby technoscientific changes and networks shape and constitute new forms of social relationships. This second position is sometimes called constructivism (that is, without the word "social"), but because I use the term "constructivism" as a family term for the entire range of constructivisms, I suggest the more appropriate label "heterogeneous constructivism." The term "heterogeneous" refers to the mixtures of social and nonsocial elements in the construction process. Note that this framework for empirical analysis can be more easily approximated to moderate or even conservative constructivism as a philosophical position.

Yet another type of constructivism is what I have called "cultural constructivism" (Hess 1995). This framework for empirical research interprets the cultural meaning and cultural politics of different scientific theories, observations, and methods through an analytic framework derived from theories in semiotics, feminism, and cultural anthropology. By beginning with the question of meaning from the actors' points of view, cultural constructivism departs from the instrumentalist rationality (practical reason) that is frequently assumed in accounts of social and heterogeneous constructivism. Rather than view technoscientific actors as motivated merely by power, status, or some other utilitarian goal, it sees them as suspended in webs of meaning that structure the possibilities of their action. Cultural analysis reveals the structures of the webs of meaning in which they act. Clearly, this type of analysis, which is explicated more in the next chapter, is complementary to the others and can be used along with them. This framework can also be linked to a variety of philosophical positions; my own preference is realistic or moderate constructivism.

Constructivist narratives of the history of science studies depict a transition from the Mertonian sociology of science to the sociology of scientific knowledge. As can be seen from the previous chapter, this narrative is not accurate because the institutional sociology of science is larger than the "Mertonian" sociology of science. Furthermore, the field had already undergone a shift in the direction of stratification studies prior to the advent of SSK, and the institutional sociology of science continued on its own trajectory well after the formation and development of SSK. It is better to think of the institutional sociology of science and the sociology of scientific knowledge as two parallel research traditions, rather than viewing SSK as a paradigm shift that replaced the institutional sociology of science with a new sociology of science. There is a long tradition in the sociology of scientific knowledge that dates back to the studies of the 1920s and 1930s by Ludwik Fleck (1979), Borris Hessen (1971), and Karl Mannheim (1952), and on to other social theorists prior to them. Furthermore, specialty studies and conflict sociology, which were also formulated by the 1970s, addressed issues of content as well. Narratives of a dramatic "scientific revolution" in the sociology of science during the 1970s therefore warrant some skepticism.

The work of the British researchers Michael Mulkay, Harry Collins, Barry Barnes, and David Bloor during the 1970s is usually flagged as the starting point of the contemporary period of the sociology of scientific knowledge. Rhetorically, the key theoretical concepts of the field were positioned against two Others: the naive realist/positivist philosopher and the naive Mertonian sociologist. As we have seen from the previous chapters, both the philosophy of science and the institutional sociology of science are diverse and sophisticated fields of inquiry, and the philosophers and institutional sociologists generally reacted negatively to the innovations and claims of the SSK researchers. Although the critique of Mertonian norms tended to go unanswered (for reasons discussed in the previous chapter), the critique of the failure of American sociology of science to develop a sociology of knowledge did draw some responses. One reply from the Mertonian camp has been the argument that if general attributes of science such as empiricism and experimentalism are regarded as content, then Merton did address content in some essays. For example, in "The Other Merton Thesis" Harriet Zuckerman (1989) argues that Merton's early work on Protestantism and science anticipated constructivism in his discussion of shifts of foci of inquiry and problems within and among sciences.

By the 1990s there had been several developments beyond the sociology of scientific knowledge, so that SSK had come to occupy a rearguard position. A major factor was the explosion of feminist, anthropological, and cultural studies of science and technology, which often began with SSK insights but moved beyond the concerns of the SSK analysts. The second was the turn to technology, policy, the environment, and public understanding of science issues as the original leaders of the SSK movement branched out into other research areas and came to be less interested in philosophical issues. Nevertheless, the arguments, concepts, and empirical research produced in the SSK field remained a major influence into the 1990s. They are an important part of the theoretical landscape that deserves to be appreciated, critiqued, and incorporated into transdisciplinary theoretical efforts.

Conflict Theory

An early approach to the sociology of scientific knowledge, and one that rarely received due credit in internalist SSK narratives of their field, focused on the construction of scientific theories as outcomes of agnostic relationships among scientists. The leading theoreticians of conflict sociology of science have been Randall Collins (1975) and Sal Restivo (e.g., 1983, 1994b). Collins distinguished four types of roles for intellectuals and scientists: political, practical, leisure entertainment, and teaching (1975: 482). From this sociology of positionality (to use a term more current today), he suggested a number of patterns, such as "The more that intellectuals occupy political positions in the state or church, the more that their intellectual productions consist of arguments over value judgments and policies," or "The more that teachers are situated in a large community of teachers and students which is relatively autonomous from outside control, the more likely they are to emphasize knowledge as general principles, or values in themselves" (520–21). As in the case of specialty studies, this research anticipated actor-network theory in some fairly precise ways, such as the following:

> The ideas that are able to sustain the most effective alliance are the ones that will be considered the firmest "knowledge"; the longest-lasting paradigm is one which serves to bind together an internal organization of the intellectual community with a hold on long-lasting material resources to support scientific investigation, communication, and careers. (505)

Conflict sociology shares with Marxism and feminism a concern with the analysis of power in science and the role of the social scientist as a critic of the outcomes of scientific conflicts, two concerns that were absent from most versions of constructivism. Daryl Chubin and Restivo (1983) formulated the "weak program" in response to the SSK endorsement of the ideal of value-neutral social science. The idea of a "weak" program was a reference to the weak force in physics, which is actually stronger than the strong force. Restivo (1988) and Restivo and Julia Loughlin (1987) later developed this perspective as a critical, profeminist, conflict sociology, pointing to the importance of feminist science studies that had emerged in the 1980s but that went largely ignored by most of the constructivist research programs.[1] There were also similarities between the critical sociology of the weak program and critical approaches that were emerging in anthropology, such as the project of anthropology as cultural critique and the emergence of feminist studies of reproductive science and technology.[2] Restivo has also been responsible for maintaining some recognition of, and interest in, the comparative sociology of Joseph Needham (Restivo 1979). Thus, conflict sociology supported many of the developments of feminist, anthropological, and critical perspectives in STS during the 1980s and 1990s that eventually came to challenge and displace SSK. Conflict sociology therefore occupied an important position as an alternative to the dominant research programs that were emerging in the sociology of scientific knowledge.

The Strong Program

In the mid-1970s, a group of researchers in Edinburgh developed some of the founding documents in the new sociology of scientific knowledge. The group included David Bloor, Barry Barnes, David Edge, and Donald MacKenzie. A highly influential framework that emerged from this group was Bloor's strong program, which he presented in 1976 in his book *Knowledge and Social Imagery*. The basic tenets of the strong program in the sociology of scientific knowledge were as follows: (1) causality: social studies of science would explain beliefs or states of knowledge; (2) impartiality: SSK would be impartial with respect to truth or falsity, rationality or irrationality, or success or failure of knowledge (and, presumably, technology); (3) symmetry: the same types of cause would explain true and false beliefs (in other words, one would not explain "true" science by referring it to nature and "false" science by referring it to society); (4) reflexivity: the same explanations that apply to science would also apply to the social studies of science. Each of those principles has subsequently been elaborated and/or criticized.

Although the causality principle has drawn probably the least criticism and discussion, the growth of anthropology and cultural studies in the 1990s has led to a more complex understanding of causality. A standard way of understanding causality in social science is to identify variables that shape or influence other variables, such as showing how class position may shape technical positions in the case of public controversies. However, it is also possible to think of technical positions as systems of meaning that can be interpreted through comparison with other systems of meaning or cultural codes, as in anthropological and cultural studies in the semiotic tradition. This type of analysis is acausal in the sense that the meaning of a text (or social action) does not "cause" the existence of the text or social action in any simple, Humean manner. However, interpretive/semiotic analyses are causal in other senses. For example, general cultural codes or systems of meaning have a causal relationship to texts and action just as linguistic structures "cause" the range of possibilities of speech. Furthermore, systems of cultural meaning implicit in scientific representations and practices can contribute to their success or failure. Thus, cultural constructivism helps clarify the causality principle as subject to a range of applications and meanings.

The impartiality and symmetry principles are the heart of the strong program. Of the two, probably the symmetry principle was the most important as well as the most controversial philosophically. I have already considered the philosophical problem of epistemological relativism that emerges from some interpretations of the symmetry principle, and I have discussed ways out of the problem through some type of realistic or moderate constructivism. Notwithstanding its philosophical problems, the symmetry principle has been enormously productive in the social studies of science. Wiebe Bijker (1993), following Steve Woolgar (1992), characterized the intellectual history of the social studies of science in terms of progressive extensions of the symmetry principle: from Merton's symmetry between science and other social institutions to Bloor's symmetry in the treatment of true and false knowledge to later developments that argue for symmetry between science and technology, the analyst and analyzed, humans and machines, and the social and the technical.

Although the impartiality and symmetry principles opened up some analytical possibilities, they foreclosed others. The weak program provided probably the first sociologically oriented critique of the assumption of value-neutrality that impartiality and symmetry suggested (Chubin and Restivo 1983). In general, the activist-oriented side of the STS community has found the impartiality and symmetry principles wanting. Furthermore, discussions led by Brian Martin and colleagues have analyzed the implications of writing an ostensibly neutral social science account of a controversy. They reveal two key aspects of what has become known as the capturing problem:

1. an epistemologically symmetrical analysis of a controversy is almost always more useful to the side with less scientific credibility or cognitive authority;
2. the side with fewer scientifically or socially credentialed resources is more likely to attempt to enroll the researcher (Scott, Richards, and Martin 1990; Martin 1997a).

In other words, in cases of controversy neutral analyses in the strong program tradition will tend to be captured, usually by the out-group. I noticed this effect in my own neutral account of the differences among skeptics, parapsychologists, and New Agers (Hess 1993), although in a reverse way: notwithstanding my clear articulation of a fourth voice (that of the social scientist), skeptics such as Carl Sagan tended to dismiss my analysis as pro-occultist. The claim struck me as bizarre, but it was consistent with the analyses of Martin and colleagues. In subsequent work, I adopted a more engaged framework for science studies analyses (Hess 1997b). If the parties of the controversy are going to read a neutral study as interested, it seems better simply to state clearly one's preferences.

The fourth principle, reflexivity, refers to social scientists' attempts to grapple with the constructed nature of their own research and theories. One approach was to flag awareness of the constructed nature of one's representations through textual devices. The new literary forms of SSK involved playful interruptions in narrative authority. For example, authors use the secondary voice device to construct a countervoice that interrupts and questions their own arguments (Woolgar, ed. 1988). This form is parallel to moves in anthropology's new ethnography of the 1980s to incorporate informant voices into ethnography by recording the anthropologist/informant dialogue or by granting large blocks of text to informants (Clifford and Marcus 1986; Marcus and Fischer 1986). The technique, as is sometimes forgotten, was pioneered in anthropology by women and feminists with knowledge-power considerations guiding its development, and it differs from that of the reflexivists' secondary voice device by giving room to other people, rather than to imagined Others. However, both techniques are subject to authorial manipulation and therefore self-legitimation, and furthermore readers often find the interruption of the authorial narrative by other voices to be an irritating nuisance. For these and other reasons, extensive use of secondary voices supplied either by the author or by informants has been of waning interest.

Another textual strategy for approaching reflexivity has been the use of the tu quoque argument, one of the many informal fallacies recognized by philosophers. This argument could be regarded as another example of the secondary voice device, except that the author remains unaware of the secondary voice and the analyst uncovers it, often to the author's chagrin. Common to deconstructionists and reflexivists, this type of analysis finds an inconsistency in the author's position (or scientific consensus), thus pointing to the interpretive flexibility of texts and the secondary voices implicit in an apparently univocal argument. Although tu quoque argumentation can be used merely to defeat an opponent, it is also useful in feminist and other critical analyses that wish to find an alternative, "supplementary" voice that has been marginalized in the account under study.[3]

An alternative approach to reflexivity has been to examine the author and Other as socially positioned actors. Under this approach reflexive commentary is directed not at the individual relationship between author and informant but instead at the author's social group(s) or analytical discursive community in relation to those described. I have developed this approach to reflexivity elsewhere in my studies that discuss how the groups in question—for example, Brazilian Spiritists—understand and appropriate social sciences such as anthropology (Hess 1991a, 1993). Woolgar (1996) has also moved in this direction in his subsequent work on reflexivity and the role of evaluation in academic institutions. The transition from "reflexive" to "positioned" accounts, led especially by feminists such as Donna Haraway (1991) and Emily Martin (1987), has become a general tendency among many science studies analysts, and it informs one alternative to the strong program that is outlined at the end of this book.

Interests Analysis

One empirical research tradition that was associated with the strong program and especially popular during the late 1970s was the analysis of scientific controversies from the perspective of interests. Barnes, MacKenzie, and other researchers affiliated with the "Edinburgh school" launched this empirical research tradition (Barnes 1977; Barnes and Shapin 1979). In the interdisciplinary STS context, "interests" is another multivocal term that requires some unpacking. According to classical Marxism, some sciences (e.g., nineteenth-century political economy) encode in a technical language the values and ideology of a class (e.g., the capitalist class). One therefore speaks of the influence or expression of class interests. Marx claimed that the two variables were related causally: bourgeois class interests had some degree of causal influence over the technical content of the standard, nineteenth-century science of political economy. (The difficulty lies in demonstrating how much influence class has in contrast with other shaping variables, including "internal" variables, such as disciplinary methodologies and observations, which themselves in turn may be socially shaped to some degree.) Marx's class analysis of interests is encapsulated in his "law" that the ruling ideas of the day are the ideas of the ruling class. In subsequent studies, the analysis of interests has been expanded very widely. First, nineteenth-century political economy is seen as the easy case, and Marx's realism on other issues suggests that his philosophical position was close to what I am calling conservative constructivism. Other scholars have subsequently argued that class interests shape a wide variety of other sciences, not simply a nineteenth-century "pseudoscience." Second, it is possible to analyze other types of interest in science other than class, for example, the interests of men in preserving patriarchal social institutions.

In addition to this expanded view of interests, one sometimes encounters a distinction between cognitive or technical interests on the one side, and social interests such as class or profession on the other side. This distinction is problematic because of the Mertonian assumptions that may underlie a discussion of purely cognitive interests. A second classification of interests appears in the post-Marxist critical theory of Jürgen Habermas (1972), who divided sciences into those with an interest in (1) technical prediction and control, as in the natural sciences and some managerial sciences; (2) communicative understanding, as in the humanities; and (3) emancipation, as in Western Marxism. However, this division across disciplines by interest is workable only if reinterpreted to apply to the ways in which all three types of interest can operate simultaneously in any single scientific discipline. In a third classification of interests, Restivo distinguishes between social interests and attributed interests:

Social interests are material or symbolic resources thought to be relevant to group survival and necessary for gaining, sustaining, or advancing advantages in relative power, privilege, and prestige. Attributed interests are social interests thought to be relevant to and necessary for a group's survival and relative power by outsiders, and may be more or less congruent with insider views. Interest attribution is itself a form of social interest. (1983)

Returning now to the simple case of class interests and the origin of controversies, a well-known example is the analysis of statistical controversies in early twentieth-century Britain. Barnes and MacKenzie (1979) used this case study material as an exemplar of the interests analysis that came to be associated with the Edinburgh school (also MacKenzie 1983). One statistical controversy involved Karl Pearson's correlation statistic r_T versus the Q statistic of his former student George Yule. Pearson's statistic assumed that a division of data into two categories (such as tall and short people) could be modeled as an arbitrary division in a normal distribution, that is, a bell-shaped curve. In other words, if one knew the height of every individual, one could plot the heights against the number of people with each height. I sometimes perform this exercise in classrooms and it usually provides a roughly bell-shaped curve. In contrast, Yule did not like to assume that there was an underlying normal distribution for the kind of data with which he worked. In the case of a population that has been exposed to smallpox, there are only two alternatives: dead or alive. Today this type of data is known as nominal data, and the controversy has been resolved by a pluralistic view that allows either statistic to be used depending on the type of data. In some cases, Pearson was right that nominal data can be interpreted as a higher form of data.

MacKenzie and Barnes analyze the difference between Pearson and Yule as more than an individual disagreement and more than a question of a technical interest in developing the best statistics. The Pearson group was associated with the biometric and eugenic laboratories of University College London, whereas Yule's following was more in the Royal Statistical Society. MacKenzie then argues that in a general way the different networks were linked to conflicts between the professional class and the established upper class. Pearson was an advocate of eugenics and Fabian socialism, both of which were programs that were seen to benefit the professional class, whereas Yule was a conservative aristocrat with no interest in eugenics. Thus, in a general way, MacKenzie claims that the background of class conflict shaped this statistics controversy.

The Edinburgh framework of interests analysis fell out of favor for a number of reasons. One major reason involves the imputation problem. Barnes described the imputation problem as "whether and how thought or belief can be attributed to social classes, or other formations, as the consequences of their particular interests" (1977: 45). His and MacKenzie's analyses of the statistics controversies were an attempt to provide a solution to the imputation problem for the sociology of science. However, various critics argued that the interests studies still suffered from the imputation problem. It was not clear how macrosociologial class interests were transformed into the microsociological accounts of the motivations that shape the action of individuals. Although the critics may have exaggerated the causal claims that MacKenzie, Barnes, and others were making, in general there was a sense that interest-based analyses risked turning scientists and other technical actors into "interest dopes" (a term borrowed from ethnomethodologist Harold Garfinkel). In other words, scientists were reduced to rather flat, puppetlike characters who were shaped by exogenous interests rather than a complex set of contingencies and motivations. Although Barnes and MacKenzie provided responses to the criticisms in this complex set of exchanges, the controversy weakened the appeal of interests analyses in SSK circles.[4]

One alternative to the Edinburgh interests analysis that maintains interests as part of the analytical framework involves, in a sense, turning the Barnes and MacKenzie analysis on its head. This alternative shows how interests can be a consequence rather than a cause of scientists' action. Actor-network theory, which will be considered in more detail shortly, examines the translation of concerns of other networks (including those involving nonscientists) into one's own interests (e.g., Callon and Law 1982). In other words, "I have a theory, technique, or technology here that will help you accomplish your goals, but you need to help me in order for me to share it with you." The analysis of the production of interests has proven very useful for an understanding of how technologies and scientific theories can succeed and fail. After the debates over the imputation problem in the Edinburgh approach to controversies, studies of interests have tended to switch from the problem of how exogenous interests shape social action to how technoscientific actors produce interested supporters. This change of focus, however, is an overcompensation, because in many cases— especially science controversies with a high public profile—it is still useful to invoke class, financial, organizational, gender, professional, and other exogenous interests as preexisting variables that constrain and structure the emergence and closure of controversies. Although the imputation problem emerges in the fine-grained analysis of controversies, interests clearly shape the overall patterns of scientific funding and research priorities.

A second alternative is to drop a claim of direct causal influence between, for example, class interests and two positions in a theoretical controversy, and instead to analyze the two domains as congruent or parallel cultural codes that share a similar structure. The advantage of this approach is that it also allows a more complex interpretation of scientific controversies. In other words, one might ask, "What did the difference between Yule's Q and Pearson's r_T mean to the different researchers?" This question may lead to general issues such as eugenics and class conflict, but it is likely that these issues will also be overlaid with other cultural differences. In other words, the controversy may turn out to have many meanings to the researchers, and class-related issues may be among them. Beyond the meaning to the researchers, there may be homologies in the cultural codes of statistics and class relations that an analyst may uncover by finding a third code to which the first two mutually translate. The cultural approach therefore provides an alternative way of exploring the relationship between macrosociological divisions (class, race, gender, etc.) and the content of science (two theories, etc.) where the imputation problem makes statements of direct causal relationship unconvincing. However, the cultural approach can be complementary to the analysis of interests and content as causally related variables; indeed, the two forms of analysis may work best when used together (Hess 1997: ch. 3).

Although both the actor-network and the cultural approach provide useful alternative frameworks for the analysis of interests, there is still a place for the causal relationships that Barnes and MacKenzie wished to draw between interests and technical positions in a scientific controversy. Harry Collins (1983) outlined one extension of interests analysis by showing the possible role of interests in the closure of a controversy rather than its origins. For example, in the debate over gravity waves, one side had access only to the minimal resources of a university department, whereas the other side had access to the resources of a large industrial company. The side with access to the industrial resources also favored the conservative position that would not throw industrial science into a state of chaos. Collins suggests that, if the empirical material is correct, this case would exemplify how industrial interests played some role in the closure of the debate by providing unequal access to resources.

Another example is the study of cancer research, where various sorts of economic and professional interests have shaped scientific research agendas in ways that can be documented with relatively little controversy. Robert Proctor's *Cancer Wars* (1995) aptly demonstrates the role of interests in shaping research agendas on carcinogens, especially when industries have a financial interest in confusing the public and causing the government to fail to enact regulations. In this case, rather than shape closure, interested parties purposely produce disinformation or destabilize a scientific research consensus in order to defuse regulatory or class action pressures. Proctor borrowed "Gibson's law" from public relations research and introduced the term "smokescreen effect" as two important techniques for inducing controversy to promote interests. Gibson's law refers to the truism, popularized in courtroom dramas that use opposing sets of expert witnesses, that "for every Ph.D. there is an equal and opposite Ph.D." The smokescreen effect refers to "the effort to tie up scientific traffic with true but trivial work, to draw attention away from what is really going on" (1995: 10–11). The analysis of interests needs more theoretical work along these lines, that is, directed toward obviously interested science in public controversies, rather than more theoretical work that frets over the imputation problem for cases of academic controversy in relatively autonomous fields of research (Hess 1997a).

The Bath School, Replication, and Controversies

A second major approach to the sociology of scientific knowledge is known as the "Bath school." The so-called Bath school was really only one person, Harry Collins, although it also included his former students Trevor Pinch and David Travis. Unlike the Edinburgh school interests analyses, which tended to focus on macrosociological interests and use historical methods, the Bath school studies focused on microsociological processes and used observational methods. However, both the Edinburgh and Bath studies examined controversies, probably because it was easier to demonstrate the social shaping of science when it enters phases of sharp internal division. Both also were empirical research traditions that were consistent with the strong program.

Collins viewed scientific controversies as neither normal science nor a scientific revolution, to use Kuhn's terms (1970). In other words, controversies represent a phase in which scientists and other actors "try to make major changes in what is taken for granted without reforming the whole structure" (Collins 1983: 93–94). Collins's empirical program of relativism

(EPOR) has three stages: (1) demonstrating the "interpretive flexibility" of experimental results, that is, their ability to be subject to more than one interpretation; (2) analyzing the mechanisms by which closure is achieved; and (3) linking the mechanisms of closure to the wider social structure. The third stage was only sketched out for the gravity waves case, as discussed above. To understand the mechanisms of closure in the second stage, Collins focused on the "core set" of experts and laboratories. The concept of a core set is one example of a network concept in SSK. However, Collins's core set is less heterogeneous than the understanding of networks in actor-network theory because it is human-centered, and furthermore the core set involves a temporary network of conflicting individuals and networks rather than a growing, large network of allies and enrolled parties.

Pinch and Bijker (1987) extended the EPOR program to technology studies in their formulation of the social construction of technology program (SCOT). They follow more or less the same stages as Collins's EPOR, but they replace some of the terms. For example, the term "relevant social group" replaces the term "core set," and "stabilization" of a technology replaces the "closure" of a scientific controversy. Their example involves the stabilization of design in the history of the bicycle. In the late nineteenth century a number of designs were available, and they meant different things to different groups (interpretive flexibility). These groups were concerned with different features of the design, such as safety, speed, and vibration. Eventually, the modern form with two wheels of equivalent size and balloon tires emerged as the stable design that met most of the concerns of the relevant groups (stabilization). As in Collins's studies, the third stage of the analysis—linking closure or stabilization to the wider social structure—remains relatively undeveloped.

Collins and Pinch (1979) also distinguished the constitutive forum—which includes theorizing, experimenting, and publishing—from the contingent forum, which includes joining professional organizations, recruiting new members, gossiping, and discussing scientific ideas in popular journals and settings. This distinction is more or less a version of content versus context. They use this distinction to question the view that action in the constitutive forum is purely rational and not subject to contingent or social factors. Thus, they contribute to criticisms of the distinction between the contexts of discovery and justification, as well as descriptive accounts of evaluation and theory choice in science that assume only Mertonian norms or Kuhnlike universalistic values.

One of the Bath school's best-known contributions to the analysis of controversies is the demonstration of the ambiguity of replication. If one asks scientists how a controversy should be resolved, they will probably say through replication. Presumably a good experiment would provide an impersonal solution to sometimes bitter controversies. Much of the appeal of science, including social science, is that we think of evidence as playing a significant role in the resolution of controversies. Collins's sociological analysis of replication is therefore important because it challenges a simplistic model of replication as a purely algorithmic process that could resolve controversies in an asocial way. Collins's ideal-typical algorithmic model of replication has six stages: (1) reject all activities that have nothing to do with replication; (2) reject all activities that are not experiments; (3) reject all remaining experiments in which the identity of the experimenter is inappropriate; (4) reject all remaining experiments that were not competent copies of the experiment that is being replicated; (5) divide the remaining set into those that generated negative results and those that generated positive results; and (6) decide whether the experiment has been replicated (Collins 1985). Although this algorithm sounds rather simple—something that could be fleshed out, codified, and written up as a set of bureaucratic standard operating procedures or as a computer program—Collins argued that in practice replication decisions depend on a number of nonformal issues that cannot be reduced to formal rules. He advocated an alternative, "enculturational" model to describe more accurately the ways in which replicating an experiment required informal knowledge, craftlike technical skills, and interpretation. For example, he found that in the case of an attempt to replicate a laser technology, those who were successful usually had the benefit of informal, personal communication.

Collins introduced the term "experimenter's regress" for a problem that emerges in controversies over replication. Consider two groups of people in a core set: the advocates of a given empirical claim and the critics. Advocates can always argue that a failure to replicate an experiment is because the replication was an incompetent copy of the original design and protocol. Likewise, critics can argue that the same experiment is a competent copy of the original design and protocol, and therefore it constitutes evidence that the original claim is false. Collins suggests that to solve the dispute over the replication design as a competent copy, one needs to know whether the original claim is true or false, but that is what the replication is intended to settle. One could perform another experiment to solve the problem, but as in the philosophical problem of induction, a negative result would still not prove that the original claim was false. The controversy could begin anew over the new experiment.

Collins argues that because experimental ability is a skill-like knowledge that cannot be reduced to an algorithm, it is always possible to disagree about which experiments constitute competent copies. Therefore, "Some 'nonscientific' tactics must be employed because the resources of experiment alone are not sufficient" (1985: 143). The descriptive claim that nonscientific factors play some causal role in the resolution of a controversy seems commonsensical. One might hypothesize that in most cases a mixture of evidence and nonevidential (social) factors plays a role in the resolution of scientific controversies; the mix of how much one side or the other influenced the outcome would vary from case to case. This view would be consistent with the constructive realism position outlined in chapter 2. However, Collins goes on to make a second, stronger argument.

In the case of a controversy over the existence of measurable gravity waves, Collins acknowledges the weight of a string of negative experiments that served to isolate the principal advocate (1985: 92–96). However, the critics themselves were not all in agreement, and many found design flaws in each of the experiments of other critics. As a result, the controversy had not yet achieved closure. Then a leader of the critics emerged who crystallized the critical mass of opinion in the core set against the proponent. This leader's experiment was not particularly well designed, but he presented a careful data analysis and a strong argument that the original claim was spurious. The group associated with the leader of the critics also circulated a paper on pathological science. The leader stated, "If we had written an ordinary paper, that just said we had a look and we didn't find [it], it would have just sunk without trace" (1985: 95). Collins suggests that the evidence is important but not determining; instead, nonevidential factors such as strong rhetoric and the circulation of the paper on pathological science were necessary to crystallize consensus.

One might even accept this second argument as far as it goes: in some cases, nonevidential factors play a determining role in the resolution of controversies, or at least in the timing of the resolution. However, Collins takes this second argument even further by generalizing it. In the conclusions to his study on replication, Collins extends his position to a strong claim of epistemological relativism. He suggests that he has found a sociological solution to the problem of induction, that is, the problem of justification for deductively invalid inferences (inferences from experimental data to general laws). Once the core set agrees on whether or not the phenomena exist, then the controversy is closed. "It is not the regularity of the world that imposes itself on our senses but the regularity of our institutionalized beliefs that imposes itself on the world" (1985: 148).

One might be inclined to dismiss this second argument as an inconsistency, but Collins makes it over and over again in his published work. For example, he argues that his framework extends the symmetry principle of the strong program as follows: "One implication of symmetry is that the natural world must be treated as though it did not affect our version of it" (1983: 88). In another essay, he describes his version of relativism as the "prescription to treat the objects in the natural world as though our beliefs about them are not caused by their existence" (Collins 1994a: 294–95). Furthermore, Collins presents a Rorschachlike drawing of "reality," which suggests that the EPOR framework assumes a highly plastic natural world (Collins 1983). As philosophers have pointed out, the EPOR framework is asymmetrical in that the social world is apparently more real, more structured, and more causally efficacious in the resolution of controversies than the natural world (Hull 1988: 4–5).

Thus, whereas Collins's first argument—that social factors or tactics play a role in the closure of some or even all controversies—is a good corrective to naive views of science as guided by purely Mertonian norms, his second argument is very problematic because it crosses over into epistemological relativism. One can see the problem by applying it reflexively to Collins's own claims. A number of studies by other social scientists claim to have replicated his claims that the resources of the experiment alone are not sufficient to resolve a controversy. However, those studies in turn raise a reflexivity issue regarding the status of a replication of a finding that problematizes replication (Ashmore 1989; Collins 1994b). One is back to the issue of prescription: how should one justify a claim that replication has been achieved?

When Collins argues that he has found a sociological solution to the problem of induction, he confuses description and prescription. Even if one were to accept Collins's argument as a valid description of how a few, some, or even all replication controversies are resolved, he does not answer the question of how they should be resolved. The problem of induction as a prescriptive problem remains unsolved, unless he is interpreted to mean that nonevidential factors should be used to resolve controversies over replication. I suggest that a prescriptive solution to the experimenter's regress—and one that may turn out to describe the closure of many controversies—is that it should be resolved by an iterative process of successive elimination of design flaws. In other words, advocates interpret a failed replication as incompetent, and the core set faces the experimenter's regress. However, the advocates outline the purported design flaws, and the experiment is performed again with the design flaws corrected. Of course, advocates may argue that a new failure has new design flaws, but the infinite regress is more like a mathematical limit that converges on a real number of either one or zero. A continued string of corrections and failed replications would suggest that the advocates' interpretation is increasingly improbable. Of course, Collins's first argument would hold because there is a social dimension to the process of negotiating the next design in the series of iterations, and there is also a social dimension to the timing of when a leader emerges to declare the controversy over. However, this approach avoids the relativism of his second argument, because the prescription for the resolution of a controversy focuses on evidence.

At roughly the same time Collins was developing his analysis of controversies, H. Tristam Engelhardt, Jr., and Arthur Caplan (1987) developed a different analysis of the closure of controversies that avoids the relativism of Collins's second argument. Synthesizing work by other researchers included in the volume they edited, they argue that closure can take place via several mechanisms: loss of interest, force, consensus, sound argument, and negotiation. By "consensus"—a term Collins uses to describe the outcome of a controversy—they appear to be thinking about a mechanism similar to Kuhnian paradigm conversion. A subsequent typology by Sharon Beder (1991) includes redefinition, negotiation, sound argument rhetoric, and loss of interest. All of these remain sociological descriptions of closure mechanisms, not prescriptions for how closure should be achieved. Under these approaches, there is no single model for closure. Collins's second argument on closure as mainly determined by social negotiation might even be descriptively valid, as long as it is pared down to reflect one type of closure mechanism that applies to some historical cases. The category of sound argument rhetoric seems to be a concession to philosophers that at least some cases of closure may follow a model similar to the prescriptive one outlined above.

A process related to closure mechanisms is sanitization, which refers less to the closure of a specific controversy than to the closure of the controversial status of an entire field of research. Roy Wallis argues that controversial sciences that face labeling as pseudosciences may follow a policy of sanitization, that is, a concerted attempt to distance the theory and practice from its more notorious proponents by means of professional associations, membership that requires high academic credentials; incorporation of the methodology of accepted scientific disciplines; and direction of funds to activities that may legitimate the knowledge claims, such as endowment of research institutes or chairs in established universities (1985: 598). Wallis cites academic parapsychology as the exemplar of a controversial field that has attempted to achieve some academic respectability by adopting a sanitization strategy. Over the years the field gradually developed journals, a scientific organization, supporting grant organizations, and institutional homes in universities such as Edinburgh and Virginia. This process is similar to the professionalization that has occurred among some alternative medical groups such as osteopaths (Baer 1987, 1989). Once again, the processes of sanitization and professionalization point to the social dimension of the resolution of controversies. However, these analyses do not imply the epistemological relativism of Collins's second argument.

Laboratory Studies and Other Microsociological Approaches

During the late 1970s and early 1980s, another alternative to the retrospective, historical accounts of the Edinburgh interests analyses was the observational study of scientists in the laboratory. This work, sometimes mistakenly called the "anthropology" or "ethnography" of science, is better referred to as "laboratory studies." The social scientists were not anthropologists and their methods did not correspond to standard ethnographic methods in anthropology. However, their observational methods were attuned to theoretical questions in the philosophy and sociology of knowledge, and a number of concepts emerged from the laboratory studies that were highly influential.

Probably the most influential concept in this area of SSK was "indexicality," a term that Karin Knorr-Cetina borrowed from the linguist C. S. Peirce via ethnomethodology. Indexicality describes local variations in research decision criteria: "General criteria are post hoc and ex ante schematizations of higher order selections which become meaningful and consequential only in their indexical forms, as circumstantially occasioned selections" (1983: 125). In other words, the actual practice of science is much messier than later reports would lead us to believe. To translate Knorr-Cetina into terms I have been using, universalistic criteria are subsequent justifications that often obscure the role of particularistic criteria in actual decisions. Formal reports tend to gloss over the ways in which scientific knowledge production is anchored in local settings, with all the local variables: office regulations, availability of lab equipment, variety in the materials used, lab assistants who have slightly different procedures, and so on. Indexicality includes not only the contextual or local aspect of research but also its "situational contingency" (1981: 33). The latter refers to how circumstances such as unplanned events (e.g., rats that escape) shape laboratory research decisions, which Knorr-Cetina characterizes as tinkering. Thus, in a general way her work is consistent with that of the Bath and Edinburgh schools by showing how particularistic criteria play a nontrivial role in the technical aspects of scientific decision making. This approach tends to show how social factors enter into decisions about what scientific knowledge gets produced, in other words, which problems are "doable" (Fujimura 1987).

Knorr-Cetina also contributed to the development of an increasing recognition of networks as the focal social units of science studies. She did this by introducing the idea of "variable transscientific fields," which refer to networks that extend beyond scientific communities or specialty groups, including equipment suppliers, grant agencies, administrators, and so on (1981: 81–83). She thus helped extend the concept of networks from a limited group of discipline-bound or problem-bound colleagues, as in Collins's core set, to something more flexible and heterogeneous approximating the actor-networks of the Paris school.

Probably the key conceptual contribution of the laboratory studies was the idea of fact construction. The discussion of fact construction has been the source of enormous misunderstandings and controversies with philosophers (and now the science studies bashers of the science wars), so it may help to introduce the topic by distinguishing a fact from an observation. I suggest that a fact is a widely accepted observation or empirical law; in other words, it is an empirical statement with a particular social status that can be analyzed independently of its epistemological status as either true or false. In this sense, there can be true facts or false facts, just as there can be observations that either do or do not have the status of facts. The distinction between fact and observation (or, better, empirical statement) may help both philosophers and social scientists see the complementary nature of their frameworks.

Bruno Latour and Steve Woolgar (1986: 77–79) distinguish five types of fact: type 1, conjectures or speculations; type 2, statements that contain modalities that refer to evidence or lack of it; type 3, claims of research finding usually attached to researchers; type 4, claims of generally accepted knowledge, usually in textbooks, but still referenced; and type 5, taken-for-granted common knowledge, so obvious that references are not given. A modality is a statement about another statement, in this case a qualifier added to claims about the truthfulness of observations. The transition toward type 5 facts linguistically involves the successive deletion of modalities. Sometimes this process is referred to as black-boxing, especially when facts become inscribed in taken-for-granted technologies. Latour and colleagues (1992) later developed this analysis with their sociotechnical graphs, that is, plots of a science controversy or technological innovation against an axis of successive statements over time and an axis of fact modalization. These graphs provide an easy visual representation of the deletion and "undeletion" of modalities in a scientific controversy.

To get some sense of how this model can provide a dynamic picture of the rhetoric of science, one might consider the gradual transformation of a fact from a starting point as type 2 status: "Research group x thinks it has found a linkage between beta-carotene and cancer prevention." This claim, perhaps after confirming studies, may eventually become a widely accepted, type 5 fact: "Given the linkage between beta-carotene and cancer prevention . . ." In this type of statement, the fact is taken-for-granted knowledge and not linked to any research group. Then, a new research group may produce a study that undermines the common knowledge, and the type 5 fact may be demoted to type 2 status: "Research group x's proposed linkage between beta-carotene and cancer prevention is undermined by . . ." This way of thinking about the social status of observations seems very useful, provided that it is clearly distinguished as a description of the history of the observation, not an evaluation of its epistemological status. Facts may achieve a type 5 social status of consensus knowledge, but it is still possible to come up with grounded reasons for why that consensus knowledge is mistaken.

Susan Leigh Star analyzes the similar transformation from "local uncertainties" to "global certainties." She develops not a set of stages, but a typology of mechanisms by which the process takes place: "attributing certainty to the results of other fields; substituting processual for production evaluations in the face of technical failures; ideal type substitutions; shifting clinical and basic evaluation criteria; ad hoc generalizing of case studies; and the subsuming of epistemological questions in internal debates" (1985: 391). Her analysis contributes to an understanding of the rhetorical moves that scientists make in order to bolster their viewpoint on the status that specific research claims should have in their communities.

A third type of laboratory study was developed from ethnomethodology. Founded in the 1950s by Harold Garfinkel, a student of Talcott Parsons and Alfred Schutz, this field of sociology studied the ways in which people in everyday life develop describing procedures that produce behavioral regularities and social structures. In contrast to Parsonian functionalism, ethnomethodologists questioned the extent to which meanings were shared across members of a social unit. In science studies, ethnomethodology is associated with laboratory studies that focused on fine-grained analyses of scientists' conversations.[5] Ethnomethodologist Michael Lynch (1992) distinguishes ethnomethodology and discourse analysis, but the two are closely related. Discourse analysis examines scientists' accounts of their work, the description of the variation of their interpretive practices, and the articulation of that variation with social context.

One of the generally important findings of ethnomethodology/discourse analysis is that the meaning or interpretation of the same theories, observations, or events often shifts across registers of discourse. For example, comparisons of spoken versus written discourse or letters versus formal write-ups often provide very different versions of the same event (Mulkay, Potter, and Yearley 1983). Although this finding is suggested in the other laboratory studies, it is developed more clearly in the ethnomethodology and discourse analysis literature. The finding is important because it renders complicated social studies of science that rely on one register or that take scientists' memoirs or interview accounts at face value.

Notwithstanding these interesting findings, discourse analysis has been faulted for being restricted to the variability of scientists' accounts. Consequently, it fails to develop more profoundly sociological or cultural analyses, a second-order move that is essential in critical and policy-oriented projects (Webster 1991: 28–32). In other words, as with some of the standpoint epistemologies, it remains too closely rooted in emic accounts and does not progress to a second-order analysis of local representations.

The laboratory studies of the 1970s and 1980s shared an emphasis on observational research that focused on what scientists actually do in the laboratory. Although laboratory studies largely disappeared from the science studies literature by the 1990s, their legacy of emphasizing what scientists do was continued in the 1990s in research on science-as-practice. For example, Andrew Pickering argues that previous studies of physics, such as

Kuhn's work on paradigm change, tend to overemphasize theory. Pickering has worked instead to show how scientific research involves a complex triangulation of three elements: "a material procedure (assembling and running a piece of apparatus), an interpretive model (a theoretical understanding of how the apparatus functioned), and a phenomenal model (a theoretical understanding of the phenomenon under investigation)" (1995: 48). Pickering argues that scientists as actors must overcome resistances posed by each of these elements. A similar model, developed by historian Peter Galison, differs from that of Pickering by viewing the resistances as more implacable "constraints."[6] The culture concept, as developed in anthropology and discussed in the next chapter, also bridges the divide between thought and practice.

Another largely microsociological framework that also emphasized practice was social worlds theory. A descendent of the Chicago school of sociology, the pragmatist emphasis of this wing of sociology leads to an emphasis on practice and work. We have already encountered the influence of one Chicago school via the pragmatist wing of the philosophy of science. Chicago was important in American sociology as the home of the first sociology department. The term "Chicago school" therefore has different meanings for philosophers and sociologists.[7] In sociology, the early twentieth-century Chicago school of Robert Park, Albion Small, W. I. Thomas, and Ernest Burgess was influential for its theorization of attitudes, studies of race relations, and use of ethnographic methods in community studies. George Herbert Mead of the philosophy department—together with sociology colleagues such as Burgess and Thomas and his student Herbert Blumer (in the sociology department from 1927 to 1952)—led the development of the symbolic interactionist wing of Chicago sociology. In turn this sociological tradition became the basis for the social worlds approach used by STS analysts such as Adele Clarke, Joan Fujimura, and Susan Leigh Star.

A social world is a unit of discourse "not bounded by geography or formal membership 'but by the limits of effective communication' " (Clarke 1990: 19). The pragmatist emphasis on work and activity distinguishes the concept somewhat from Collins's core set or Knorr-Cetina's transscientific fields. STS researchers associated with social worlds theory have introduced several concepts into the interdisciplinary conversation. In an analysis of "doable" problems in science, Fujimura shows how scientists negotiate disparate demands from different social worlds, such as those of their employer and their scientific discipline (1987). To achieve success, scientists must find problems that crosscut or align different social worlds in a process similar to the enrollments of actor-network theory. "Boundary objects," as scientific objects that "inhabit several intersecting social worlds . . . and satisfy the informational requirements of each of them," become crucial to this process of aligning different social worlds (Star and Griesemer 1989: 393).

Fujimura also introduced the idea of a scientific bandwagon, which occurs "when large numbers of people, laboratories, and organizations commit their resources to one approach to a problem" (1987: 261). More than a network, it describes an increasing returns phenomenon in the selection of scientific problems such that researchers tend to flock to "hot" areas. An example is the snowballing of research, researchers, and institutions that entered molecular biology cancer research in the United States by the early 1980s. Fujimura argues that the success of the bandwagon was due to several factors, including a theory-method package that made "doable" problems (normal science) possible, the existence of new DNA techniques, the realization that novel information could be rapidly produced, and the support of funding institutions. Again, the concept of a bandwagon articulates with network theories; a bandwagon might be viewed as a particular type of rapid network growth.

In summary, the Bath school, the laboratory studies, ethnomethodology/discourse analysis, and social worlds theory all provided alternatives to the interests analyses of the Edinburgh school. They also moved science studies methods away from reliance on historical records to a variety of sources including observations, interviews, and all sorts of other records that are usually not archived. The result was that these studies provided detailed insights into how particularistic values and local contingencies permeated the knowledge-making process, and they provided a new vocabulary for conceptualizing various aspects of the construction process. However, the great macrosociological issues opened up by the Edinburgh school—class, the state, race, gender, colonialism, historical transformations—were largely irrelevant for a kind of analysis that focused on the making of science in small groups, networks, and shifting institutional fields. As a result, the critical potential of SSK was limited. It is interesting that subsequent analyses by Star (1995), Clarke (Clarke and Montini 1993), and to some extent Fujimura (1995) have moved away from social worlds theory to analyses that reveal a greater concern with these broader issues. Likewise, subsequent work by the former discourse analyst Steven Yearley (1996) reveals a change in problematics to broader political and societal issues. For this reason, their subsequent work could be classified more as contributing to the postconstructivist wave of critical and cultural studies of science and technology that will be discussed in the next chapter. However, other SSK researchers dismiss the argument that there is a need to retain some concept of society or culture as part of a good theory of science; the actor-network theorists advocate instead that the analysis should focus on individuals and networks.

Network Theories

The network concept can be viewed broadly to cover a wide range of studies that recognize the fundamental insight that informal social linkages play an important part in the making of science. For example, the previous chapter included a discussion of invisible colleges, specialty groups, cocitation networks, and other forms of network analysis. In this chapter the agnostic alliances of Restivo and Randall Collins, the core set and relevant social groups of the EPOR/SCOT programs, the transscientific fields of Knorr-Cetina, and the social worlds of Clarke, Fujimura, and Star are all examples of attempts to think about the social units of science beyond formal organizational terms such as laboratories, departments, research institutions, and disciplines. Likewise, some historians have developed an interest in research schools, or groups within science that are usually larger than a laboratory, that often but not always include teachers and students or former students, and that are united by a common doctrine, method, or style (Geissen and Holmes 1993). In this sense, one could argue that some version of a network is at the core of the major theories of the sociology of scientific knowledge, just as it has been at the core of many of the empirical research projects of the institutional sociology of science.

In technology studies, network theories have also been highly influential, and not only in the SCOT program described above. Perhaps the best-known development of the network concept in technology studies is the work of historian Thomas Hughes (1987), who extended his research on the history of electric power systems to a general model of large technological systems. These systems are hierarchically organized and include diverse components such as people, machines, organizations, scientific research, regulatory laws, and natural resources. Hughes recognizes an exogenous environment that can influence systems or that systems in turn can control. An example of the former is fossil fuels, on which electric systems are dependent, and an example of the latter is a fully owned subsidiary corporation. Hughes also distinguishes between human and nonhuman components of the system because humans have "degrees of freedom not possessed by artifacts" (54).

These large technological systems tend to go through phases of growth. As Hughes outlines,

> During invention and development inventor-entrepreneurs solve critical problems; during innovation, competition, and growth manager-entrepreneurs make crucial decisions; and during consolidation and rationalization financier-entrepreneurs and consulting engineers, especially those with political influence, often solve the critical problems associated with growth and momentum. (1987: 57)

Systems acquire momentum over time, but Hughes cautions against the mistaken view that the systems are autonomous and not subject to human control (76). Systems may also encounter reverse salients, or "components of a system that have fallen behind or out of phase with the others" (73). Reverse salients are something like bottlenecks in a network; these lagging components often require adjustments or compensation from other components in the system. Finally, systems acquire distinctive styles, particularly national styles, which he noticed in his comparative studies of electric power systems.[8]

Another sustained and detailed attempt to theorize networks is actor-network theory. The theory is largely the product of Michel Callon, Bruno Latour, and colleagues at the École des Mines, and sometimes their work is called the Paris school of STS. However, many others have used, supported, or extended actor-network theory. For example, John Law formulated the concept of heterogeneous engineering to refer to the process by which "the stability and form of artifacts should be seen as the function of heterogeneous [social, natural, and technical] elements as these are shaped and assimilated into a network" (1987: 113). The concept of "heterogeneity" bridges many of the approaches in network theory, including the work of Hughes, Law, Callon, and Latour. As formulated in actor-network theory, a principle of extended symmetry is the basis for treating social agents, objects, and texts as "entities" on the same level in a heterogeneous, sociotechnical network. In general, the term "heterogeneity" has come to mean any mixture of social and ostensibly nonsocial elements, usually via a network. The concept of a heterogeneous ensemble also appears in Michel Foucault's discussions of the apparatus of power (1979). Likewise, Donna

Haraway's discussions of hybrids and cyborgs also point to similar crossings of nature/culture or technical/human boundaries (1989).

In one of the many critiques of actor-network theory, historian of science Yves Gingras argues that actor-network theorists may confuse identities and relations in their accounts of heterogeneous entities (1995). Gingras argues that in practice actor-network analyses maintain distinctions between technical and social, or natural and cultural, entities, which therefore have separate identities and are linked via networks. Gingras's criticism is similar to that of others who have pointed out that heterogeneous explanations of scientific events provide a way of letting nature back in to constructivist accounts of how theories come to be accepted (e.g., Giere 1993). The extent to which the constraints or resistances of the material world are granted a causal role in heterogeneous accounts varies among the actor-network theorists; some accounts are moderate constructivist and others are closer to what I call radical constructivism. However, actor-network theory has the advantage over earlier frameworks, such as EPOR and the laboratory studies, in that it tends to sidestep the philosophical confusion over relativism by providing a way for nature or evidence to influence the outcome of scientific disputes and technological controversies.

In actor-network theory, agency is a matter of attribution; in this sense things can have agency based on their position in a network. Thus, actor-network theory calls for a new sociology that follows the attribution of agency. A number of terms to describe this new sociology have emerged. An "actant," sometimes used instead of the "actor" of classical social theory such as Parsonian functionalism, is defined alternatively as any entity endowed with an ability to act or "whoever or whatever is represented" (Callon 1994: 53; Latour 1987: 84). Representations are the designation of someone or something as a spokesperson for an actant (another person, object, institution, or network).

The theory of actants is confusing to many people and remains controversial. Because action in classical Parsonian social theory involves the idea of a goal state or intention, nonhuman entities cannot be actors because they do not have intentions and goals. Furthermore, as some critics have pointed out, any theorists who put humans on par with things need to be careful of maintaining prescriptive/descriptive distinctions; otherwise, they might soon run into legal arguments about the rights of things over people. It seems more fruitful to think of actor-network theory as attempting to give a name to the common processes whereby things are endowed with an ability to influence human actions through delegation or representation. A traffic light is a mundane but credible example; in most situations the machine has "agency" in the sense that it "causes" people to stop and go in an orderly way.

The general framework of actor-network theory is called a sociology of translation. The metaphor seems to bridge linguistic/semiotic analysis with molecular biology. Translation refers to the means by which one entity gives a role to others.[9] The four "moments" of translation are problematization, interessement, enrollment, and mobilization. Problematization refers to the process of defining the issue in such a way that other actors accept one's definition of the problem. They gradually come to accept one's knowledge claims or technology as an obligatory point of passage, that is, as a necessary means to solving their problem. In Callon's terms, "We want what you want, so ally yourselves with us by endorsing our research and you will have a greater chance of obtaining what you want" (1994: 52). Interessement means imposing and stabilizing the roles of the other actors defined by one's problematization, and enrollment, the result of interessement, is the device by which actors/entities are anchored to the network in interrelated roles. Finally, mobilization is the achievement of desired representatives to act as spokespersons of other entities (Callon 1986).

In actor-network theory, context/content are not distinct but instead the mutual products of networks. Facts and technologies flow along networks, and as networks expand and become more robust, knowledge claims become more accepted (more "factual") and technologies more successful. Likewise, social structure changes. In what actor-network theorists view as a kind of Copernican shift, social structure is no longer a causal shaping factor for networks but the outcome of previous networks and their conflicting relations in an agonistic field.

An example of the elegance of this framework is seen in Latour's analysis of Louis Pasteur (1983, 1988). In "Give Me a Laboratory and I Will Raise the World," Latour (1983) focuses on one aspect of Pasteur's career, his successful intervention into the anthrax disease. Pasteur problematizes the disease by defining it as a potential bacterial infection, rather than a condition imposed by bad airs or bad fields. Therefore, Pasteur proposes that he may be able to find a solution to the problem. By moving his laboratory out into the field, Pasteur learns from the local knowledge of the veterinarians and translates that knowledge into his own bacteriological framework:

> For instance, the spore of the bacillus (shown by Koch) is the translation through which dormant fields can suddenly become infectious even after

many years. The "spore phase" is the laboratory translation of the "infected field" in the farmer's language. (1983: 145)

Pasteur then returns with this knowledge, and the bacterial pathogen, to his laboratory, where he succeeds in producing the disease in experimental animals. He has now translated the disease into his bacteriological framework, and he is able to interest his potential allies by making his laboratory an obligatory point of passage: "If you wish to solve your anthrax problem, you have to pass through my laboratory first" (146). Although the laboratory is small in comparison with the scale of the disease, the veterinarian profession, and the agricultural industry, Pasteur's translation of the disease serves as a fulcrum that redistributes the configuration of forces or entities. In other words, the power equation is altered, and the small laboratory becomes more powerful. However, to enroll the allies—to secure them in his network—Pasteur must return to the field and demonstrate the efficacy of his vaccine. Pasteur's theory and vaccine now become available all over France; the small laboratory is now multiplied in scale to include all of France. "French society, in some of its important aspects, has been transformed through the displacements of a few laboratories" (153).

One can see the appeal and elegance of actor-network theory as a description of successful scientific and technological entrepreneurship. It is also possible to understand the claim that Pasteur in some sense changes French society. Indeed, today we live in a "pasteurized" world. However, there is no compelling evidence that networks are the cause of fundamental aspects of society such as the class structure, the patriarchy, and colonialism. Pasteur is less like a social revolutionary than a friendly digestive tract bacterium that finds a place for itself in its host. The actor-network account is excellent as a story of a great man and the network he erected; it is also a fine how-to manual for technical entrepreneurs who want to build an empire by ingratiating themselves to existing interests. As a theory of science, the analysis is a lucid explanation of why the winners win, even why would-be winners lose.

However, the theory is not very good at explaining why some actors are excluded from the game and why the playing field is not level. Likewise, the account provides no ground for analyzing pasteurization as a social and technological phenomenon, considering its shortcomings, and developing alternatives. Perhaps for this reason categories such as race, class, gender, colonialism, and industrial interests tend to be absent from actor-network analyses. A whole range of questions remain outside the horizon of the framework. For example, what are the implications of a culture of germs for social relations between in-groups and out-groups? Do we want to be living in a world where concern with germs gets translated into carcinogenic household cleansing products? Or, from alternative medicine circles that I study, does the pasteurization of milk denature proteins and lead to chronic disease?

A related problem is the tendency for actor-network accounts to explain social action instrumentally, that is, without recourse to the noninstrumental cultural meanings attributed to action by actors. In some actor-network accounts scientists appear to be relatively unidimensional actors who are somewhere between power-hungry monsters and the rational optimizers of neoclassical economics. In this sense the theory tends to fall victim to the flattening kinds of accounts that were originally raised against neo-Marxist interests analyses that reduced scientists to interest dopes. The antidote to this approach is a more cultural approach that begins with the webs of meaning in which scientists are suspended and their own views of the world. However, unlike discourse analysis and ethnomethodology, the analysis would not end with actors' viewpoints but instead would connect them to larger structures and values. Thus, without rejecting the achievements of actor-network theory, I contend that social studies of scientific knowledge needs to move in a different direction that grants power and culture a more prominent role: power as it is embedded in historical structures of class, race, gender, and so forth, and culture as a contested system of meanings for actors. These concepts constitute major points of departure for cultural studies and critical social studies of science and technology.

5

Critical and Cultural Studies of Science and Technology

Cultural studies is an interdisciplinary conversation that, like STS, defies easy definition. In Britain cultural studies was historically associated with the Birmingham Centre for Cultural Studies. The key features of British cultural studies include (1) theoretical frameworks that first drew on Western Marxism (such as Gramsci) and semiotics, followed by feminism and other frameworks; (2) a focus on contemporary popular culture, subcultures, and the mass media rather than high culture, as in traditional literature and art studies; (3) a range of social science and humanities methods (archival, ethnographic, textual criticism); and (4) a politically engaged perspective.[1] In North America cultural studies tends to draw more on some type of language theory (e.g., poststructuralism) and to be more concerned with feminist, queer, antiracist, and postcolonial identity issues. North American cultural studies also tends to be dominated by humanities scholars in literature studies, film studies, and interdisciplinary departments such as women's studies.[2]

In STS circles in the United States, some researchers view cultural studies of science and technology as the successor to the various constructivisms considered in the previous chapter. The growing participation of women, people of color, new professional organizations, and new disciplines (anthropology, literary studies) supports this contention. However, the definition of cultural studies of science and technology is complicated and ambiguous. In science studies, the participation of anthropologists and historians is probably greater than in North American cultural studies as a whole. Some anthropologists and historians reject the label cultural studies because of its associations with poststructuralist literary criticism and identity politics. Those who accept the label or at least see themselves as friendly to cultural studies have tended to redefine the field along lines that are similar to British cultural studies. Therefore, social theory tends to occupy a greater place in the cultural studies of science and technology than in

American cultural studies as a whole. Feminist and queer theory often serves as a bridge between the two, as in the work of Donna Haraway. Likewise, the STS context tends to favor fieldwork, ethnographic interviews, and archival research over the text-oriented critical methods or impressionistic observational methods that are characteristic of American cultural studies in general. In my opinion, cultural studies of science and technology therefore tends to be more rigorous theoretically and methodologically—and more toward the social science/history ends of the humanities/social sciences arena—than North American cultural studies as a whole. Additional features of cultural studies of science and technology include the tendencies to focus on questions of culture and power (particularly as theorized from feminist, postcolonial, and antiracist standpoints), to problematize contemporary science and technology historically as part of the postmodern condition, to examine how nonexperts and historically excluded groups reconstruct science and technology, and to forge alliances between researchers and activist/interventionist social agendas.[3]

The term "critical" is equally ambiguous and complex in the contemporary STS context. In the humanities the term "critical theory" usually refers to a theory of literary or cultural criticism, in other words, a theory that helps guide the interpretation of texts. In the social sciences the same term often refers to the Western Marxist tradition associated with the Frankfurt school and post-Marxist researchers influenced by the school, such as Jürgen Habermas (Held 1980). In STS the term is sometimes used to describe the confluence of research traditions that includes feminist/antiracist studies, critics of the technological society, radical science researchers, and various other scholars who are concerned with issues of social justice and democracy. The category of critical STS therefore overlaps with but is not continuous with cultural studies of science and technology. As is evident, the terminology is confusing even for a reasonably well placed native speaker like myself, and even this attempt at a nonpolemical mapping is likely to be contested.

Critical science studies per se can be traced to the radical science movements within science that began in the 1930s and 1940s and grew substantially during and after the events of the 1960s. Some of the movements and journals include the British Society for Social Responsibility in Science (*Science for People*), Scientists and Engineers for Social and Political Action (*Science for the People*), and *Radical Science Journal* (now *Science as Culture*), as well as organizations such as the Radical Science Collective and the women's health movement organizations. The Rensselaer Science and

Technology Studies Department is one of the oldest STS programs to achieve departmental status and has played an important role as a haven for graduate students who wish to study successors of this variant of STS in critical and cultural studies of science and technology. Many of the department members share a concern with a critical inspection of science and technology from the perspective of democratic values defined in the widest sense.

Some Key Background Concepts

The Frankfurt school was a group of mid-twentieth-century German intellectuals influenced by Marx and Freud and led by Max Horkheimer, Theodor Adorno, and Walter Benjamin. As in the case of the Vienna Circle, many were forced to leave central Europe after the rise of Nazi power, and many came to the United States. The debates that continue today between philosophers and social studies researchers in science studies therefore have some historical precedence in the differences between the two European schools. The Frankfurt school members in the United States influenced the transition from the Old Left of the 1930s—which was linked to labor and was generally procommunist until the 1950s—to the American New Left that blossomed with the civil rights and antiwar movements of the 1960s. New Left social theory generally drew on Western Marxism to critique "bourgeois" or functionalist sociology such as that of Talcott Parsons and Robert Merton. Jürgen Habermas is considered the most influential European heir to the Frankfurt school, and some of his work informed the interest-based analysis of the Edinburgh school. In the United States, Herbert Marcuse probably had a greater influence on New Left social theory, at least during the 1960s and 1970s.

Although the Frankfurt school was probably the most influential of the Western Marxist traditions of social theory (that is, non-Soviet and non-Chinese), two concepts associated with Georg Lukács and Antonio Gramsci—reification and hegemony—have probably been the most influential Western Marxist concepts in contemporary STS analysis. Marx analyzed commodity fetishism as the situation in capitalist production whereby relations among people take on the character of relations among things and therefore acquire a phantom objectivity. In Lukács's reading (1968), when a world of objects and relations among things comes into being, subjectively the workers are alienated from their labor, which becomes a commodity. Thus, Lukács's concept of reification involves the transformation of social and human relationships into commodities and things; in other words, workers' labor is no longer creative work because it becomes a commodity they sell in the labor market. Lukács argued that the historical process of mystification of human relationships developed alongside capitalism and culminated in the development of philosophical idealism.

The concept of reification can be used in science studies as a way of describing how general cultural values can come to be seen as natural after they have been encoded in scientific representations. For example, Donna Haraway describes gender as "a concept developed to contest the naturalization of sexual difference" (1989: 290). Feminists have shown how science reifies cultural values and categories by attributing to them a naturalness that in fact may not be there. Historically, this has often occurred in descriptions of natural differences among human groups according to race, gender, and sexuality. Biological or genetic differences (such as skin color or sex) have sometimes been used to explain purported social differences (such as intelligence or rationality), even when there is little evidence for such claims.

A second key concept is hegemony. Usually credited to Gramsci although latent in Marx, the idea of hegemony provides an antidote to the economic determinism of simplistic or vulgar Marxism. Moreover, the concept of hegemony helps explain the stability of the unequal distribution of wealth and power in apparently democratic societies. Unlike Marx's concept of ideology, which roots beliefs in class position, and Weber's legitimacy, which describes a general belief in the right of the rulers to rule, hegemony describes the process whereby the ruling class(es) support the creation and diffusion of a general system of values and ideas that percolates through the major institutions of society.[4] Other belief and value systems are allowed to exist, and therefore an illusion of democratic pluralism can be maintained, an illusion that is useful to legitimate the ruling class. The hegemonic system manages to achieve support from many members of the middle sectors and even some members of oppressed classes and groups. Likewise, it is not necessary to delegitimate the system by repressing its critics; it is only necessary to ensure that the critics are marginalized and ineffective. Gramsci was especially interested in the role of the Catholic Church in preserving hegemony, but the institution of science also plays an important role. Although Marxists generally see science as a potentially liberating force, it can also be used to suppress counterhegemonic political and intellectual movements by attacking them as pseudoscientific. This side of science is particularly evident in environmental conflicts between communities and large corporations or the state. Here, the wealthy institutions often amass large quantities of well-funded and well-credentialed science as part of an overall political strategy to undermine the claims of communities.

In general, Marxist social theory tends to draw a distinction between science and ideology, with ideology representing false knowledge or false consciousness. Although Marx's clear recognition of the need to distinguish true from false knowledge was laudable, it seems unnecessary to waste the term "ideology" on this distinction. It seems better to define ideology as discourses or systems of ideas considered in their cultural/political dimension apart from their status as true or false (e.g., Lynch 1994). Louis Dumont (1977) provided one profound example of an analysis of the cultural dimension of ideology. In a controversial analysis that is supported by a keen anthropological eye for comparison, Dumont showed how modern economics—both conventional and Marxist—encoded the modern Western value of individualism. It is useful to distinguish ideology in this general sense—systems of ideas viewed in their cultural dimension—from the term "political ideology," such as Thatcherism or Reaganism.

Although the Dumontian formulation of ideology provides a profound cultural critique of the universalizing pretensions of some Western social sciences, it does not clearly focus the analysis of scientific disciplines and discourse on the question of power. For this reason many researchers have found Michel Foucault's theorizing of knowledge and power to be more appropriate to their concerns. Before introducing Foucault's conceptualization (1970) of knowledge and power, it is helpful first to explain his concepts of episteme and apparatus. The former refers to an "epistemological grid" that for the present purposes can be glossed as the general, implicit assumptions that underlie a range of disciplines at a given time period. In his terms, the episteme is "the total set of relations that unite, at a given period, the discursive practices that give rise to epistemological figures, science, and possibly formalized systems" (1972: 191). Examples help clarify this rather abstract definition. In *The Order of Things,* Foucault charted a transition that began with the Renaissance episteme in which thought was based on "resemblances," as in astrological similarities between heavenly bodies and earthly behavior. In contrast, during the classical episteme— that of knowledge in the period following the scientific revolution and antedating the industrial revolution—thought was based on "representation" in a table of possibilities. Examples of this style of organizing thought include the plant and animal taxonomies of early botany and zoology. Finally, the "modern" episteme, which began in the late eighteenth century, brought time, function, and dynamism into many scientific disciplines.

Foucault subsequently developed a more encompassing analysis of the apparatus ("dispositif"), a term for a "heterogeneous ensemble" of elements that includes "discourses, institutions, architectural forms, regulatory decisions, laws, administrative measures, scientific statements, philosophical, moral, and philanthropic propositions—in short, the said as much as the unsaid" (1980: 194). From an STS angle, Foucault's apparatus is very similar to the subsequent formulations of heterogeneous networks. In terms of his own thought, the apparatus marks a shift from his concept of the episteme toward a focus on nondiscursive practices and the analytics of power.

Foucault developed a framework for analyzing the modern form of power that he described as exercised "within the social body, rather than from above it" (1980: 30). He used the metaphor of a "capillary" to describe the dispersed nature of modern power throughout the society. Although Foucault worked on power in the state and the legal–juridical system, his overall corpus tended to shift attention to practices associated with institutions such as asylums, prisons, barracks, schools, and hospitals (1980: 30–31). Modern power produced new objects of knowledge and new scientific disciplines, mostly in the social and managerial sciences. Contra Merton, Foucault argues that claims for the existence of or even the goal of the autonomy of science are naive: "The exercise of power perpetually creates knowledge and, conversely, knowledge constantly induces effects of power" (52). Modern power, that is, the form of power that emerged roughly after the industrial revolution, operated largely through normalization and surveillance rather than repression. "Normalization" describes a process of moving the population toward norms or standards via disciplinary technologies, particularly in the areas of education, the military, public and mental health, criminality, and sexuality. Disciplinary technologies separated and confined deviants, and these technologies acted in numerous ways directly on the regimentation and control of the body to produce docility. The emergence of biopower shifted power away from public displays of repression to a regimentation of (1) the social body, such as by segregating the sick, mad, or criminal and by developing measures and norms for the population, especially in the area of public health; and (2) the individual body, by regimenting behavior through direct control of the bodily habits, work, or pleasure.

In the opening pages of *Discipline and Punish,* Foucault provides a memorable description of punishment prior to the nineteenth century. A convict was subjected to painful, public torture that involved ripping away his flesh and pouring molten lead and oil in his wounds, before his body was finally drawn and quartered. Foucault contrasts this form of punishment with more modern forms, such as the panopticon of nineteenth-century utilitarian philosopher Jeremy Bentham. In this model, prison guards stood at the center and could see into the cells of the inmates who encircled them. Foucault (1979, 1980) used the panopticon as a metaphor for a technology of modern power that solves the problem of surveillance by developing disciplinary procedures that are internalized by the population, as in the internalization of public health regulations through body care practices. One might be tempted to invoke the metaphor of the surveillance cameras in banks, but probably a better metaphor for this type of power is the numerous files and dossiers that are kept on individuals by government agencies, employers, and health care providers. Thus, there is no longer a reliance on stocks and public torture—remnants of which can still be found in the historic sites of colonial America; instead, the population is controlled through monitoring and evaluation.

An alternative approach to the analysis of power in science appears in the work of Pierre Bourdieu. Some researchers have found Bourdieu's concepts of symbolic capital and doxa to be particularly useful. One might think of symbolic capital as status viewed through a political economy lens. Symbolic capital can be saved and spent, hoarded and wasted, accumulated and invested, and transformed into financial capital. In terms of science, symbolic capital might be operationalized as a scientist's CV and rolodex, that is, a set of career achievements and a network. In other words, symbolic capital is similar to the concepts of reputation and recognition in the sociology of science. However, Bourdieu's analysis (1975) of symbolic capital in science is somewhat different from reputation or recognition because it allows for analyses of science in terms of owning and nonowning scientific classes. Bourdieu's work has influenced some science studies scholars, such as Bruno Latour and Steve Woolgar (1986), who extended his work in their analysis of cycles of credit. Nevertheless, the concept is still subject to the criticisms that have been made of other economic models; in other words, those models tend to flatten accounts of scientists by portraying them as optimizers (Knorr-Cetina 1981).

Of more general use is Bourdieu's analysis of doxa, the presuppositions that opponents in a controversy or other disputes disregard as self-evident and therefore beyond dispute (1975: 34). To some extent, the concept of doxa can be compared with Foucault's episteme, but the purposes and uses of the two concepts are different. Doxa points to the undisputed assumptions in a field characterized by controversy and disagreement, whereas the episteme—while often undisputed and perhaps unconscious—is more historically rooted and specific to a set of disciplines. In general, Bourdieu's work brings out questions of strategies and actors, whereas Foucault's work allows for a more long-term view of historically emergent structures.

Concepts from Feminist and Antiracist Theory

So far, the critical theorists considered have been men, and feminist concerns have been largely excluded from their horizon of inquiry. Feminist theory intersects with STS in a number of ways, including topics already discussed for the philosophy and sociology of science. One result of the feminist contributions to the critical/cultural studies wings of STS is that problem areas and frameworks as defined by male theorists have been extended to gender-related technology areas. For example, Anne Balsamo (1996) has extended the Foucauldian concern with the body and disciplinary technologies to the intersection of these topics with gender. In an analysis of women bodybuilders, she reveals the crosscurrents at work in a corporeal disciplinary practice that appears to confront traditional male stereotypes of the weak or frail female body. She argues that even while the practice appears to confront male stereotypes, representations of the practice (such as photos) reinscribe the stereotypes of the sexy female body. A somewhat different extension of the Foucauldian problematic is David Horn's work (1994) on reproduction in interwar Italy. Horn examines the emergence of new sciences, professions, and policies that made population dynamics and reproduction the focus of state intervention.

In addition to concepts that have emerged from extensions of existing frameworks, a number of more general feminist concepts are also important for critical science and technology studies. Primary among them is the concept of gender. Although "gender" is so widely used today that the term may not need elaboration, this was not always the case. Originally developed in contrast with sex, the idea of gender was useful for critiquing accounts of gendered behavior that reduced social action to biology. (Note that the meanings of the terms "sex" and "gender" sometimes are reversed across disciplines; I am following the usage in anthropology and cultural studies.) "Gender" refers to cultural differences between what it means to be masculine and what it means to be feminine, whereas "sex" refers to understandings of biological differences between male and female. The key development from feminist science studies is the way in which the "sex" side of the sex/gender division has come to be seen as socially constructed. In other words, the hierarchical relationship of sex and gender has been reversed, such that the supplementary term (gender) has been shown in some ways to underlie the formerly uncontested term (sex). Whereas some early accounts left biological descriptions of sexual difference as given and merely pointed to the irreducibility of the cultural (gender) to the biological (sex), contemporary feminist accounts of biological understandings of sexual difference reveal sexist bias and therefore the cultural (gendered) aspect of some biological descriptions of sex (e.g., Hubbard 1990; Tuana 1989).

Other key concepts from feminist science studies include androcentrism (accounts developed from a male-centered perspective), sexism (degradation of one sex), and misogyny (discourse or action directed against women). Harding (1986) identified five major areas of androcentrism in the social sciences, some of which can be extended to biology: (1) ignoring areas of inquiry; (2) focusing on public and visible actors rather than private and less visible ones; (3) assuming a single society or a single biology (ignoring gendered divisions); (4) not taking sex/gender distinctions into account as a factor in analyzing social action or biological processes; and (5) preventing the elicitation of some types of information due to methodological preferences (Harding 1986; following Millman and Kanter 1975).

Another key concept in feminist STS is "essentialism." One heavily criticized example of essentialism is the argument that women or indigenous groups—especially women members of indigenous groups—are closer to nature and therefore have an especially privileged viewpoint in the critique of Western science (e.g., Shiva 1989). Another example of essentialism is the view that because, for example, women have the childbearing function in the sexual division of labor, they are naturally associated with more empathetic methods in science. Although feminists now recognize the strategic value of essentialist rhetoric in some political contexts, as a theoretical or philosophical position essentialism is highly problematic (Haraway 1991: 255–57). Even when one uses essentialist arguments to privilege historically excluded groups, they can rapidly be turned on their head to maintain exclusionary practices. In other words, if one applies the argument that women may make a specific contribution to science because of their special powers of empathy, this can rapidly be turned against women by those who wish to make the classic association of the female and irrationality.

Haraway (1991) has introduced another key concept: "oppositional groups" or "oppositional practices," which might be viewed in Gramscian terms as counterhegemonic movements and practices. The concept goes beyond the traditional idea of coalition politics because it recognizes the contradictions among historically excluded groups and therefore the possibility for a range of oppositional positions. For example, Haraway (1989) reviews the different ways in which women have brought women's perspectives, feminism, or gender issues into the reassessment of methods and theory in primatology. She cautions against the easy form of oppositional practice that merely inverts the existing terms of a relationship, such as the replacement of a man-the-hunter theory of human origins with a woman-the-gatherer theory. She shows instead that women brought about a variety of shifts in primatology that were at times in conflict with each other. In general, she argues that the oppositional groups did not invert the terms of the field but instead brought about more profound changes "by restructuring the whole field" (1989: 303).

Haraway's case study of primatology provides the outlines of a theory of scientific change that can be posed as an alternative to Thomas Kuhn's (1970, 1993) description of linguistic change in scientific revolutions as well as to the actor-network theory of gradual enrollment and stabilization. She suggests that in order to destabilize a field, one must "write computer programs, argue for different data collection protocols, take photographs, consult on national science policy bodies, write high school texts, publish in the right journals, etc." (1989: 303). In other words, Haraway acknowledges the heterogeneous, network-building work that the actor-network theorists have highlighted, work that would encompass the much more vague process of developing anomalies that Kuhn described. She also recognizes that "destabilization is a collective undertaking," that is, not the work of an individual genius or scientific revolutionary. This point is more evident in Michel Callon's work (1986), less so in Bruno Latour's example of Pasteur (1988), and mostly implicit in Kuhn's paradigm concept. However, Haraway points to a third, crucial element that the actor-network theorists and Kuhn both miss: "Even to imagine destabilization, one must be formed at a social moment when change is possible, when people are producing different meanings in many other areas of life" (1989: 303). For example, the demise of the man-the-hunter theory of human origins was not merely the work of a heterogeneous network of women scientists, but part of a broader social transition that involved dramatic changes in the role of women in society and social thought. This emphasis highlights the cultural contexts of historical processes that are missed in the alternative theories.

Another issue that can be brought under the rubric of oppositional practices is the delicate relationship between race and gender in science. Although women in Western societies and men from non-Western societies face similar issues of out-group status in science, their interests and perspectives do not necessarily coincide. In some cases, such as primatology, the coincidences are tantalizing. For example, very much like Western white women, Japanese primatologists developed subjective methods, and they also made observations that highlighted the importance of females in primate societies. Yet, just when one may begin to speak of unity rooted in out-group perspectives, Haraway questions a discourse of unity. "What is the generative structure of oppositional discourse," she asks, "that insists on privileging 'unity' at the expense of painful self-critical analyses of power and violence in one's own politics?" (1989: 257). In other words, she is very conscious of the processes of hegemony that occur within oppositional groups, such as that of men over women in the labor movement or that of white women over women of color in the feminist movement.

Other race-oriented studies have examined the egregious cases of racism that science has legitimated. An example is nineteenth-century craniometry, or the measurement of cranial capacity to prove intelligence differences among the races. The early studies had huge methodological flaws, and the consensus soon shifted to the idea that one could not relate cranial capacity to intelligence in human populations. The school of Franz Boas—the Columbia school of anthropology, which should be distinguished from the Columbia school of the sociology of science (Merton)—devoted substantial resources to criticizing various racist assumptions in science. Probably the key theoretical concept that has emerged from research on racism in science is the incoherence of race as a biological concept. One can demonstrate the incoherence of the concept from a cultural approach or a biological approach. Culturally, it is easy to demonstrate the variation in racial classification systems over time and across cultures. Comparison of the mainly bipolar North American system—one is either black or white— with the myriad categories in the Brazilian system soon leaves one with the insight that the everyday concept of race is culturally constructed. Likewise, from a biological perspective, race is incoherent because of the lack of covariance of genes across human population groups.[5]

Environmental racism is another key concept that has emerged from race-related science and technology studies. Robert Bullard (1990) has shown that in the United States NIMBY (not-in-my-backyard) struggles often translate into PIBBY (put-in-blacks'-backyard) politics. Research on environmental justice and environmental racism involves a number of interesting general issues. One is the analysis of the way in which issues of social and economic justice are rendered invisible and difficult to contest when they are translated into highly technical discourse. Thus, environmental justice studies provide an opportunity for a general study of hegemony through the analysis of the processes by which social and economic issues are made resistant to challenges by becoming highly technical and difficult to contest. In turn, this topic leads to the related issue of understanding resistance, technology, and the dumping of unwanted technologies on poor communities and countries. The whole area of technology and resistance by workers, communities, and poor countries warrants more research and theorizing.[6]

Critical and Feminist Technology Studies

Critical technology studies involves a somewhat different lineage of concepts as applied to the analysis of technology. Lewis Mumford (1964a, 1964b) is the grandfather of critical technology studies, and on occasion his distinction between authoritarian and democratic technics is still invoked. This distinction contrasts system-centered, powerful, and unstable technologies with human-centered, relatively weak, but resourceful and durable ones. Mumford clearly favored the latter, low-tech world, and he worried about the general direction of human "progress."

Jacques Ellul developed a similar critique of the technological society. He borrowed from Marcel Mauss the term "technique" to distinguish a rationalizing, technical principle from the machine or technology per se. He defined technique as "the totality of methods, rationally arrived at and having [as a goal] absolute efficiency (at a given stage of development) in every field of human endeavor" (Ellul 1965: xxv). The end result of the growth of technique, as in Max Weber's world history that ends in the iron cage of rationalization, is the technological society.

Both Mumford and Ellul were highly critical of the massive rush toward new technologies that characterized modernist culture. One outcome of the optimistic view of new technologies is the "technological fix," that is, an attempt to find a technological solution to a social and/or political problem (Ellison 1978). The technological fix is usually doomed to failure or at best mixed success, as in the case of some of the new biomedical technologies or some aspects of the Green Revolution (Pfaffenberger 1992). Likewise, one sometimes encounters rosy predictions that a new technology will lead to a much more just society. This view is particularly evident regarding computerization and the global information infrastructure. David Hakken and Barbara Andrews (1993) criticized two essentialist camps: the computopians, those who believe that computerization will result in a better society; and computropians, those who believe that it will contribute to a dystopian future. Hakken and Andrews advocate instead an alternative "computing studies" perspective that views the relationship between computerization and social change as a topic for empirical research that recognizes local variations. This position can be extended to a large number of claims of simple causal relationships between technology and society.

Technological determinism is the slightly more general view that "societal development is determined by technology" (Bijker 1994: 238). Some versions of Marxism (so-called vulgar Marxism) have taken one of Marx's most famous pronouncements—the hand mill leads to society with the feudal lord, the steam mill to society with the industrial capitalist—and turned it into a license for technological determinism (Marx 1963: 109). Theories of technological determinism often rest implicitly on the assumption of what Langdon Winner (1977) has called "autonomous technology." This term describes the widely held belief that in advanced capitalist societies technological development had taken on a life of its own as if it were an out-of-control Frankenstein monster.

Winner developed the alternative perspective that technology and technological design are the products of interested human decisions. His work suggests that citizens should awaken from their "technological somnambulism" and explore, critique, and protest the uncritical embracing of new technologies. They should also challenge the assumption that technological design choices are not politically driven, without economic and political consequences, and beyond control or refashioning. In an often-cited essay, Winner (1986) asks the question, "Do artifacts have politics?" and answers it in the affirmative. One major exemplar is the work of the New York state public works mogul Robert Moses, who built Long Island parkway bridges to block bus access to Jones Beach and therefore to preserve segregated beaches. By making design decisions that were difficult or costly to get around, producers of artifacts can construct built-in politics that limit interpretive flexibility (Winner 1993).

In another analysis of the politics of design, Brian Pfaffenberger developed the concept "technological regularization," which he describes as follows: "A design constituency creates, appropriates, or modifies a technological artifact, activity, or system that is capable of signifying and coercively implementing a constructed vision of a stratified society, one in which power, wealth, and prestige is differentially allocated" (1992: 291). Pfaffenberger then developed a typology of regularization strategies that includes processes such as centralization, standardization, marginalization, and disavowal. This development of the analysis of the politics of technology has obvious potentials for hybrid theorization utilizing Foucauldian concepts such as normalization.

Technology critics have sometimes been accused of being Luddites, that is, throwbacks to the workers who broke the machines in England during the industrial revolution (for contemporary variants, see Lyon 1989). One attempt to go beyond criticism of the technological society to a more positive program was the appropriate technology movement (also known as intermediate technology). Associated with E. F. Schumacher (1973) and especially popular during the 1960s, this movement called for the development of technology that was consistent with the local ecology and culture, especially of poor countries. As Winner notes, the idea of appropriate technology became more problematic when applied to Western, industrialized societies (1986: 63).[7] More recently, discussions have turned toward green technologies or sustainable technology, vague terms for appropriate technology that somehow shifts human ecology toward relationships that are not likely to crash from unsustainable effects such as global warming, excess population growth, or rampant pollution.

Two other contemporary areas of critical technology studies are technology in the military and technology in the workplace. For example, "dual use" refers to the design of technologies to have applications in both military and civilian sectors. Generally used in the context of post–Cold War budget maneuvering, such proposals warrant careful inspection because they may be cleverly disguised ways of preserving military budgets without providing optimal civilian benefits. Dual use technologies are unlikely to have a significant impact on the economy, and they are likely to entangle technology policy in national security issues (Sclove 1994). Regarding technology in the workplace, Harry Braverman (1974) developed a critique of modernist managerial practices by showing how Taylorism "deskilled" workers by breaking down the craftlike nature of manufacturing. David Noble (1984) extended this type of analysis by showing how automation and machinery were introduced in ways that enhanced this process and therefore transferred power from the skilled worker to management.

Feminist STS analysts have examined the implications of new domestic technologies and new reproductive technologies for women. Critical studies of domestic technologies such as the work of Ruth Schwartz Cowen (1976, 1983) have shown how labor-saving devices have coincided with changing domestic arrangements that resulted in "more work for mother." Others in the appropriate (domestic) technology vein have examined the potential of altered domestic spatial design for women's liberation projects (Doorly 1985). The best studies of women's reproductive technologies have methodologically begun with an interpretation of patients' or users' perspectives, pointed to the diversity of women's experiences and therefore the fragmented nature of the category "woman," and shown how technologies are constructed in interaction with health care professionals in ways that cannot be captured by simple models of patriarchal domination.[8] In short, these studies bring a cultural perspective into the analysis of technology.

An example of a fieldwork-based cultural approach to new reproductive technologies is the work of Robbie Davis-Floyd (1992a, 1992b) on birth technologies. She shows a range of approaches from the natural birth model with lay midwives to high-tech hospital birth. As in some of the other studies of new reproductive technologies, Davis-Floyd challenges the simplistic feminist view that the male-dominated world of high-tech hospital birth is alienating and disempowering for women. Instead, she points to the tremendous variety among pregnant women and the fact that some find the high-tech setting empowering. Thus, choice is crucial to the issue of empowerment. Nevertheless, the broader culture of choice itself is problematic. Marilyn Strathern (1992) examines the wide ranges of choices opened up by surrogacy, artificial insemination, amniocentesis, and other new reproductive technologies. Kinship has always been constructed as something one cannot do anything about; one is "stuck" with one's family. In contrast, the new reproductive technologies encompass the world of kinship relations in the entrepreneurial culture of choice. These complexities raise questions about the nature of identity and social relationships in an increasingly commodified world (see also Edwards et al. 1993).

Concepts from the History of Science

Although the history of science is largely descriptive or idiographic, there are some crucial theoretical issues that have emerged from historical studies. Consequently, the history of science deserves recognition in any review of key concepts in science studies. Three examples of conceptual contributions are the critique of whig history, the analysis of the scientific revolution, and the problem of periodization in science. All three provide tools for critical, cultural analyses in science studies.

"Whig history" refers to a type of history that interprets the past from the scientific perspectives of the present and often adopts the teleological view that scientific discoveries and technological innovations were bound to happen because they were there in nature. Whig history therefore represents an asymmetrical approach to the social studies of knowledge for which the strong program's symmetry principle provided one alternative. From a whig historical perspective, one can speak of premature and postmature discoveries. Postmature discoveries appear to be behind their time rather than ahead of it, as judged by present knowledge (Zuckerman and Lederberg 1986). A related methodological issue is presentism, an approach to history that values the past in terms of the present. Although the term overlaps with whig history, presentism refers to the attempt to reduce the task of history to providing lessons for the present such as policy insights. An alternative is to view the past as another culture, and to use the past as a point of reference to develop comparative studies that provide the basis for a more profound cultural analysis of the assumptions of science in the present.

The critiques of whig history and presentism are closely related to the former debate between internalism and externalism. Internalist accounts of science and technology explained innovation by examining intellectual genealogies and puzzle-solving ventures, and they focused on the origin and growth of scientific ideas by studying how ideas were influenced by other ideas. In contrast, externalist accounts examined the interaction of society and scientific ideas by charting the social factors that shaped the origin and development of those ideas. In many ways this distinction was parallel to the realist/constructivist controversy between some philosophers and SSK theorists. The internalist/externalist controversy seems to have lost much of its appeal as historians increasingly write heterogeneous accounts that show how content/context, intellectual/social, or universalistic/particularistic factors operate simultaneously in the making of knowledge, technology, and society.

Another set of key concepts in the history of science has emerged from debates over the interpretation of the scientific revolution, that is, the emergence of modern science associated with the work of early modern natural philosophers such as Copernicus, Galileo, Boyle, and Newton. The study of the scientific revolution provided one setting for an interdisciplinary exchange between historians and social scientists in which historians contributed, often implicitly, to a general theory of scientific change. Debates over the causes of and meaning of the scientific revolution imply a theory of scientific revolutions that situates them in broader transformations taking place in the society and culture. As in the case of Haraway's discussions of primatology, these debates suggest an alternative to Kuhn's intellectualist emphasis on the buildup of anomalies as the driving force behind scientific revolutions. Likewise, they suggest an alternative to the actor-and-strategy models of SSK. Therefore, studies of the scientific revolution of the seventeenth century (*the* scientific revolution) can be mined to provide an alternative theoretical framework for analyzing other scientific revolutions, consensus shifts, and scientific change in general.

Early sociological accounts of the scientific revolution tended to focus on its location in the emergence of Western modernity as conceptualized by Weber and Marx. The Merton thesis is probably the best-known account of the scientific revolution in these terms. Robert Merton's analysis (1970) is built on Weber's diagnosis of modernity as a general process of rationalization in which institutions tend to become more bureaucratized and specialized, and practices tend to become more standardized. Weber (1958) also argued that the ascetic, Calvinist wing of Protestantism contributed to the development of the rationalized, bureaucratic capitalism characteristic of the modern West. The Merton thesis adds to this theory the footnote that Puritan religious values served as a spur to the values of modern science. Frequently misunderstood on this point, Merton did not claim that a quantitative tally of early natural philosophers in England or other countries would show them to be mostly Puritans, nor did he claim that Puritan values constituted a necessary and sufficient cause for modern science.[9] Rather, he argued that Puritan values provided a fertile soil, or a spur, to the scientific revolution. For example, he argued that the Puritan concern with good works and work in general helped spur the use of the experimental method of early modern science.

Related to the Merton thesis in terms of its comparative perspective are the Needham and Hessen theses. Joseph Needham (1974) adds a diagnosis of the comparative factors that led to the surge of scientific developments in the West, even when China had been ahead of the West for centuries prior to the modern period. The set of factors is a complex one that changes over the course of this scholar's prolific career, but it includes factors of social organization that are roughly consistent with a Weberian account.[10] The Hessen thesis (1971) was an alternative, Marxist account developed by Boris Hessen, a Soviet physicist and historian whose work on the scientific revolution was contemporary with that of Merton. Hessen held that Newtonian mechanics can be explained instrumentally as a response to contemporary problems of water transport, mining technology, and ballistics. In a particularly elegant argument, Hessen suggests that the development of thermodynamics, especially the law of conservation of energy, had to await the problems encountered with the development of the steam engine.[11]

Two other influential accounts are provided by Steve Shapin and Simon Schaffer (1985) and Margaret Jacob (1988). The former review the Boyle/ Hobbes controversy over experimental science and argue that the emergence of the experiment and laboratory as a social space contributed to the making of modern society. Jacob showed that Boyle's corpuscular philosophy, which from a presentist perspective is seen as the antecedent to the modern atomic theory of chemistry, was developed in a divisive religious context that included radical pantheistic views of nature. Boyle's view supported the orthodox religious doctrine of dualism of matter and spirit. Jacob adds, as a refinement if not correction of the Merton thesis, that by the time of Newton science was less an expression of Puritanism than of the liberal or "latitudinarian" Protestantism typifying the Anglican Church of the late seventeenth century. She also developed an account of the science/society relationship that she calls "social framing," an alternative to social constructivism that, like "realistic constructivism," recognizes some of the arguments of the realist position (Jacob 1994).

Increasingly scholars have developed cultural accounts of the scientific revolution that have expanded the scope of analysis from an emphasis on capitalism, Protestantism, and the emergence of modernity to questions of countercultural values, gender, colonialism, and international exchanges. For example, Frances Yates (1972) argues that modern science emerged from the cocoon of occultist and magical practices known as Renaissance magic, Neoplatonism, and Rosicrucianism. The Yates thesis is generally considered overstated, but she provides a valuable reminder that many of the first natural philosophers, including Newton, were not as modern as some standard accounts of the scientific revolution would suggest. Even the term "scientist" is an anachronism; the term in use at the time was "natural philosopher." Likewise, some of the key concepts of early modern science, such as gravity, involved quasi-occultist notions such as action at a distance. These were echoes of what Foucault would call the Renaissance episteme of resemblances.

The Merchant (1980) thesis adds the argument that the origins of modern science were deeply shaped by, as it shaped, the modernization of the Western patriarchy. Early modern scientists envisioned science as a process of dominating a disorderly nature, just as men dominated women (perceived as closer to nature) and excluded them from science and the emerging arenas of market-based capitalism. A key proponent of a patriarchal science and society was Francis Bacon, whose writings Carolyn Merchant analyzes for their sometimes violent metaphors of science as a project of masculinist domination.[12] A number of other researchers have explored the role of early modern science in colonialism, and Islamic researchers have also shown how many of the apparent novelties of early modern science were in fact the result of Western/non-Western exchanges. As a result, the stature of the Western scientific revolution diminishes the more one examines its non-Western predecessors.[13]

A third area of historical research that has resulted in general conceptual work is the discussion of periodization. Science and technology, like literature and the arts, have sometimes been categorized historically with the period concept. This practice can be useful for gaining a better understanding of the implicit assumptions shared by sciences today, and possibly for proposing alternatives to some of the current fads in science (such as chaos and complexity theory). "Modernity" is the term given to the general transformation of Western society since about 1500. This transformation included the emergence of religious pluralism, capitalism, parliamentary democracy, the modern bureaucratic state, colonialism, the modernization of the patriarchy and fragmentation of kin-based communities, and the scientific revolution. I use the term "early modernity" to refer to the period up to about 1800. The terms "modern" and "modernization" are extended to non-Western societies that have adopted some or all of the major features of Western modernity.

Foucault's view of modernity (1970) was somewhat different from the standard usage; he emphasized the break that occurred roughly after the industrial revolution and the French Revolution. Certainly, during the nineteenth century there was a distinctive cultural style among many of the sciences. It is important to remember that the world of Newtonian physics was in a sense timeless and reversible. It was not until the development of thermodynamics in the nineteenth century that time—in a sense, history—entered physics. Although, as Hessen argued, the emergence of steam power provided instrumental reasons for the development of thermodynamics, the theoretical innovation was also part of a general cultural transition that conceptualized the world in grandly evolutionary terms. Evolutionary theory and historical perspectives loomed large in a number of disciplines, including biology, geology, anthropology, sociology, political economy, and philology. The general society at the time has sometimes been characterized as the "age of revolutions," that is, an age when reform and revolutionary movements attempted to bring about human-guided transitions in society and the state. These political movements were guided by a similar value system that viewed history as a progressive process that could be shaped by human reason. To some extent this optimistic view of history and politics remained intact until the world wars of the twentieth century.

Elsewhere I have argued that one can also demarcate two subsequent temporal cultures in science (Hess 1995: ch. 3). In cultural studies "modernism" usually refers to the period running roughly from the 1870s to the 1960s, with the high period generally seen as between the two world wars. In technology studies, modernism is characterized by the second industrial revolution. During this period iron production gave way to steel, and steam engines were replaced by electrical and internal combustion power. Likewise, during the modernist period transportation and communication were also transformed as railroads gave way to roads and airways, and telegraphs were replaced by telephones, radio, and later television. In manufacturing, assembly-line systems and Taylorism became increasingly prevalent, and in architecture functionalist projects were popular. One of the most influential studies of modernist science is by historian Paul Forman, who argued that physicists in Weimar Germany readily accepted the indeterminacy principle because of the strong current in German intellectual culture of the time that was critical of the overly mechanistic, mechanical, and deterministic assumptions of science.[14]

More generally, the modernist sciences tended to share a few general patterns: they developed theories that conceptualized their objects in terms of closed system dynamics, often with equilibrium principles. Concepts of equilibrium and homeostasis were central in a number of fields, including economics, biology, linguistics, chemistry, psychology, and sociology. For example, the emergence of atomic physics was built around fundamental assumptions regarding equilibrium dynamics and closed systems. These developments did not occur simultaneously across the disciplines; they occurred to varying degrees at varying times. However, together they mark a modernist style in science that was consistent with the modernist culture of the surrounding societies.

As a descriptive term, "postmodernism" generally refers to social changes that have occurred during the second half of the twentieth century, accelerating after the 1960s and even more so during the 1990s. These changes include computerization, the emergence of biotechnologies, globalization, and the demise of the nation-state. In the economy, flexible accumulation—that is, lean production and the use of new managerial technologies—has come to replace assembly-line production and hierarchical management. Likewise, in the sciences there is a tendency for the closed systems and equilibrium thinking of the modernist period to give way to open systems models and nonlinear dynamics of self-organization. Generally, the term "postmodern" in this sense is assumed to be equivalent to "late modern" or "postmodernist." The global economy remains capitalist and therefore postmodernity is in some fundamental sense continuous with the early modern period. "Post-Fordism" refers to the postmodern organization of the workplace, including post-Taylorist managerial methods, flexible accumulation, and a rhetoric of labor-capital partnership.[15] David Harvey's discussion (1989) of flexible accumulation has occupied a significant place in theories of the economic and technical side of the postmodern period. Emily Martin (1994) has argued that the flexible workers and workplaces of post-Fordist production are characteristic of other manifestations of flexibility in postmodern culture, including new ways of thinking about disease and the immune system.

The term "postmodern" is also used to describe a type of theoretical framework in the social sciences and humanities usually associated with cultural studies and poststructuralist semiotic theory. Opponents of this approach frequently accuse it of irrationalism, which, when the smoke clears, usually amounts to a charge of epistemological or ontological relativism. However, careful reading of frequently cited figures such as Jacques Derrida and Donna Haraway reveals that such labels are inaccurate and highly polemical. It is possible that such labels apply meaningfully to philosophers such as Paul Feyerabend, but there is little evidence to suggest that a so-called postmodern science studies theorist and analyst like Haraway supports irrationalism or antiscience positions. Instead, she provides interesting new ways to think about the historical phenomenon of the postmodern society.

One of Haraway's conceptual contributions has been to develop the idea of the cyborg as the icon of postmodern culture. Although the common use of the term is any human-machine hybrid, Haraway's definition is more complex: "Linguistically and materially a hybrid of cybernetic device and organism, a cyborg is a science fiction chimera from the 1950s and after; but a cyborg is also a powerful social and scientific reality in the same historical period" (1991: ch. 8). She argues that a cyborg exists "when two kinds of boundaries are simultaneously problematic: 1) that between animals (and other organisms) and humans, and 2) that between self-controlled, self-governing machines (automatons) and organisms, especially humans (models of autonomy). The cyborg is the figure born of the interface of automaton and autonomy" (1989: 138–39). However, Haraway's word is not the last on the topic; by the mid-1990s cultural studies of cyborgetic aspects of the postmodern society had become a growth industry (Gray et al. 1995).

One salient feature of postmodern culture is the juxtaposition of previously separate cultural domains or the crossing of previously unblurred boundaries. Haraway has popularized the term "implosion" to describe this process (1989). The rise of interdisciplinary studies, such as STS, is one example of the level of increased complexity and communication of the postmodern world. Paul Rabinow (1992) argues that another type of implosion is also occurring in postmodern culture: biosociality, in which "nature" becomes a manufactured object that is no longer outside society, as is occurring with the genetic engineering of plants and animals (see also Strathern 1992). Interdisciplinarity and biosociality are but two examples of the postmodern condition in which previously stable boundaries are transgressed with relative ease and frequency.

In the sciences, outlines of postmodern theorizing are seen in a number of fields. In biology the evolutionary theory of the nineteenth century has undergone another shift from the equilibrium models of the modernist period to new theories based on computer simulation and nonlinear dynamics. Likewise, molecular biology destabilizes conventional species categories by focusing on genes, their recombination, and their transmission. In physics there is less sense that an ultimate foundation particle will be found, and chaos/complexity theory has provided a new framework for the analysis of areas previously seen as merely random. In general, the shift in emphasis toward open systems and patterns of self-organization marks a "postmodern" style in scientific theorizing. As in the past, this style is quite in synch with the economic and social changes in the national and international cultures. Viewing postmodern thought historically makes it easier to question its applications to social phenomena. The history of social Darwinism and functionalist social theories from earlier periods suggests that these applications may obfuscate as much as they clarify. In a sense, we are back to the key concept of reification: changing social processes are projected onto nature in new scientific models (that may also be "true" in the sense that they represent part of the world that had not been seen previously), and in turn these new models are fed back into theories of society. These theories of society may point to new aspects of the social world that had not been seen previously, but at the same time they may deflect attention from a more critical inspection of the fundamental continuities of modernity and capitalism.

Concepts from Anthropology

My tweaking of the period concept and epistemes toward the idea of temporal cultures reflects my background as an anthropologist. Anthropology's contribution to STS has historically been seen as merely methodological: the use of ethnography as a research method. This view of the field's contribution is doubly wrong, not only because it tends to reduce anthropology to ethnography, but also because it usually involves a misunderstanding of the term "ethnography." In science studies "ethnography" has historically applied loosely to any kind of fieldwork-based method, including short-term observational studies. Thus, in science studies circles the term has a considerably looser usage than in anthropology, where ethnography usually requires learning the language, developing key informants, and spending at least one to two years of more-or-less continuous participant-observation in a community, organization, or social movement. For this reason, the term "laboratory studies" is preferable for the first wave of ethnographic studies in science studies. The first wave of ethnographic studies, or laboratory studies, focused on the laboratory, addressed questions about theoretical issues in the sociology and philosophy of knowledge, and was the product largely of Europeans with training in sociology and philosophy.[16] The second wave works with larger field sites such as transnational disciplines or geographic regions, addresses questions defined largely by a concern with various social problems (e.g., sexism, racism, colonialism, class conflict, ecology) that are theorized with hybrid feminist/cultural/social theories, and is much more the product of Americans with professional training in anthropology.

Sharon Traweek's ethnographic studies of physicists, based on over a decade of ethnographic fieldwork, are often regarded as a landmark for the beginning of the second wave of ethnography.[17] Her first book, *Beamtimes and Lifetimes* (1988), provides a marked contrast with the older laboratory "ethnographies" of the SSK wing of science studies. Rather than focus on the fact-making process, Traweek explores the meaning of spatial arrangements, machine design, the life cycle (or career cycle), social groups, and cultural change. Furthermore, by comparing Japanese and Western physicists, Traweek explores the role of national and gender cultures in the shaping of scientific institutions and practices. She also shows how scientists maneuver among the cultural differences and even use those differences as strategic resources (1992).

Sustained, ethnographically based anthropological studies of modern science and technology are of such recent origin that by the middle of the 1990s a well-developed dialogue with other branches of STS had not yet been achieved. However, several key concepts inform current anthropological research and are beginning to have some impact on STS as a whole. One area of innovation is the tendency for anthropologically informed cultural studies and ethnographic analyses to work with a larger unit than an actor-network, field of power, or social world. One term for this larger unit is an "arena," that is, a field of interactions among scientific, governmental, industrial, religious, and other domains of society. A variety of anthropologists and some sociologists adopt this approach as they examine the introduction of a new technology or science through the shifting lenses of the various sides involved.[18] Rather than follow scientists through society, to use the SSK prescription, this approach looks over the shoulders of diverse groups at the prism of science and technology. This approach begins with the diverse points of view of experts and laypeople, defenders and debunkers, producers and consumers, men and women, managers and workers, and so on. This form of ethnography is therefore more like the EPOR/SCOT programs of SSK and social worlds theory than the laboratory studies. In other words, the meaning-oriented approach of EPOR/SCOT and social worlds theory provides a point of continuity with the cultural approach of anthropological ethnography.

The term "culture" has multiple meanings associated with the diverse disciplinary constituencies that use it, and it is therefore useful to preface an attempt to explicate the anthropological culture concept with its use in related fields. In cultural studies the term generally refers to print and electronic media, the arts, and other representations of cultural practices. These representations include high, low (popular), and folk cultures, and therefore cultural studies is positioned in contrast to older disciplinary frameworks that limited the object of study to high culture, such as English literature. However, because cultural studies tends to focus on mediated popular culture, it also remains continuous with fields such as literary and film criticism.

In sociology and political science, "culture" usually means the norms and values of a social unit such as a nation-state, region, or local community. In this sense, "culture" is used in opposition to the state, economy, and social structure, as in the Parsonian distinction between the cultural and the social system. Cultural institutions in this sense are limited to those institutions responsible for socialization and pattern maintenance such as education, the arts, and religion. For sociologists, "society" is often the encompassing term, and "culture" is used as a descriptor for a narrower field of norms and values.

For anthropologists (at least many in North America), "culture" tends to be the more encompassing term. It refers to the total learned knowledge, beliefs, and practices, both conscious and unconscious, of a social unit (ranging from multinational regions to microsociological units). In this sense, culture permeates and includes all social institutions and practices associated with a given social unit, including the polity, economy, social organization, religion, arts, and education. The term "cultural institutions" is an oxymoron because all institutions are cultural. More than a system of norms and values, culture is an interwoven system of symbolic meanings. Culture is structured like a language; thus, it is possible to delineate symbolic structures that permeate the range of social institutions, practices, discourses, and so forth that are associated with the culture. Also like a language, culture provides the conditions of action, the dispositions (to use Pierre Bourdieu's term) that incline people to act and react in certain ways.[19] Unlike the unitary view suggested by the norms and values formulation, culture is contested, changing, and distributed; thus, different individuals and groups within a social unit have different areas of expertise and contrasting values. Culture is recursive and crosscutting; one may therefore speak of cultures within cultures (as in the case of high-energy physics within the culture of physics) and cultures crossing cultures (physics as a transnational culture that crosscuts Japanese and American national cultures). Sometimes culture is thought of as divisible into cultural systems, a term popularized by Clifford Geertz (1973) and borrowed from Parsonian sociology. Thus, the religion, political ideology, science, and arts of a society are examples of cultural systems or systems of symbolic meaning.

Usually, anthropologists begin their accounts with the perspective of communities. The starting point of a "cultural account" is therefore not very different from a standpoint epistemology. Ironically, anthropologists tend not to use the word "culture" among themselves. Rather, it tends to surface in interdisciplinary conversations when they encounter others who are using the term in ways that anthropologists consider to be overly narrow, or they are making assumptions about actors' perspectives without doing the necessary empirical research to substantiate those assumptions.

Anthropologists who study science and technology have occasionally applied the culture concept by extending categories of traditional cultural analysis. For example, Hugh Gusterson (1996) examines the role of rituals and secrecy in the culture of a nuclear weapons laboratory. By viewing nuclear weapons testing as ritual, he shows how participation in the tests changes the social status of the nuclear weapons designers. Likewise, the culture of secrecy and the institutional insulation of the nuclear weapons community separate scientists from the world and from the anxieties of responsibility associated with nuclear weapons production. Another category of traditional cultural analysis is material culture, which covers all human-made physical objects produced in a selected culture: buildings, clothing, machines, equipment, furniture, and so on. Anthropologists have long recognized that different cultures have different styles of material culture. By comparing material culture across nations, anthropologists have revealed interesting differences in design. For example, in Japan high-energy physics detectors are reliable and durable, whereas in the United States Traweek (1988) found a design that emphasized open architecture. She demonstrates that the different designs reflect different funding patterns, training of technicians, and research problems and styles.

Structuralism and Poststructuralism

In a good example of scientific innovation by idea hybridization, Claude Lévi-Strauss (1966) developed the culture concept by applying the structuralist theory of linguistics to phenomena such as kinship and myths. He followed the linguistic model of breaking down phonemes (basic sound units that listeners hear, such as the "p" and "b" of "pit" and "bit") into phonetic features that linguists generalized from observations of phonemes (such as plus or minus voice, or plus or minus aspiration). When translated into anthropology, this distinction of phoneme and phonetic feature became known in some quarters as emic versus etic levels of analysis. Emic analyses represented the categories of the local culture, whereas etic analyses were categories produced by the anthropologist based on comparative analysis (something like the distinction between observational and theoretical terms).

The structuralism of Lévi-Strauss and other anthropologists is now considered outdated for reasons such as its excessive formalism and its failure to theorize actor/structure relationships. Nevertheless, structuralism has influenced anthropology and cultural studies by providing a way of interpreting the meaning of action, texts, and institutions by mapping one code of meanings onto others. For example, one can interpret categories of nature and culture in myths by showing how they map onto codes of cooking. (In most circumstances raw food is natural and cooked food is cultural.) In this analysis women often mediate nature and culture, and the general argument was raised that cultural codes often involve the symbolic equation that women are to nature as men are to culture, a cultural structure that was found to be nearly universal.[20] Although Lévi-Straussian analysis has been faulted for androcentrism, the basic method of interpreting the coding of nature/culture divisions against gender divisions has been highly influential in feminist science studies. For example, many of Haraway's analyses in *Primate Visions* make much more sense when read against the background of the structuralist-influenced debates of the feminist anthropology of the 1980s.

A second important aspect of Lévi-Straussian structuralism is his analysis of totemism. Totems are categories of social difference that are coconstituted with categories of natural difference. The previous example of gender provides one type of analysis of totemism in the most general sense. However, anthropological discussions have focused on totemic relationships in premodern societies. For example, a set of natural differences (bears, eagles, wolves) is related to a set of social differences (the bear clan, the eagle clan, the wolf clan). Some anthropologists have suggested that totemism may be a useful metaphor for modern societies and even science. For example, Marshall Sahlins (1976) argued that science may be the highest form of totemism, as in the parallel—first noticed and critiqued by Marx—between Darwinian evolutionary theory and capitalist competition. Darwin's delineation of mechanisms of variation and selection is quite similar to the capitalist world of product innovation and market competition. I have extended this discussion by arguing that the analysis of "technototems"— temporally and culturally localized alignments of technical and social meanings—provides a useful alternative to the Edinburgh school interests analyses of the relationship between thought and social categories (Hess 1995: ch. 2).

Yet another area where anthropologists and cultural studies researchers have distinguished themselves is the study of reconstruction. One aspect of reconstruction involves the processes by which new social groups in expert communities (such as women scientists) challenge existing theories and methods. However, reconstruction can also include the tendency for non-expert groups (or groups with different professional expertises) to reinterpret and remake science and technology as they pass out of expert producer groups and into other groups, either in domestic or workplace settings.[21]

Reconstruction is comparable to a process that Lévi-Strauss described as bricolage. A French word for a jack-of-all-trades, *bricoleur* entered social theory via Lévi-Strauss's comparison with the engineer (1966). Lévi-Strauss argued that the engineer worked from a plan or first principles, whereas the bricoleur worked with the objects at hand under an opportunistic or tinkering "logic of the concrete." After laboratory studies revealed the indexical nature of laboratory science as tinkering (e.g., Knorr-Cetina 1981), scientists began to look more like bricoleurs than ideal-typical engineers in the Lévi-Straussian formulation. More generally, as new groups enter into scientific disciplines, or as science passes into the general public, theories and knowledge are sometimes subject to a general process of reconstruction akin to bricolage.

For a better understanding of reconstruction, the interpretive methods of deconstruction are more appropriate than those of structuralism. Deconstruction is often introduced via Derrida's critique of logocentrism, an ethnocentrism of the philosophical subject that he attributed to a long line of thinkers, including de Saussure (1966). Derrida (1974) argued that the logocentric primacy of speech over writing reflects the erroneous Western assumption of the primacy of the subject over language. In more STS terms, one might translate Derrida as critiquing the assumption of the primacy of actors over networks or, in more social theoretical terms, of individuals over society and actors over structure. Of more importance to the cultural studies of science and technology than Derrida's critique of logocentrism is his way of thinking about cultural codes that departs from the structuralist analysis of symbolic oppositions (e.g., male/female). Instead, Derrida developed an analysis of implicit hierarchies in which one term is supplementary and the other is, to borrow a term from Louis Dumont (1980), the encompassing term. This way of thinking about symbolism can be a powerful tool for detecting phallocentrism and other kinds of cultural biases in scientific representations, texts, and language in general.

For example, in the conventional patriarchal use of most Western languages, the pair of terms "man/woman" is also a hierarchy in which "man" is the encompassing term that stands for the species. In turn the species category "man" includes the gendered division "man/woman," with woman as the supplemental term. In turn, "woman" as the female of the species includes the terms "woman" for the adult and "girl" for the child, the new supplemental term. Deconstructive interpretations show how an apparently neutral opposition is in turn a hierarchy, which in turned can be inverted by showing how the supplemental term (or theory) can be reinterpreted as the conditions of possibility of the first. A major use of this strategy is in feminist literary studies, which provide new readings of old texts that bring out an overlooked viewpoint such as the submerged perspective of a woman character. A similar strategy underlies some accounts of gender and science, in which hidden female perspectives are brought out to undermine sexist or androcentric male accounts.

A classic example is the critique of the master molecule theory of DNA, with its implicit cultural mappings onto hierarchies of race and gender. A number of scholars have pointed out the cultural subtext of the master molecule theory of early molecular biology, which involves a sort of chain of command from the DNA to the RNA to the manufacture of protein.[22] This view of the cell assigns activity to the nucleus and passivity to the cytoplasm, and the cultural categories of activity/passivity are extremely gender-laden. As Emily Martin (1991) argues, the gendering of these spaces in the cell occurs not only through general association with assignments of activity and passivity, but also through the traditional theory that the egg is the passive vehicle that the active sperm fertilizes. This is because sperm contributes to the nucleus of the egg and transforms it, whereas the cytoplasm remains in a sense a female space. Of course, accuracy issues are distinct from issues of cultural meaning, and theories of the master molecule or the active nucleus and sperm may or may not be justifiable. However, feminist theory and deconstructive analysis help to set off alarm bells that make it possible to question those representations as potentially inaccurate.

It turns out that the active sperm model has been discredited as inaccurate, but as Martin shows, the new active egg model soon accumulated equally gendered and negative associations.

Public Understanding of Science and Technology

Cultural and anthropological studies of supplemental terms and reconstruction put a new twist on the study of the public understanding of science (PUS or PUST, to include technology). In a review essay on PUS literature, Brian Wynne (1994) divided the empirical studies into three main groups: large-scale quantitative surveys of selected samples of the public, cognitive models of lay understandings of science, and field studies of how people in different social contexts experience and construct the meaning of scientific expertise. As Wynne notes, surveys frequently "reinforce the syndrome . . . in which only the public, and not science or scientific culture and institutions, are problematized" (370). In contrast, field studies tend to emphasize the processes of how lay groups actively reconstruct science. Here, we see a hierarchical configuration of terms—scientists and the lay public—that field studies tend to question.

Scientists who were concerned with loss of taxpayer support for their research projects were early supporters of research on the PUS. Surveys revealed that lay understandings of most scientific concepts and research are very poor. In other words, "scientific literacy" is low. From the scientists' perspective the problem is therefore one of transmitting science to the public. Some social scientists share this concern and point to the troubling implications of low scientific literacy for a viable democracy. For example, Merton worried that the public was "susceptible to new mysticisms expressed in apparently scientific terms" and therefore subject to totalitarian ideology (1973: 277). Drawing on theories and methods from cultural anthropology, Christopher Toumey analyzes cases in which "the *appearance* of scientific authority can be easily conjured from cheap symbols and ersatz images like an actor's white coat" (1996: 6). Toumey discussed the troubling implications of the "conjuring" of scientific authority for a democratic culture.

Sociologist Dorothy Nelkin and colleagues have contributed a somewhat different approach to PUS issues in a democratic culture through their studies of scientific and technical controversies (Nelkin 1992, 1994). Examples include fetal research, animal rights, ozone depletion, nuclear energy, and creation science. Nelkin and colleagues tend to approach these controversies as articulations of wider conflicts between values and social groups, not as simple cases of rational scientists and irrational publics. Often the clashes involve two "goods," such as political priorities versus environmental values, economic interests versus health risks, and individual rights versus social goals. Nelkin has also tracked how the technical controversies have changed over time. For example, she noted, "By the end of the 1980s protesters increasingly framed their attacks on science in the moral language of rights" (1992: xii). Nelkin's research reveals that these technical conflicts are a continuation of fundamental value conflicts in the broader society. This framework suggests a much more sophisticated analysis of the PUS than the transmission model held by some scientists.

A number of studies by sociologists and anthropologists demonstrate that lay groups develop fairly sophisticated understandings of science when it is in their interest to do so. For example, Brian Wynne (1996) examined the local understandings of radiation pollution in the Lake District of northern England. The Chernobyl incident was accompanied by high levels of rainfall in this region, and sheep farmers subsequently learned that their flocks were contaminated. However, the government intervention came via a series of mixed messages, and scientists did not take local knowledge into consideration as they developed their analyses. As a result, some of the scientists' recommendations were ludicrous in light of lay knowledge about grazing patterns, local ecology, and local soil types. Furthermore, longstanding suspicions about contamination from the nearby Sellafield Nuclear Plant reemerged as farmers began to suspect that the Chernobyl incident was being used to cover up a local radioactive contamination problem. Thus, Wynne demonstrates not only that lay groups can develop a relatively sophisticated skepticism of expert knowledge (provided that it is worth their while to do so), but also that expert groups can fail—both technically and politically—when they do not take into account local knowledge. If the scientists had listened to the farmers, they would have produced better scientific models of the radiation as well as better policy recommendations for handling the contamination.

Wynne's approach is somewhat similar to the lessons of development anthropologists who have examined local responses to technical change. A classic example is Lauriston Sharp's "Steel Axes for Stone Age Australians" (1952), which demonstrates the impact of an apparently innocuous technology transfer: steel axes. Sharp shows that the transfer accelerated the disintegration of the social structure and cosmology that was accompanying missionary work and contact with whites in general. As in the case of Wynne's sheep farmers, Sharp attempts to show how the failure to take local knowledge into account can be disastrous. In fact, Sharp founded Cornell's anthropology department with the hope that anthropologists could help avoid some of the disasters that often occurred in development projects that were planned without considering local knowledge.

In the decades since "Steel Axes," some grassroots groups in the third world, as well as some anthropologists, have come to question even an enlightened pro-development position such as Sharp's vision of development projects that were guided by anthropological knowledge. As Arturo Escobar points out, "The authors in this trend state that they are interested not in development alternatives but in alternatives to development, that is, the rejection of the paradigm altogether" (1995: 215). Escobar analyzes and critiques development sciences, including their history, institutional practices, methods, and relations to alignments of global power.

A related expansion of PUS via anthropology would be to rethink the study of ethnoscience as a version of PUS studies. The term "ethnoscience" sometimes refers to a method for a relatively formal analysis of classification systems, usually local and non-Western. However, the term can also be used for the study of any of the various non-Western or folk Western knowledge systems. Used in this way, which seems preferable, "ethnoscience" is a general term that can include disciplinary divisions that mirror those of Western knowledge, for example, ethnoastronomy, ethnobotany, ethnomedicine, ethnopsychiatry, and so forth. (Hess 1995: ch. 7). Study of indigenous and non-Western knowledge systems can lead to a rethinking of some Western sciences from a non-Western perspective. Non-Western approaches have been particularly prevalent in the medical field; for example, they have provided ways of rethinking standard psychiatric categories and assumptions (Kleinman 1988). Studies of ethnosciences also have implications for rethinking development projects that do not take into consideration local knowledges. One application has been the use of local games, kinship knowledge, and other formal systems as a means for improved mathematics pedagogy in schools (Borba 1990; Watson-Verran 1988).

An additional step in PUS research is to follow native groups and poor communities as they develop their own technologies and articulations with the global capitalist system. For example, one group in India developed a snake farm that sells venom to laboratories, and another group has developed a way to produce paper from the pod of a tree rather than from harvesting softwood forests (Hess 1995: ch. 8). In the United States, Paula

Treichler's research (1991) on the AIDS community and alternative medicine demonstrates how lay groups sometimes take steps toward doing their own research that poses a direct alternative to official medical research. In the AIDS movement this has taken the form of guerrilla clinics that offer and test alternative medicines. I am currently examining reconstructions of medicine in the alternative cancer therapy movement. This form of PUS can be particularly powerful because lay groups—or mixes of lay groups and marginalized scientists—can put together successful coalitions of alternative science. In the areas of medical treatment for chronic disease and research on environmental toxins, these coalitions can provide an important impetus for badly needed reforms in established research agendas.

More generally, PUS studies reveal the shortcomings of the transmission model that characterizes the lay anthropology of scientists and medical researchers. The idea that the main problem in the public understanding of science is that there is not enough of it is similar to the old colonialist narrative that it was the white man's burden to civilize the natives and domesticate the females. When applied to scientific literacy, this approach will lead to policy failures, just as the top-down development models led to disasters in the field. The alternative reconstruction model suggests that "the public" is often the possessor of profound knowledges. How well would scientists do if they were given literacy tests on automobile mechanics, mail delivery procedures, hairdressing, and so on? The public is not illiterate as much as busy. Research outlined above suggests that public groups are capable of understanding science when it touches their lives in significant and sustained ways. When this happens, lay groups often develop opinions and sometimes research that are at odds with the experts. For example, I have found that cancer patients who go "off-grid" into the world of alternative medicine often develop very sophisticated understandings of the relevant science. Although the PUS in this case may be narrowband in the sense that it is restricted to a small area of science, it is often very deep and enveloped in a sophisticated understanding of the politics and sociology of knowledge. In this situation a condescending approach of uplifting the illiterates will only lead to further polarization. Instead, relatively literate lay models of science need to be understood, analyzed, and tested empirically, and in some cases incorporated into expert science. Environmental and medical issues are two areas where lay knowledges point to substantial shortcomings in officially sponsored research programs.

Rethinking Values

The analysis of culture—comparatively across groups, genders, places, and times—provides one way to expand the discussion of values in science that was opened in previous chapters. To review, I began with the technical values for theory choice outlined by Kuhn, then examined the complementary list of Mertonian norms. However, the sociological studies of cumulative advantage theory and the SSK literature demonstrated the widespread importance of various types of particularistic values. These values play a variable role in key decisions such as the evaluation of personnel, choice of research problems and materials, and theoretical and methodological preferences. Subsequent work in cultural and critical studies of science and technology has helped generalize the analysis of values to show how sciences and theories are shaped by general cultural values even as they provide representations of or instrumental predictions for the world. The term "general cultural values" refers to values linked to ways of seeing the world associated with particular time periods, nations, classes, genders, ethnic groups, and so forth. Some researchers in the STS field (myself included) think of general cultural values not as contaminating forces that should be eliminated but as productive resources for theoretical, methodological, design, and other innovations. The question is not how to eliminate cultural values but instead how to find out which cultural values structure science and whether different or better sciences would result if other values replaced the ones currently in place.

For example, in the nineteenth century scientists tended to view the world in terms of grand temporal narratives that were consistent with the expansionary industrial and colonial cultures of the time. According to the contemporary view, the societies of the time were—and should be—expanding in a never-ending, onward-and-upward flow of progress. Values such as progress over time were not contaminations that prevented scientists from deriving accurate pictures of the world; instead, they were productive in that they provided the conditions of possibility for such theories as evolution, linguistic change, and the second law of thermodynamics. At the time those theories seemed more all-encompassing than they do today, when grand temporal narratives meet with greater skepticism in the general culture and scientists produce theories that are more consistent with the cultures they live in. By examining science comparatively across temporal cultures, it becomes easier to perceive the values that underlie the general contours of theories, including those of the present period. As a result, one is in a better position to propose alternatives and to understand current technocultural phenomena, such as the way in which complexity and chaos theory has tended to sweep across the intellectual landscape. Although these new theories may seem particularly attractive, it is exactly at the moment when they exert their attraction that they should be questioned from the distant view of a comparative perspective.

The key methodological issue in discussions of values is a comparative perspective. It is difficult to see the biases of existing theories until there is an alternative to which they can be compared. In the case of primatology as studied by Haraway (1989), several of the most profound alternatives emerged when previously excluded social categories — South Asians, Japanese, and Western women — entered the field. They were able to see what the Western men could not see, to go (sometimes boldly) where no white man had gone before. What appeared previously as pure representation now was revealed to be only partial representation that was grounded in cultural values. No doubt as new groups continue to enter the field (such as gay and lesbian scientists), there will be additional revisions that will reveal the doxa of the apparently very disparate views being debated today.

Similar insights occur when comparing the social organization of scientific research units across, for example, national cultures.[23] The organizational structure of academic departments and laboratories varies tremendously from one country to another, and the variation is part of a wider pattern of general social structural variation. In the United States the system tends to be based on competition, promotion via mobility, and the emergence of rising stars. In other countries promotion occurs more within comparatively rigid hierarchical structures that are part of a wider pattern of hierarchical models of family and social organization. These differences are not of mere scholarly interest; they can lead to substantial cross-cultural miscommunication in international meetings and projects of collaboration. They can also provide the conditions for different styles of national theory and research interests (Harwood 1993).

Finally, because science and technology policy itself is part of a broader political culture, values also structure policy processes. In a review of descriptive research on national values and policy, Andrew Webster delineated two key differences in national science and technology policy styles (1991: 62–65). In countries such as the United States, the policy process is open, competitive, and agonistic, rather than relatively closed and with limited experts and limited public scrutiny, as in Britain. Furthermore, in the United States and Britain the policy process is pluralistic rather than state-planned, as in the open, competitive Dutch system or the closed, limited Japanese system. In all cases, there are different styles of democratic participation, and one country may have lessons to offer others. Richard Sclove's work (1995a) is probably the primary exemplar of how to alter science and technology policy processes from the perspective of democratic values.

In short, the question of values remains central to STS, but that question has shifted to involve a more sophisticated and comparative understanding of values than in the Mertonian model of technical and institutional norms. Contemporary STS research opens up the problem to temporal, national, gender, democratic, and a range of other values as they ground institutions, theories, design, methods, policy, and other dimensions of science and technology. Furthermore, because values emerge from the actions of historically situated social actors, values are no longer seen as monolithic, but as contestable, contested, and subject to change. The wide range of values and contexts studied shows how scientific knowledge is part of culture even as it represents the world.

6

Conclusions

What good is science studies, technology studies, or STS as a whole? What is the value of all the terms, concepts, schools, and frameworks? In today's academy, this question has sinister undertones, particularly when it is asked in the context of science wars and budget cuts. All disciplines—and especially the very vulnerable interdisciplinary programs—are forced to justify themselves, and not merely in the philosophical or Calvinist sense of the word. We are asked to provide a reason for our continued existence. It is the most brutal form of justification: budgetary justification.

Perhaps the oldest answer to the question is that students need some appreciation of the history of science and technology. This has been the traditional justification for programs in the philosophy and history of science and technology. These programs are valuable because they provide all students, not only science students, with an understanding of the basic principles and history of science and technology. Presumably courses of this sort will help make students become better scientists or, if they do not become scientists, better supporters of science and more willing taxpayers. Langdon Winner (1996) appropriately calls this approach "HSTS," or the hooray for science and technology school.

Another apparently uncontroversial approach is the scientometric study of science, which has policy implications for the management of science. This branch of science studies is justified in terms of national policy goals such as making better decisions on which areas of science should receive public funding, rather than improving the public appreciation of science. Policy implications can also be fine-tuned to focus on local managerial issues such as organizing scientific work and workers in ways that enhance productivity. Scientometrics also looks familiar to scientists and engineers; it uses similar quantitative methods and styles of presentation. For the sake of a parallel, I will call this approach MSTS: managing science, technology, and society.

However transparent their justification seems, both HSTS and MSTS ultimately will run into conflict with scientists, engineers, and physicians. As in any field that professionalizes, historical, philosophical, or managerial studies of science and technology will become increasingly autonomous from the sciences and technologies that they study. In the process, their researchers will come to have representations of science and technology that differ from those of the scientists, engineers, and medical researchers. Managerially oriented social science will become increasingly intrusive, just as the philosophy of science will become more irrelevant and the history of science and technology more sacrilegious. Those who are even more extreme—the purveyors of SSK, cultural studies, feminism, radical science, or some version of a critical STS—will be seen as dangerous heretics who should be lined up and detenured in the science wars.

A better way to justify STS is to make the potential of conflict explicit, or even to capitalize on it by defining STS in terms of a widespread public concern with science, technology, and values. The concerned public includes many scientists, engineers, and physicians who themselves have developed organizations dedicated to ethics, values, and social responsibility issues. Thus, categories such as "scientists" and "STS scholars" need not be defined oppositionally. Instead, there are merely researchers and citizens who are concerned with preserving an institutional location for debate on science, technology, and values. From this perspective, STS is justified as the badly needed site where people who are concerned with the place of science and technology in a democratic society can debate these complicated issues. The issues may focus on the internal institutional dynamics of science, such as more equitable recruitment and retention of women and other historically excluded groups. Alternatively, the issues may involve the general place of science and technology in society: How can societies move toward a more "sustainable" ecological relationship? How can democratic principles be incorporated into the science policy process? How can the design of technology and urban space be reshaped in more equitable ways?

The very phrasing of these questions requires an exit from the neutrality and relativism of the constructivist period, and also from the dead-horse debates such as relativism versus realism. However, unlike some of my colleagues I believe that much of the previous research of STS can be made relevant to debates on values. For example, the philosophers' concerns with developing good prescriptive evaluation criteria can be helpful for public debates on which research and development programs should be funded. The quantitative sociology of science provides a good empirical basis for discussions of how to reform institutions. Even the constructivists have left a legacy of resources that make it easier to find those points in the history of a research program or technology where one pathway was chosen over another. They also help make it possible to find the roads no longer traveled by and to ask whether those roads deserve another try.

Intervention as Research and Action

It is also possible—and valuable—to translate the general question of a concern with values into concrete research agendas. One approach is a different kind of policy studies: one that focuses on how concerned citizens—both within their fields of expertise and outside them—intervene to change science and technology. The many types of intervention include the institutions of science and technology, technology use patterns, policy processes, and even the "content" of science itself. To flesh out this alternative type of policy studies, I will focus on one form of intervention, one that the lessons of feminism, cultural/critical studies, and constructivism teach us to regard as crucial: intervention into the "content" of science or the knowledge-making process itself. I divide research on the topic into three types of intervention: by experts in their own fields, by nonexperts, and by social scientists and humanities scholars.

Regarding the first area, SSK research provides an important resource for strategies. Studies of the rhetoric of fact construction and the mechanisms of controversy provide resources for scientists who wish to reform some aspect of their field. Furthermore, actor-network theory provides a potentially useful resource for reformers within scientific fields. Problematization would well describe the case of primatologist Jeanne Altmann, discussed by Haraway (1989), who intervened in a strategic way by focusing on methodology. In a classic paper, this primatologist reviewed several major sampling methods and pointed out when to use and not use each of them. Focusing on methodological reforms rhetorically puts the reformer on the side of "better science," but it also serves to translate potentially contentious theoretical issues into less dramatic technicalities. As Haraway describes it, "Her feminism was operationalized as a keen sense of critical method, with consequences for allowable narratives about women scientists and about animals" (1989: 307). Altmann's methodological strictures became an obligatory point of passage, and, to use the lingo of chapter 3, her paper on the topic reached the level of a citation classic before it faced obliteration by incorporation. However, Haraway's studies of feminist reconstructions of primatology suggest that while problematization and enrollment are important, intervention is a more complex process. As discussed in chapter 5, she points to the collective and social nature of intervention, and the importance of linkages to broader social movements.

Regarding the second type of intervention, by lay citizens, in several European countries citizen review panels provide a means of direct participatory policy making in which laypersons examine science and technology policy in the making. Although the results of these panels usually are nonbinding, citizen review panels do provide a potential mechanism for direct, participatory democracy in the science policy process and they do sometimes have an impact on national agendas (Sclove 1996). Environmental disputes are another area where nonexperts frequently develop alternative accounts of science. These disputes often take the form of accounts of environmental safety that are developed by well-financed corporations or the government and are in conflict with the knowledge of local citizens' activist groups. Gary Downey (1988) has explored some of the mechanisms that lay groups can use for developing alternative scientific interpretations in environmental disputes: reconstructing official data and pointing to internal contradictions in official accounts, recruiting renegade scientists and therefore destabilizing scientific consensus, and drawing on local knowledge to destabilize official accounts. They must also fight against what Brian Martin and Pam Scott (1992) call nondecision-making, or the operation of power "through issues never being thought of enough to warrant formal attention."

Probably more developed than the lay epidemiology of the environmental groups is the science that is emerging from alternative medical communities. Treichler's work on AIDS patients holds out the promise of a "democratic technoculture" in which basement science examines the efficacy of alternatives that official medicine refuses to consider. In the alternative cancer therapy movement, the outcomes research of the Gerson Research Organization promises an even higher level of sophistication in the making of science by groups outside the establishment (e.g., Hildenbrand et al. 1995).

Regarding the third area, intervention into scientific controversies by STS researchers, Downey and Juan Rogers (1995) have suggested "partner theorizing." Under this form of intervention, STS researchers work together with scientists or engineers and take their views into account in building strategies for change, as in the case of engineering curriculum reform (see also Woolgar 1996). This strategy has great potential, although it risks appropriation when one partner has greater prestige and power. It may be a more appropriate strategy in the case of support for community groups, and the Dutch model of science shops provides a possibly more productive site for partner theorizing. In science shops, faculty, students, and other university members provide research for unions, environmental- ists, and other nonprofit groups that do not have the resources to do their own research but do have the resources to act on the research provided by the scientists (see Sclove 1995a, 1995b, 1995c). These partnerships help bridge town/gown splits in ways that involve academic researchers directly in community struggles for improvement.

Similar to partner theorizing is the work of Brian Martin and colleagues (1986; also Martin 1997b) as activists in cases of intellectual suppression. According to Martin, suppression usually occurs when the research, teach- ing, or public statements of intellectuals threaten the vested interests of a corporation, government, or profession. The direct mechanisms of suppres- sion involve denying funds or work opportunities; blocking appointments, tenure, promotion, courses, and/or publication; preventing free speech; dismissal; harassment; blacklisting; and/or smearing reputations. The indi- rect mechanisms involve implied sanctions, a general climate of fear, or pressures for conformity. Usually complaints are made to a person's supervi- sor rather than the person directly. Martin and colleagues also distinguish suppression from repression, which involves physical violence such as beat- ings, imprisonment, torture, and murder; and oppression, which they de- fine as an institutionalized lack of justice or freedom. In a fascinating case study that reveals a new type of policy role for the STS analyst, Brian Martin (1996) has developed a partnership, in coalition with a journalist and a lawyer, with representatives of a marginalized AIDS theory. His publication of a working paper through the STS Department at the Univer- sity of Wollongong helped get a hearing for a viewpoint that he believed deserved more attention in the scientific community: the theory that AIDS emerged from bad polio vaccines.

Aspects of a Postconstructivist Science Studies

I have been developing an analytical framework for intervention-oriented research that takes advantage of the third-party position of the social scien- tist to provide an outside evaluation of the scientific merits of different positions in a controversy (Hess 1997a). Even framing the issue in this way reveals the distance from the classical controversy studies of the sociology of scientific knowledge. This alternative, which evaluates the scientific merits of different positions in a controversy rather than merely analyzing them sociologically, requires spending a great deal of time to acquire competency in the sciences in question. To paraphrase one of Marx's theses on Feuerbach, one must attempt to understand how the world is represented if one is to attempt to change it. In developing this framework, I have focused on one theory in the huge world of alternative medicine: the theory that bacterial infections play an overlooked role in cancer etiology.

This case study of an alternative cancer theory provides the empirical material with which I develop an alternative to the strong program and its successors in the sociology of scientific knowledge. It is far too easy to find faults in the strong program and its successors; much more difficult is the project of articulating an alternative and applying it to a concrete research problem. Thus, rather than provide yet another critique of the strong program, constructivism, and the sociology of scientific knowledge in general, I develop an alternative analytical framework that involves four basic steps that double as principles of analysis. The principles are as follows:

1. The analysis is political; it explores the operation of power in the history of a field of knowledge that becomes constituted by a consensus and attendant heterodoxies. Thus, I begin with an examination of the historical record on the suppression of one theory in cancer research and how that theory became part of the heterodoxy of the field of cancer research.

2. The analysis is cultural in the sense that it develops a sophisticated, noninstrumentalist explanation and explication of the dynamics of power that have been described in the first step. Although some researchers may prefer the term "sociological" or "social," I use the term "cultural" to flag a kind of analysis that does not reduce the explanation of consensus knowledge and heterodoxy to what Marshall Sahlins (1976) calls practical reason. In other words, it is far too easy to explain the history of suppression as the result of a coalition of interested parties who act in a mechanical way to attain status, enhance symbolic capital, protect their interests, or simply gain and maintain power. Instead, emphasis is placed on the role of evidence and efficacy in shaping the field of possibilities; thus, a picture of science as a rational activity is maintained. However, within this field of possibilities, sociocultural factors contribute to the structuring of preferences and the

crystallization of consensus. Interest theory is welded to a more complex interpretation of (1) the growth of the autonomy of research cultures that respond with some internal integrity to ecological changes in the political economy; (2) the role of gender in the construction of consensus knowledge; and (3) the place of transcultural movements in the destabilization of a consensus and associated suppressive apparati.

3. The analysis is evaluative; it draws on the philosophy of science to weigh the accuracy, consistency, pragmatic value, and potential social biases of the knowledge claims of the consensus and alternative research traditions. This principle assumes that a fully interdisciplinary STS analysis steps out of the traditional plane of social scientific analysis/critique (here formulated around the two strands of culture and power) to a prescriptive level. At this level, two types of evaluation take place: the evaluation of knowledge claims and the evaluation of proposed policy or political changes. The first type of evaluation is based on the standards of the best available scientific knowledge at the time of the evaluator's analysis, but it also assumes that those standards may themselves be biased against the research under analysis due to the same political and cultural processes already analyzed. The evaluation examines the content of the science itself from the philosophical perspective of constructive realism, that is, a position that recognizes both the constructed and the representational aspects of knowledge but that bases evaluation on the best available knowledge of cancer research. The view of knowledge is neither relativist (as for the ideal typical radical constructivist who does not allow for the power of the world to constrain evidence) nor algorithmic (as for the ideal typical naive realist who believes that the crucial experiment can generally resolve disputes over evidence). Rather, the nature of knowledge is assumed to be more like that of the legal profession and the qualitative social sciences, in which evidence can be established but always within a social situation that recognizes the power of cross-examination and interpretation. To establish criteria for evaluating the alternative research program, I draw on a wide range of sources in the philosophy of science, including the work of feminists as synthesized by Longino (1994).

4. The analysis is positioned; it provides an evaluation of alternative policy and political goals that could result in beneficial institutional and research program changes. As a social scientist, I assume that I will be positioned inside the controversy. The capturing literature demonstrates that this situation is inescapable, and therefore I am better off positioning

myself rather than letting someone else do it for me. In the terminology of the STS field, this level of analysis can be described as a type of reflexivity, but one that is more profoundly sociological or anthropological than previously discussed forms.

In my previous books (e.g., Hess 1993) I argued against a mere epistemological reflexivity of the strong program and suggested a culturally oriented reflexivity that operated at the level of the relations between the researcher's academic communities and the groups researched. As a next step, positioning is achieved not through the confessional (why I believe what I believe or how I did my research) or through deconstructive literary devices (such as secondary voices), but through the evaluation of agendas for potentially beneficial institutional changes and investments for future research. Because the analysis evaluates concrete policy recommendations, as a social scientist I am automatically positioned inside the controversy and therefore become part of it. Nevertheless, as a social scientist I also bring a unique perspective and position that does not mean complete alliance with any single position within the controversy.

In the process of developing this alternative vision for STS, I found many of its constituent disciplines—history, sociology, anthropology, philosophy, and policy—fundamental as points of reference. Empirically, the end result is a contribution to a growing national debate on the failure of the war on cancer and the need for a reformed cancer research agenda. Cancer will soon strike one in two Americans at some point during their lifetime, and nearly always someone among one's friends or relatives is facing the life-threatening disease. In this situation, decisions need to be made both personally about which therapies to use and nationally about a failed policy of research investments. When decisions of this magnitude are looming, relativism is impossible and the basic principles of a politically neutral philosophy, history, or social science are not viable. Nevertheless, there is still a great value in bringing a level of disciplined inquiry to the many pressing social issues that involve science and technology.

The principles I have outlined represent only one attempt to grapple with the issue of repositioning science studies inquiry after the constructivist period. A number of colleagues who could roughly be classified as affiliated with the cultural/critical studies wings of STS share at least some of the principles articulated here. The future of STS lies in its ability to provide a site for public debates on issues of social importance, and for the evaluation of major research programs and technological decisions. Far from the caricature of postmodern irrationalism that appears among some of the science war detractors, at its best STS provides intellectual tools and resources for injecting research and reasoning into debates of great public importance.

For Additional Information

For those interested in the attacks on STS known as the "science wars," a good place to start is issue 46–47 of *Social Text* (1996, vol. 14, nos. 1 and 2), which itself became part of the controversy. For an introduction to the philosophy of science, I have found Fuller (1993a), Hacking (1983), and Kourany's reader (1987) to be the most useful, and Idhe (1993) is a useful guide to the philosophy of technology. Callebut's collection of interviews (1993) gives a good taste of some contemporary debates in the field. For feminist philosophy of science, the standard starting points are philosophers such as Longino (1994) and Harding (1986, 1992). The journals *Social Epistemology* and *Studies in the History and Philosophy of Science* are examples of philosophically oriented journals where one tends to find an interdisciplinary orientation.

For the sociology of science, the classic text is Merton (1973), but the survey by Cole (1992) is more up-to-date and it provides one example of how American sociologists of science have responded to the sociology of scientific knowledge. The other main line of American sociologists includes Allison, Hagstrom, Hargens, Long, McGinness, and Reskin, whose work is cited in the bibliography. There is no equivalent introductory book for them, but their articles are reviewed in the chapter on the sociology of science, and Hagstrom (1965) may be a good starting point. The psychology of science literature is undeveloped and largely irrelevant to the other STS social sciences, but its use of variables and quantitative methods overlaps in some cases with the sociology of science, as in productivity studies and creativity studies. See Fuller et al. (1989) and Shadish and Fuller (1994) for introductions to the psychology of science.

For the sociology of scientific knowledge (sometimes called the new sociology of science), one might begin with introductions by Woolgar (1988), whose book is more programmatic; Webster (1991), whose book is more general and includes policy discussions; or Restivo (1994a), whose introductory chapter surveys a variety of sociological frameworks in science studies. For the SSK approach to technology, key articles are found in the reader by Bijker, Hughes, and Pinch (1987) and a subsequent collection by Bijker and Law (1992). There are also detailed reviews of work in the sociology of science and scientific knowledge in the huge *Handbook of Science and Technology Studies* (Jasanoff et al. 1994). For those who prefer to learn about a field by flipping through journals, I suggest *Scientometrics* for the quantitative end of the spectrum, *American Sociological Review* and *Social Forces* for the sociology of science, *Social Studies of Science* for the social studies of knowledge, and *Science, Technology, and Human Values* for a more general range of interdisciplinary social science articles.

There are some general surveys of the history of science and technology (e.g., Bernal 1969 or Pacey 1990), but I would encourage the reader to follow up the specialty literature in a specific area of interest. The conceptual debates tend to occur more around interpretations of specific historical events rather than around general theoretical issues, as in sociology and philosophy. The major American journals in the field are *Isis* and *Culture and Technology*, but there are many other journals in the history of science, technology, and medicine.

For critical science and technology studies, one would do well to survey the past issues of *Science as Culture*, but there are sometimes interesting articles on technology in the issues of *Research in Philosophy and Technology* and in *Science, Technology, and Human Values*. The reader by MacKenzie and Wajcman (1985) contains a general sample of technology studies, with some citation classics in critical technology studies included. Richard Sclove's Loka Institute is a good way to hook up with relevant activist groups. It can be reached at http://www.amherst.edu/~loka/.

For cultural studies and the anthropology of science and technology, I have written a survey book that focuses on cultural aspects of science and technology, including cross-cultural, multicultural, and temporal cultural issues (Hess 1995). I have used this book in my advanced undergraduate courses along with the excellent reader by Harding (1993). A volume edited by Downey, Dumit, and Traweek (1997) brings together some contributions by anthropologists and provides helpful information to newcomers to the field. Anthropology journals that occasionally include STS-related essays are *Cultural Anthropology, Current Anthropology,* and, for more applied and development-oriented material, *Human Organization*. The journal *Minerva* is another source of cross-cultural studies of science and technology. Irwin and Wynne (1996) provide a survey of public understanding of science issues; a journal by that name is also now available. For the literary/postmodern side of cultural studies, the journal *Configurations* is a good place to start, as is the reader by Gray et al. (1995). For the rhetoric of science, one might start with scholars such as Bazerman (1988) and Myers (1990), or Fuller (1993b) on philosophy and rhetoric. For feminist social and cultural studies of science, starting points are the journal *Signs*, collections such as Tuana (1989), and general books by scholars of influence such as Haraway (1991), Keller (1992), Martin (1987), and Rose (1994).

Notes

NOTES TO CHAPTER 2

1. Fuller (1993a), Gillies (1993), Hacking (1983), Kourany (1987), Losee (1993), and Rouse (1996).

2. I am following Popper's interpretation of Russell and Wittgenstein here (Popper 1963: 69).

3. See Saussure (1966) or Culler (1986) on semiotics, and Rouse (1996) on contemporary philosophical debates on meaning.

4. Fuller notes that the distinction has a history that dates back to the nineteenth century, especially to William Whewell, who coined the term "scientist" and was a founder of the history and philosophy of science. The distinction had a social basis in Whewell's attempt to define a place for science and to ensure a privileged role for universities (Fuller, personal correspondence, January 2, 1996; citing Yeo 1993; see also Hoyningen-Huene 1987).

5. Fuller (1994: 255; and personal correspondence, January 2, 1996).

6. The term "Duhem-Quine thesis" may be a bit of a misnomer because Duhem's and Quine's versions are different (Gillies 1993: 98). See Duhem (1982), Quine (1980), and Hesse (1980a).

7. Laudan (1977: 114). It is helpful to keep in mind the difference between ad hoc theorizing and post hoc analyses. The latter are statistical analyses made after data come in and reported in the discussion section of a paper. Often researchers perform post hoc analyses to find out why negative results were obtained. As a clearly labeled exploratory exercise for future hypothesis generation and research, they can be useful. However, when used with post hoc explanations and when multiple post hoc analyses are made on the same data, post hoc analyses are considered methodologically unsound. When post hoc analyses are not labeled and are reported as "pre hoc" hypotheses in the results section, they are fraudulent.

8. See Solomon and Hackett (1996), Yearley (1995), and, for an applied discussion in the context of alternative medicine, Jaffe (1996).

9. Fuller (1992: 245); on Kuhn as a sociologist, see Hesse (1980b: 32) and Restivo (1983: 294).

10. Although the term "anomaly" is widely associated with Kuhn, there are other uses in the literature. For example, historians have frequently pointed out that

researchers who pay attention to anomalies rather than ignore them have occasionally made major theoretical or empirical breakthroughs. Another example is anomalistics, the term for the scientific study of anomalies defined as claims of phenomena not generally accepted by the bulk of the scientific community. In the United States, the Society for Scientific Exploration studies anomalistics. Probably the Kuhnian theory of anomalies influenced the researchers' choice to position and name their field as anomalistics.

11. In addition to the Lakatos and Musgrave volume (1970), see Hacking (1983: ch. 5), who distinguished among topic-incommensurability, dissociation, and meaning-incommensurability, and Fuller (1988: ch. 5), who distinguished between textual and ecological incommensurability.

12. Laudan also proposed a solution to the metamethodological problem of justifying justification strategies. In other words, justification strategies often have a hierarchical structure in which theories are justified by methodological rules, which in turn are justified by more general aims, but the justification of general aims opens the door to social and cultural contamination. To escape this problem, Laudan proposed a reticulated model of an interacting triad in which the three categories of theories, methods, and aims are set in motion to justify each other (1984: ch. 3). However, the reticulated model itself then faces the problem of how to justify the complex triangle of relationships.

13. As Rouse (1996) clarifies, this is the first of three programs developed by Laudan, for which the reticulated model served as the second phase. Because Laudan's second and third approaches did not contribute to the theory-choice criteria debate with the specificity that his first program did, I focus only on the first program.

14. See Hacking (1983: ch. 4) for a discussion of the relationship between pragmatism and realism.

15. Constructive empiricism, Van Fraasen's reply (1980) to ontological realism, holds that instead of thinking of theories as either true or false, they should be deemed only empirically adequate or not.

16. The principle of common cause holds that when two events are correlated, either one causes the other or the two are caused by a third event. Salmon (1989: 110) defended the principle of common cause as well as an account of causality as a mechanism for the transmission of marks or structures in the world. Kitchner added the idea of the unification of causes to a comprehensive theory (Losee 1993: ch. 15). Van Fraasen has criticized the common cause principle and defended a more pragmatic, "erotetic" approach to explanation, in which explanation is understood as an answer to a why question (1980). For an introduction that includes essays by Hempel, Salmon, and van Fraasen, see Kourany (1987).

17. Giere (1993, 1995), Fuller (1993a: 5), and probably Haraway (1989). On how evolutionary theory could be reframed according to temporal cultures, see my discussion in Hess (1995: ch. 4).

18. Some of the work in the social studies of science and the philosophy of science in the 1990s has shifted attention from science as representation to science as practice (e.g., Pickering 1992; Rouse 1995). The general philosophical implications of this shift have yet to be determined. For the purposes of the discussion here, moderate constructivism could also be extended to cover practices, much as culture includes both myth and ritual. Furthermore, regarding the general issue of theory-choice criteria to which this chapter is dedicated, the turn to practices has not contributed to the debate by providing grounds for an alternative set of theory-choice criteria.

19. The term "cognitive cronyism" is from Travis and Collins (1991), and "cognitive particularism" is from Cole (1992: 184).

20. For example, see the constructive realism of Giere (1988) or the "hard program" of Schmaus et al. (1992).

21. Fuller (1993a: 59–61), following Redner (1986).

NOTES TO CHAPTER 3

1. I am greatly indebted for this and other background historical information, as well as many specific comments, to Lowell Hargens. Although he cannot be held responsible for the ideas in this chapter, as an "informant" on the history of the sociology of science community, he has provided invaluable help.

2. The Wisconsin-Berkeley-Cornell axis had the following genealogy: Warren Hagstrom's students included Paul Allison and Lowell Hargens, and Hargens's students included Barbara Reskin. At Cornell, where Allison and Robert McGinness were on the faculty, McGinness, Allison, and Scott Long worked on the scientific career, and Daryl Chubin, Ken Studer, and Carl Backman worked on specialties. McGinness was the committee chair for Long and Edward Hackett. Merton's students during the earlier period also included Bernard Barber and Diana Crane (Ben-David 1978: 198–200).

3. On SSK critiques of norms, see Barnes and Dolby (1970) and Mulkay (1976); on SSK interest theory, see Barnes and MacKenzie (1979).

4. Merton's other teachers included George Sarton, Pitirim Sorokin, and L. J. Henderson (Crothers 1987: 25).

5. Barnes and Dolby (1970), Long et al. (1979), McGinness et al. (1982), Mitroff (1974), Mulkay (1976), and Reskin (1976).

6. On the historical importance of the Merton essay (1957) for the sociology of science, see Hargens (1978: 124) and Ben-David (1978: 200).

7. For subsequent work on autonomy, see Cozzens (1990).

8. Fox (1994: 205), citing Bayer and Astin (1975), Reskin (1976), and Zuckerman and Cole (1975).

9. See Long (1978); Long et al. (1979); Long and McGinness (1981); and Reskin (1977). See also Knorr et al. (1979).

10. Earlier literature is reviewed by Merton and Zuckerman in Merton (1973: ch. 22), and subsequent developments are reviewed by Fox (1983) and Stephan and Levin (1992). Because the variables "creativity" and "productivity" sometimes overlap, this literature tends to overlap with psychological studies of creativity (see Shadish and Neimeyer 1994: 16–17).

11. Research in the 1970s and earlier is reviewed by Stankiewicz (1979) and Cohen (1981).

12. See Merton (1973: ch. 16) and research notes by Westrum, Simonton, and Constant (1979).

13. See Hackett (1994), discussing Stephan and Levin (1992).

14. The hypothesis at one point received so much interest that a special issue of *Scientometrics* was devoted to it (1987, vol. 12, nos. 5–6), but results are still not consistent. See Kretschmer and Müller (1990); Kretschmer (1993).

15. For recent discussions, see Gupta (1987) as well as Allison et al. (1976).

16. The group was built around three initial members (Gernot Böhme, Wolfgang van den Daele, and Wolfgang Krohn) and three later members (Wolf Schäfer, Rainer Hohlfeld, and Tilman Spengler).

17. For a discussion of productivity measures for multiple authorship and whether adjustments for multiple authorship are necessary, see Long and McGinness (1982a, 1982b) and Lindsey (1982).

NOTES TO CHAPTER 4

1. See Haraway's essays that later appeared in Haraway (1989, 1991), as well as Harding (1986), Keller (1985), and Merchant (1980).

2. On the former, see Marcus and Fischer (1986); on the latter for this same period, see Martin (1987) and Rapp (1988, 1990).

3. For a survey of supplementarity and other deconstructive concepts and reading techniques for the recovery of gendered and other subaltern perspectives, see Culler (1982).

4. On the problem in the interests theory debate, see Barnes (1981), MacKenzie (1981, 1984), Woolgar (1981a, 1981b), and Yearley (1982). Kim (1994) makes a more realist-oriented critique.

5. See Mullins (1973a, 1973b) for a sociological account of ethnomethodology and Michael Lynch (1985) for an example of ethnomethodology in science studies.

6. Galison (1995). See also Baigrie (1995) and Pickering (1992).

7. Furthermore, in anthropology the term refers to the mid-twentieth-century studies of peasant societies, civilizations, and the folk/urban continuum associated with Robert Redfield, the son-in-law of Robert Park, and Milton Singer. In economics during the 1970s and 1980s the term referred to the free-market school of Milton Friedman.

8. On other studies of large technical systems, see LaPorte (1994), and on macroengineering, see Hori (1990).

9. Of translation, Callon writes, "From marks to diagram, from table to graph, from graph to statement, and from statement to statement—each is a translation" (1994: 51). Inscription is the reduction or translation of complex observable processes to features represented in two-dimensional spaces (Latour, Mauguin, and Teil 1992). "Inscription" therefore refers to all written marks, which "include graphic displays, laboratory notebooks, tables of data, brief reports, lengthier and more public articles and books" (Callon 1994: 50).

NOTES TO CHAPTER 5

1. For an introduction, see During (1993) and Turner (1992). Oxford University Press now has a series of cultural studies readers for other European countries.

2. See Grossberg et al. (1992) on cultural studies in general, and Rouse (1991) and Traweek (1993) for two reviews oriented toward STS issues.

3. Examples of this tradition include Downey et al. (1997), Haraway (1989), Martin (1994), Penley and Ross (1991), and Traweek (1992).

4. See Bocock (1986) for a review of the concept.

5. For an introduction to studies of race, craniometry, and related topics in science, see the essays collected in Harding (1993).

6. For more on resistance in the context of the poor countries and indigenous groups, see Hess (1995: ch. 8). For resistance in the context of developed countries and controversies involving nuclear power, information technology, and biotechnology, see Bauer (1995). Also watch for forthcoming research by Ron Eglash of Ohio State University.

7. For a review of the appropriate technology movement in the United States, see Pursell (1993).

8. E.g., Davis-Floyd (1992a), Edwards and Franklin (1993), Layne (1992), Martin (1987), and Rapp (1991).

9. Merton (1973: ch. 11; 1984); also Abraham (1983) and Shapin (1988).

10. See Restivo (1979) for an introduction to Joseph Needham's massive, multivolume work.

11. Hessen's work dates back to the 1930s, and like that of Fleck (1979) and Mannheim (1952), is considered a precursor to the contemporary sociology of scientific knowledge. For a sociological account of Hessen's theory in the context of Soviet science, see Graham (1985).

12. See also Keller (1985) on Bacon, and Noble (1992) and Schiebinger (1989) on women and the early history of modern science.

13. Cohen (1994) reviews these and other accounts of the scientific revolution. See also Hess (1995: ch. 5) for a review that emphasizes the multicultural aspects of scholarship on the scientific revolution.

14. On the Forman thesis, see Forman (1971), Fuller (1988: ch. 10), and Hendry (1980).

15. See the special issue of *Science as Culture* (1990, vol. 8).

16. Sample laboratory studies were Knorr-Cetina (1981), Latour and Woolgar (1986, orig. 1979), Lynch (1985), and to some extent Collins and Pinch (1982), although the latter was more a study in controversy that moved outside laboratories and was much more like anthropological ethnography.

17. Traweek (1988, 1992). See Hess (1991a, 1997b) for an articulation of the methodological background of the second wave and a more detailed analysis of ethnography in STS.

18. Examples include Clarke and Montini (1993: 44), Clarke (1990), Hess (1991b), Martin (1994), Rapp (1990), and Traweek (1992).

19. See Bourdieu (1991). Because the contemporary anthropological use of the culture concept in American anthropology is flexible enough to recognize the dialectic of actors and structures, there seems to be little need to clutter up the vocabulary with similar concepts such as Bourdieu's "habitus."

20. E.g., Ortner (1974), MacCormack and Strathern (1980).

21. For introductions to these literatures, see Hess (1995: ch. 6) and Irwin and Wynne (1996).

22. See, for example, Gilbert (1989) and Keller (1985). For a more detailed summary of the studies, see Hess (1995: 27–32).

23. For a review, see Hess (1995: ch. 5), which builds on a research tradition that dates back at least to Ben-David (1971).

Bibliography

Abir-Am, Pnina
1987 *Uneasy Careers and Intimate Lives: Women in Science, 1789–1979.* New Brunswick: Rutgers University Press.

Abraham, Gary
1983 "Misunderstanding the Merton Thesis." *Isis 74:* 368–87.

Allison, Paul, and J. Scott Long
1987 "Interuniversity Mobility of Academic Scientists." *American Sociological Review* 52: 643–52.

Allison, Paul, Derek de Solla Price, Belver Griffith, Michael Moravcsik, and John Stewart
1976 "Lotka's Law: A Problem in Its Interpretation and Application." *Social Studies of Science 6:* 269–76.

Angier, Natalie
1995 "Why Science Loses Women in the Ranks." *New York Times,* May 14, section 4, p. 5.

Ashmore, Malcolm
1989 *The Reflexive Thesis.* Chicago: University of Chicago Press.

Baer, Hans
1987 "Divergence and Convergence in Two Systems of Manual Medicine: Osteopathy and Chiropractic in the United States." *Medical Anthropology Quarterly 1 (2):* 176–93.

1989 "The American Dominative Medical System as a Reflection of Social Relations in the Larger Society." *Social Science and Medicine 28 (11):* 1103–12.

Baigrie, Brian
1995 "Scientific Practice: The View from the Tabletop." In Jed Buchwald (ed.), *Scientific Practice: Theories and Stories of Doing Physics.* Chicago: University of Chicago Press.

Balsamo, Anne
1996 *Technologies of the Gendered Body.* Durham: Duke University Press.

Barber, Bernard
1952 *Science and the Social Order.* New York: Macmillan.

Barnes, Barry
1977 *Interests and the Growth of Knowledge.* London: Routledge.
1981 "On the 'Hows' and 'Whys' of Cultural Change." *Social Studies of Science 11:* 481–98.

Barnes, Barry, and R. G. A. Dolby
1970 "The Scientific Ethos: A Deviant Viewpoint." *Archives Européenes de Sociologie 11:* 3–25.

Barnes, Barry, and Donald MacKenzie
1979 "On the Role of Interests in Scientific Change." In Roy Wallis (ed.), *On the Margins of Science.* Sociological Review Monograph No. 27. Keele, Staffordshire: University of Keele.

Barnes, Barry, and Steven Shapin (eds.)
1979 *Natural Order.* Beverly Hills: Sage.

Bauer, Martin (ed.)
1995 *Resistance to New Technology.* New York: Cambridge University Press.

Bayer, Alan, and Helen Astin
1975 "Sex Differentials in the Academic Reward System." *Science 188:* 796–802.

Bazerman, Charles
1988 *Shaping Written Knowledge.* Madison: University of Wisconsin Press.

Beder, Sharon
1991 "Controversy and Closure: Sydney's Beaches in Crisis." *Social Studies of Science 21:* 223–56.

Ben-David, Joseph
1960 "Roles and Innovations in Medicine." *American Journal of Sociology 65:* 557–68.
1971 *The Scientist's Role in Society: A Comparative Study.* Chicago: University of Chicago Press.
1978 "Emergence of National Traditions in the Sociology of Science: The United States and Great Britain." In Jerry Gaston (ed.), *Sociology of Science.* San Francisco: Jossey-Bass.

Ben-David, Joseph, and Randall Collins
1966 "Social Factors in the Origins of a New Science: The Case of Psychology." *American Sociological Review 31 (4):* 451–65.

Bernal, J. D.
1969 *Science in History.* Cambridge: MIT Press.

Bijker, Wiebe
1987 "The Social Construction of Bakelite: Toward a Theory of Invention." In Wiebe Bijker, Thomas Hughes, and Trevor Pinch (eds.), *The Social Construction of Technological Systems.* Cambridge: MIT Press.
1993 "Do Not Despair: There Is Life after Constructivism." *Science, Technology, and Values 18 (1):* 113–38.

1994 "Sociohistorical Technology Studies." In Sheila Jasanoff, Gerry Markle, James Peterson, and Trevor Pinch (eds.), *Handbook of Science and Technology.* Beverly Hills: Sage.

Bijker, Wiebe, Thomas Hughes, and Trevor Pinch (eds.)
1987 *The Social Construction of Technological Systems.* Cambridge: MIT Press.

Bijker, Wiebe, and John Law (eds.)
1992 *Shaping Technology/Building Society.* Cambridge: MIT Press.

Bleier, Ruth
1986 *Feminist Approaches to Science.* New York: Pergamon.

Bloor, David
1991 *Knowledge and Social Imagery.* 2nd edition. Chicago: University of Chicago Press.

Bocock, Robert
1986 *Hegemony.* New York: Tavistock.

Böhme, Bernot, Wolfgang van den Daele, and Wolfgang Krohn
1976 "Finalization in Science." *Social Science Information 15:* 307–30.

Borba, Marcelo
1990 "Ethnomathematics and Education." *For the Learning of Mathematics 10 (1):* 39–43.

Bourdieu, Pierre
1975 "The Specificity of the Scientific Field and the Social Conditions of the Progress of Reason." *Social Scientific Information 14 (6):* 19–47.

1991 *Language and Symbolic Power.* Cambridge: Harvard University Press.

Bradie, Michael
1986 "Assessing Evolutionary Epistemology." *Biology and Philosophy 1:* 401–50.

Braverman, Harry
1974 *Labor and Monopoly Capital.* New York: Monthly Review.

Broadus, R. N.
1987 "Toward a Definition of 'Bibliometrics.'" *Scientometrics 12:* 373–79.

Bullard, Robert
1990 *Dumping in Dixie: Race, Class, and Environmental Equity.* Boulder: Westview.

Bunge, Mario
1982 "Demarcating Science from Nonscience." *Fundamenta Scientiae 3:* 369–88.

Burrell, Q. L.
1991 "The Bradford Distribution and the Gini Index." *Scientometrics 21:* 181–94.

Callebut, Werner
1993 *Taking the Naturalistic Turn, or How Real Philosophy of Science Is Done.* Chicago: University of Chicago Press.

Callon, Michel
1986 "Some Elements of a Sociology of Translation: Domestication of the Scallops and Fishermen." In John Law (ed.), *Power, Action, and Belief.* Sociological Review Monograph No. 32 (University of Keele). London: Routledge.
1994 "Four Models for the Dynamics of Science." In Sheila Jasanoff, Gerry Markle, James Peterson, and Trevor Pinch (eds.), *Handbook of Science and Technology.* Beverly Hills: Sage.

Callon, Michel, J. P. Courtial, and F. Laville
1991 "Co-Word Analysis as a Tool for Describing a Network of Interactions between Basic and Technological Research: The Case of Polymer Chemistry." *Scientometrics 22:* 155–205.

Callon, Michel, and John Law
1982 "On Interests and Their Transformation: Enrollment and Counterenrollment." *Social Studies of Science 12:* 615–25.

Callon, Michel, John Law, and Arie Rip (eds.)
1986 *Mapping the Dynamics of Science and Technology.* London: Macmillan.

Campbell, Donald
1979 "A Tribal Model of the Social System Vehicle Carrying Scientific Knowledge." *Knowledge: Creation, Diffusion, Utilitization 1:* 181–201.

Cano, V., and N. C. Lind
1991 "Citation Life Cycles of Ten Citation Classics." *Scientometrics 22:* 297–312.

Carnap, Rudolf
1995 *An Introduction to the Philosophy of Science.* Mineola, N.Y.: Dover Books.

Chubin, Daryl
1983 *Sociology of Sciences: An Annotated Bibliography on Invisible Colleges, 1972–81.* New York: Garland.
1990 "Scientific Malpractice and the Contemporary Politics of Knowledge." In Susan Cozzens and Thomas Gieryn (eds.), *Theories of Science in Society.* Bloomington: Indiana University Press.

Chubin, Daryl, and Sal Restivo
1983 "The 'Mooting' of Science Studies: Research Programmes and Science Policy." In Karin Knorr-Cetina and Michael Mulkay (eds.), *Science Observed.* Beverly Hills: Sage.

Clarke, Adele
1990 "A Social Worlds Adventure." In Susan Cozzens and Thomas Gieryn (eds.), *Theories of Science in Society.* Bloomington: Indiana University Press.

Clarke, Adele, and Theresa Montini
1993 "The Many Faces of RU486: Tales of Situated Knowledges and Technological Contestations." *Science, Technology, and Values 18 (1):* 42–78.

Clifford, James
1988 "On Ethnographic Authority." In *The Predicament of Culture*. Cambridge: Harvard University Press.

Clifford, James, and George Marcus
1986 *Writing Culture*. Berkeley: University of California Press.

Cohen, H. Floris
1994 *The Scientific Revolution: A Historiographical Inquiry*. Chicago: University of Chicago Press.

Cohen, J. E.
1980 "Publication Rate as a Function of Laboratory Size in a Biomedical Research Institution." *Scientometrics 2*: 35–52.

1981 "Publication Rate as a Function of Laboratory Size in Three Biomedical Research Institutions." *Scientometrics 3*: 467–87.

Cole, Jonathan
1987 *Fair Science*. New York: Columbia University Press.

Cole, Jonathan, and Stephen Cole
1973 *Social Stratification in Science*. Chicago: University of Chicago Press.

Cole, Stephen
1992 *Making Science*. Cambridge: Harvard University Press.

Cole, Stephen, Gary Simon, and Jonathan Cole
1988 "Do Journal Rejection Rates Index Consensus?" *American Sociological Review 53 (1)*: 152–56.

Collins, Harry
1983 "An Empirical Relativist Programme in the Sociology of Scientific Knowledge." In Karin Knorr-Cetina and Michael Mulkay (eds.), *Science Observed*. Beverly Hills: Sage.

1985 *Changing Order: Replication and Induction in Scientific Practice*. Beverly Hills: Sage.

1994a "Science Studies and Machine Intelligence." In Sheila Jasanoff, Gerry Markle, James Peterson, and Trevor Pinch (eds.), *Handbook of Science and Technology*. Beverly Hills: Sage.

1994b "A Strong Confirmation of Experimenter's Regress." *Studies in the History and Philosophy of Science 25 (3)*: 493–503.

Collins, Harry, and Trevor Pinch
1979 "The Construction of the Paranormal: Nothing Unscientific Is Happening." In Roy Wallis (ed.), *On the Margins of Science: The Social Construction of Rejected Knowledge*. Sociological Review Monograph No. 27. Keele, Staffordshire: University of Keele.

1982 *Frames of Meaning*. London: Routledge.

Collins, Randall
1975 *Conflict Sociology*. New York: Academic Press.

Collins, Randall, and Sal Restivo
1983 "Robber Barons and Politicians in Mathematics: A Conflict Model of Science." *Canadian Journal of Sociology 8 (2):* 199–227.

Cowen, Ruth Schwartz
1976 "The 'Industrial Revolution' in the Home: Household Technology and Social Change in the Twentieth Century." *Technology and Culture 17:* 1–23.

1983 *More Work for Mother.* New York: Basic Books.

Cozzens, Susan
1988 "Derek Price and the Paradigm of Science Policy." *Science, Technology, and Values 13 (3 & 4):* 361–72.

1990 "Autonomy and Power in Science." In Susan Cozzens and Thomas Gieryn (eds.), *Theories of Science in Society.* Bloomington: University of Indiana Press.

Crane, Diana
1965 "Scientists at Major and Minor Universities: A Study of Productivity and Recognition." *American Sociological Review 30:* 699–714.

1967 "The Gatekeepers of Science: Some Factors Affecting the Selection of Articles of Scientific Journals." *American Sociologist 2:* 195–201.

1972 *Invisible Colleges.* Chicago: University of Chicago Press.

Crothers, Charles
1987 *Robert K. Merton.* London and New York: Tavistock.

Culler, Jonathan
1982 *On Deconstruction.* Ithaca: Cornell University Press.

1986 *Ferdinand de Saussure.* Ithaca: Cornell University Press.

Davis-Floyd, Robbie
1992a *Birth as an American Rite of Passage.* Berkeley: University of California Press.

1992b "The Technocratic Body and the Organic Body: Cultural Models for Women's Birth Choices." In David Hess and Linda Layne (eds.), *Knowledge and Society. Vol. 9: The Anthropology of Science and Technology.* Greenwich, Conn.: JAI Press.

Derrida, Jacques
1974 *Of Grammatology.* Baltimore: Johns Hopkins University Press.

Dewey, John
1903 *Studies in Logical Theory.* Chicago: University of Chicago Press.

Doorly, Moyra
1985 "A Woman's Place: Dolores Hayden on the 'Grand Domestic Revolution.' " In Donald MacKenzie and Judy Wajcman (eds.), *The Social Shaping of Technology.* Philadelphia: Open University Press.

Downey, Gary
1988 "Structure and Practice in the Cultural Identities of Scientists: Negotiating Nuclear Wastes in New Mexico." *Anthropological Quarterly 61 (1):* 26–38.

Downey, Gary, Joe Dumit, and Sharon Traweek (eds.)
1997 *Cyborgs and Citadels.* Santa Fe: School for American Research Press.

Downey, Gary, and Juan Rogers
1995 "On the Politics of Theorizing in the Postmodern Academy." *American Anthropologist 97 (2):* 269–81.

Duhem, Pierre
1982 *The Aim and Structure of Physical Theory.* Princeton: Princeton University Press.

Dumont, Louis
1977 *From Mandeville to Marx.* Chicago: University of Chicago Press.

1980 *Homo Hierarchicus.* Chicago: University of Chicago Press.

Durbin, Paul
1988 *Dictionary of Concepts in the Philosophy of Science.* New York: Greenwood.

During, Simon (ed.)
1993 *The Cultural Studies Reader.* New York: Routledge.

Earman, John
1993 "Carnap, Kuhn, and the Philosophy of Scientific Methodology." In Paul Howich (ed.), *World Changes: Thomas Kuhn and the Nature of Science.* Cambridge: MIT Press.

Edge, David, and Michael Mulkay
1976 *Astronomy Transformed: The Emergence of Radio Astronomy in Britain.* New York: John Wiley and Sons.

Edwards, Jeannette, Sarah Franklin, Eric Hirsch, Frances Price, and Marilyn Strathern
1993 *Technologies of Procreation: Kinship in the Age of Assisted Conception.* Manchester: Manchester University Press.

Egghe, L.
1987 "An Exact Calculation of Price's Law for the Law of Lotka." *Scientometrics 11:* 81–97.

Elkana, Yehuda, Joshua Lederberg, Robert Merton, Arnold Thackery, and Harriet Zuckerman
1978 *Toward a Metric of Science.* New York: John Wiley and Sons.

Ellison, David
1978 *The Bio-Medical Fix: Dimensions of Bio-Medical Technologies.* Westport, Conn.: Greenwood.

Ellul, Jacques
1965 *The Technological Society.* New York: Knopf.

Engelhardt, H. Tristram, Jr., and Arthur Caplan
1987 *Scientific Controversies.* New York: Cambridge University Press.

Escobar, Arturo
1995 *Encountering Development: The Making and Unmaking of the Third World.* Princeton: Princeton University Press.

Feyerabend, Paul
1978 *Against Method.* London: Verso.

Fidell, L. S.
1975 "Empirical Verification of Sex Discrimination in Hiring Practices in Psychology." In Rhoda K. Unger and F. L. Denmark (eds.), *Women: Dependent or Independent Variable.* New York: Psychological Dimensions.

Fleck, Ludwik
1979 *Genesis and Development of a Scientific Fact.* Chicago: University of Chicago Press.

Forman, Paul
1971 "Weimar Culture, Causality, and Quantum Theory, 1918–1927: Adaptation by German Physicists and Mathematicians to a Hostile Intellectual Environment." In Russell McCormach (ed.), *Historical Studies in the Physical Sciences.* Philadelphia: University of Pennsylvania Press.

Foucault, Michel
1970 *The Order of Things.* New York: Vintage.

1972 *The Archaeology of Knowledge.* London: A. M. Sheridan Smith.

1979 *Discipline and Punish.* New York: Vintage.

1980 *Power/Knowledge.* Edited by Colin Gordon. New York: Pantheon.

Fox, Mary Frank
1983 "Publication Productivity among Scientists: A Critical Review." *Social Studies of Science 13:* 285–305.

1994 "Women and Science Careers." In Sheila Jasanoff, Gerry Markle, James Peterson, and Trevor Pinch (eds.), *Handbook of Science and Technology.* Beverly Hills: Sage.

Franklin, Jeffrey
1988 "Testing and Using Quantitative Methods in Science Policy Contexts." *Social Studies of Science 18:* 365–75.

Fujimura, Joan
1987 "Constructing Do-able Problems in Cancer Research: Articulating Alignment." *Social Studies of Science 17:* 257–93.

1995 "Ecologies of Action: Recombining Genes, Molecularizing Cancer, and Transforming Biology." In Susan Leigh Star (ed.), *Ecologies of Knowledge:*

Work and Politics in Science and Technology. Albany: State University of New York Press.

Fuller, Steve
1988 *Social Epistemology.* Bloomington: University of Indiana Press.
1992 "Being There with Thomas Kuhn: A Parable for Postmodern Times." *History and Theory 31 (3):* 241–75.
1993a *Philosophy of Science and Its Discontents.* 2nd edition. New York: Guilford.
1993b *Philosophy, Rhetoric, and the End of Knowledge.* Madison: University of Wisconsin Press.
1994 "Mortgaging the Farm to Save the (Sacred) Cow." *Studies in the History and Philosophy of Science 25 (2):* 251–61.

Fuller, Steve, Marc De Mey, Terry Shinn, and Steve Woolgar (eds.)
1989 *The Cognitive Turn: Sociological and Psychological Perspectives on Science. Sociology of Sciences Yearbook, Vol. 13.* Boston: Kluwer Academic Publishers.

Gage, Matilda
1882 *Woman as Inventor.* Boston: O. Everett.

Galison, Peter
1995 "Context and Constraints." In Jed Buchwald (ed.), *Scientific Practice: Theories and Stories of Doing Physics.* Chicago: University of Chicago Press.

Garfield, Eugene
1955 "Citation Indexes for Science." *Science 122:* 108–15.

Geertz, Clifford
1973 *The Interpretation of Cultures.* New York: Basic Books.

Geissen, Gerald, and Frederic Holmes (eds.)
1993 *Research Schools: Historical Reappraisals. Osiris Vol. 8, 2nd Series.*

Giere, Ronald
1988 *Explaining Science.* Chicago: University of Chicago Press.
1993 "Science and Technology Studies: Prospects for an Enlightened Postmodern Synthesis." *Science, Technology, and Values 18 (1):* 102–12.
1995 "Viewing Science." Presidential address, Philosophy of Science Association.

Gieryn, Thomas
1983 "Boundary-Work and the Demarcation of Science from Non-Science." *American Sociological Review 48:* 781–95.
1994 "Boundaries of Science." In Sheila Jasanoff, Gerry Markle, James Peterson, and Trevor Pinch (eds.), *Handbook of Science and Technology.* Beverly Hills: Sage.

Gieryn, Thomas, and Richard Hirsch
1983 "Marginality and Innovation in Science." *Social Studies of Science 13:* 87–106.

1984 "Marginalia: Reply to Simonton and Handberg." *Social Studies of Science* 14: 624.

Gilbert, Scott (Biology and Gender Study Group)
1989 "The Importance of Feminist Critique for Contemporary Cell Biology." In Nancy Tuana (ed.), *Feminism and Science*. Bloomington: Indiana University Press.

Gillies, Donald
1993 *Philosophy of Science in the Twentieth Century*. Cambridge, Mass.: Blackwell.

Gingras, Yves
1995 "Following Scientists through Society? Yes, but at Arm's Length!" In Jed Buchwald (ed.), *Scientific Practice: Theories and Stories of Doing Physics*. Chicago: University of Chicago Press.

Graham, Loren
1985 "The Sociopolitical Roots of Boris Hessen: Soviet Marxism and the History of Science." *Social Studies of Science* 15: 702–22.

Gray, Chris Hables, Heidi Figueroa-Sarriera, and Steven Mentor (eds.)
1995 *The Cyborg Handbook*. New York: Routledge.

Griffith, Belver, Henry Small, Judith Stonehill, and Sandra Dey
1974 "The Structure of Scientific Literatures II: Toward a Macro- and Microstructure for Science." *Science Studies* 4: 339–65.

Grossberg, Lawrence, Cary Nelson, and Paula Treichler (eds.)
1992 *Cultural Studies*. New York: Routledge.

Gupta, D. K.
1987 "Lotka's Law and Productivity Patterns of Entomological Research in Nigeria for the Period 1900–73." *Scientometrics* 12: 33–46.

Gusterson, Hugh
1996 *Nuclear Rites: A Weapons Laboratory at the End of the Cold War*. Berkeley: University of California Press.

Habermas, Jürgen
1972 *Knowledge and Interests*. London: Heinemann.

Hackett, Edward
1994 "Review of Striking the Mother Lode in Science." *Science, Technology, and Values* 19 (2): 247–53.

1995 "Dynamics of Research Groups: Initial Findings and Future Directions." Paper presented at the colloquium series of the Science and Technology Studies Department, Rensselaer Polytechnic Institute, March 22.

Hacking, Ian
1983 *Representing and Intervening*. Cambridge: Cambridge University Press.

Hagstrom, Warren
1965 *The Scientific Community*. New York: Basic Books.

Hakken, David, and Barbara Andrews
1993 *Computing Myths, Class Realities: An Ethnography of Technology and Working People in Sheffield, England.* Boulder: Westview.

Haraway, Donna
1989 *Primate Visions.* London: Routledge.

1991 *Simians, Cyborgs, and Women.* London: Routledge.

Harding, Sandra
1986 *The Science Question in Feminism.* Ithaca: Cornell University Press.

1992 "After the Neutrality Ideal: Science, Politics, and 'Strong Objectivity.' " *Social Research 59 (3):* 567–87.

Harding, Sandra (ed.)
1993 *The Racial Economy of Science.* New York: Routledge.

Hargens, Lowell
1978 "Theory and Method in the Sociology of Science." In Jerry Gaston (ed.), *Sociology of Science.* San Francisco: Jossey-Bass.

1988a "Further Evidence on Field Differences in Consensus from the NSF Peer Review Studies." *American Sociological Review 53 (1):* 157–60.

1988b "Scholarly Consensus and Journal Rejection Rates." *American Sociological Review 53 (1):* 139–51.

Hargens, Lowell, and Diane Felmlee
1984 "Structural Determinants of Stratification in Science." *American Sociological Review 49:* 685–97.

Harvey, David
1989 *The Condition of Postmodernity.* Oxford: Blackwell.

Harwood, Jonathan
1993 *Styles of Scientific Thought: The German Genetics Community, 1930–1933.* Chicago: University of Chicago Press.

Held, David
1980 *Introduction to Critical Theory: Horkheimer to Habermas.* Berkeley: University of California Press.

Hempel, Carl
1965 *Aspects of Scientific Explanation and Other Essays in the Philosophy of Science.* New York: Free Press.

Hempel, Carl, and Paul Oppenheim
1948 "Studies in the Logic of Explanation." *Philosophy of Science 15:* 135–75.

Hendry, John
1980 "Weimar Culture and Quantum Causality." *History of Science 18:* 155–80.

Hess, David
1991a "The New Ethnography and the Anthropology of Science and Technology."

In David Hess and Linda Layne (eds.), *Knowledge and Society. Vol. 9: The Anthropology of Science and Technology*. Greenwich, Conn.: JAI Press.

1991b *Spirits and Scientists*. University Park: Pennsylvania State University Press.

1993 *Science in the New Age*. Madison: University of Wisconsin Press.

1995 *Science and Technology in a Multicultural World*. New York: Columbia University Press.

1997a *Can Bacteria Cause Cancer? Alternative Medicine Confronts Big Science*. New York: New York University Press.

1997b "If You're Thinking of Living in STS . . . A Guide for the Perplexed." In Gary Downey, Joe Dumit, and Sharon Traweek (eds.), *Cyborgs and Citadels*. Santa Fe: School for American Research Press.

Hesse, Mary

1980a "Duhem, Quine, and a New Empiricism." In Harold Morick (ed.), *Challenges to Empiricism*. Cambridge: Hackett.

1980b *Revolutions and Reconstructions*. Bloomington: Indiana University Press.

1994 "How to Be Postmodern without Being a Feminist." *Monist 77 (4)*: 445–61.

Hessen, Boris

1971 *The Social and Economic Roots of Newton's Principia*. New York: Howard Fertig.

Hicks, Diana

1987 "Limitations of Co-Citation Analysis as a Tool for Science Policy." *Social Studies of Science 17*: 295–316.

1988 "Limitations and More Limitations of Co-Citation Analysis/Bibliometric Modeling: A Reply to Franklin." *Social Studies of Science 18*: 375–84.

Hicks, Diana, and Jonathan Potter

1991 "Sociology of Scientific Knowledge: A Reflexive Citation Analysis or Science Disciplines and Disciplining Science." *Social Studies of Science 21*: 459–501.

Hildenbrand, Gar, L. Christeene Hildenbrand, Karen Bradford, and Shirley Cavin

1995 "Five-Year Survival Rates of Melanoma Patients Treated by Diet Therapy after the Manner of Gerson: A Retrospective Review." *Alternative Therapies 1 (4)*: 29–37.

Hori, Hiroshi

1990 "Macro-Engineering: A View from Japan." *Technology in Society 12*: 45–63.

Horn, David

1994 *Social Bodies: Science, Reproduction, and Italian Modernity*. Princeton: Princeton University Press.

Hoyningen-Huene, Paul

1987 "Context of Discovery and Context of Justification." *Studies in the History and Philosophy of Science 18 (4)*: 501–15.

Hubbard, Ruth
1990 *The Politics of Women's Biology.* New Brunswick: Rutgers University Press.

Hughes, Thomas
1987 "The Evolution of Large Technological Systems." In Wiebe Bijker, Thomas Hughes, and Trevor Pinch (eds.), *The Social Construction of Technological Systems.* Cambridge: MIT Press.

Hull, David
1988 *Science as a Process.* Chicago: University of Chicago Press.

Ihde, Don
1993 *Philosophy of Technology: An Introduction.* New York: Paragon House.

Irwin, Allan, and Brian Wynne (eds.)
1996 *Misunderstanding Science? The Public Reconstruction of Science and Technology.* Cambridge: Cambridge University Press.

Jacob, Margaret
1988 *The Cultural Meaning of the Scientific Revolution.* New York: Knopf.

Jacob, Margaret (ed.)
1994 *The Politics of Western Science, 1640–1990.* Atlantic Highlands, N.J.: Humanities Press.

Jaffe, Richard
1996 "Evolving Evidentiary Standards for Expert Witnesses: Is There Trouble Ahead?" *Townsend Letter for Doctors and Patients,* January, pp. 119–20.

Jasanoff, Sheila
1990 *The Fifth Branch: Science Advisors as Policy Makers.* Cambridge: Harvard University Press.

Jasanoff, Sheila, Gerald Markle, James Peterson, and Trevor Pinch (eds.)
1994 *Handbook of Science and Technology Studies.* Beverly Hills: Sage.

Keller, Evelyn Fox
1985 *Reflections on Gender and Science.* New Haven: Yale University Press.
1992 *Secrets of Life, Secrets of Death.* New York: Routledge.

Kim, Kyung-Man
1994 *Explaining Scientific Consensus: The Case of Mendelian Genetics.* New York: Guilford.

Kleinman, Arthur
1988 *Rethinking Psychiatry.* New York: Free Press.

Knorr, Karin, Roland Mittermeir, Georg Aichholzer, and Georg Waller
1979 "Individual Publication Productivity as a Social Position Effect in Academic and Industrial Research Units." In Frank Andrews (ed.), *Scientific Productivity.* New York: Cambridge University Press.

Knorr-Cetina, Karin

1981 *The Manufacture of Knowledge*. New York: Pergamon.

1983 "The Ethnographic Study of Science: Towards a Constructivist Interpretation of Science." In Karin Knorr-Cetina and Michael Mulkay (eds.), *Science Observed*. Beverly Hills: Sage.

Knorr-Cetina, Karin, and Michael Mulkay

1983 "Introduction: Emerging Principles in Social Studies of Science." In Karin Knorr-Cetina and Michael Mulkay (eds.), *Science Observed*. Beverly Hills: Sage.

Kourany, Janet

1987 *Scientific Knowledge: Basic Issues in the Philosophy of Science*. Belmont, Cal.: Wadsworth.

Kretschmer, Hildrun

1993 "Measurement of Social Stratification: A Contribution to the Dispute of the Ortega Hypothesis." *Scientometrics 26*: 97–113.

Kretschmer, Hildrun, and Renate Müller

1990 "A Contribution to the Dispute on the Ortega Hypothesis." *Scientometrics 18*: 43–56.

Kuhn, Thomas

1970 *The Structure of Scientific Revolutions*. 2nd edition. Chicago: University of Chicago Press.

1977 *The Essential Tension*. Chicago: University of Chicago Press.

1989 "Possible Worlds in the History of Science." In S. Allen (ed.), *Possible Worlds in the Humanities, Arts, and Sciences*. Berlin: W. de Gruyter.

1993 "Afterwords." In Paul Howich (ed.), *World Changes: Thomas Kuhn and the Nature of Science*. Cambridge: MIT Press.

Lakatos, Imre

1978 *The Methodology of Scientific Research Programmes*. Cambridge: Cambridge University Press.

Lakatos, Imre, and A. Musgrave (eds.)

1970 *Criticism and the Growth of Knowledge*. Cambridge: Cambridge University Press.

LaPorte, Todd

1994 "Large Technical Systems, Institutional Surprises, and Challenges to Political Legitimacy." *Technology in Society 16 (3)*: 269–88.

Latour, Bruno

1983 "Give Me a Laboratory and I Will Raise the World." In Karin Knorr-Cetina and Michael Mulkay (eds.), *Science Observed*. Beverly Hills: Sage.

1987 *Science and Action*. Cambridge: Harvard University Press.

1988 *The Pasteurization of France*. Cambridge: Harvard University Press.

Latour, Bruno, Philippe Mauguin, and Genevive Teil
1992 "A Note on Sociotechnical Graphs." *Social Studies of Science 22:* 33–57.

Latour, Bruno, and Steve Woolgar
1986 *Laboratory Life: The Social Construction of Scientific Facts.* 2nd edition. Princeton:
Princeton University Press.

Laudan, Larry
1977 *Progress and Its Problems.* Berkeley: University of California Press.

1983 "The Demise of the Demarcation Problem." In Rachel Laudan (ed.), *The
Demarcation between Science and Pseudoscience.* Blacksburg: Virginia Polytechnic
Institute and State University, Center for the Study of Science and Society.

1984 *Science and Values.* Berkeley: University of California Press.

1990 *Science and Relativism.* Chicago: University of Chicago Press.

Law, John
1987 "Technology and Heterogeneous Engineering." In Wiebe Bijker, Thomas
Hughes, and Trevor Pinch (eds.), *The Social Construction of Technological Systems.*
Cambridge: MIT Press.

Layne, Linda
1992 "Of Fetuses and Angels: Fragmentation and Integration in Narratives of
Pregnancy Loss." In David Hess and Linda Layne (eds.), *Knowledge and Society.
Vol. 9: The Anthropology of Science and Technology.* Greenwich, Conn.: JAI Press.

Lenoir, Timothy
1979 "Quantitative Foundations for the Sociology of Science: On Linking Block-
Modeling with Cocitation Analysis." *Social Studies of Science 9:* 455–80.

Lévi-Strauss, Claude
1966 *The Savage Mind.* Chicago: University of Chicago Press.

Lindsey, Duncan
1982 "Further Evidence for Adjusting for Multiple Authorship." *Scientometrics 4:*
379–87.

Long, J. Scott
1978 "Productivity and Academic Position in the Scientific Career." *American
Sociological Review 43:* 889–908.

1990 "The Origins of Sex Differences in Science." *Social Forces 68:* 1297–1315.

1992 "Measures of Sex Differences in Scientific Productivity." *Social Forces 70:*
159–78.

Long, J. Scott, Paul Allison, and Robert McGinness
1979 "Entrance into the Academic Career." *American Sociological Review 44:* 816–30.

Long, J. Scott, and Robert McGinness
1981 "Organizational Context and Scientific Productivity." *American Sociological
Review 46:* 422–42.

1982a "Further Evidence for Adjusting for Multiple Authorship." *Scientometrics 4:* 397–98.

1982b "On Adjusting Productivity Measures for Multiple Authorship." *Scientometrics 4:* 379–87.

1985 "The Effects of the Mentor on the Academic Career." *Scientometrics 7:* 255–80.

Longino, Helen

1990 *Science as Social Knowledge.* Princeton: Princeton University Press.

1994 "In Search of Feminist Epistemologies." *Monist 77 (4):* 472–85.

Losee, John

1993 *A Historical Introduction to the Philosophy of Science.* New York: Oxford University Press.

Lotka, Alfred

1926 "The Frequency Distribution of Scientific Productivity." *Journal of the Washington Academy of Sciences 16:* 317–23.

Lukács, Georg

1968 "Reification and the Consciousness of the Proletariat." In *History and Class Consciousness.* Cambridge: MIT Press.

Lynch, Michael

1985 *Art and Artifact in the Laboratory.* London: Routledge.

1992 "Extending Wittgenstein: The Pivotal Move from Epistemology to the Sociology of Science." In Andrew Pickering (ed.), *Science as Practice and Culture.* Chicago: University of Chicago Press.

Lynch, William T.

1994 "Ideology and the Sociology of Scientific Knowledge." *Social Studies of Science 24:* 197–227.

Lyon, David

1989 "New Technology and the Limits of Luddism." *Science as Culture 7:* 122–34.

MacCormack, Carol, and Marilyn Strathern

1980 *Nature, Culture, and Gender.* Cambridge: Cambridge University Press.

McGinness, Robert, Paul Allison, and J. Scott Long

1982 "Postdoctoral Training in Bioscience: Allocation and Outcomes." *Social Forces 60:* 701–22.

MacKenzie, Donald

1981 "Interests, Positivism, and History." *Social Studies of Science 11:* 498–501.

1983 *Statistics in Britain.* Edinburgh: University of Edinburgh Press.

1984 "Reply to Yearley." *Studies in the History and Philosophy of Science 15 (3):* 251–59.

MacKenzie, Donald, and Barry Barnes
1979 "Scientific Judgment: The Biometry-Mendelism Controversy." In Barry Barnes and Steve Shapin (eds.), *Natural Order.* Beverly Hills: Sage.

MacKenzie, Donald, and Judith Wajcman (eds.)
1985 *The Social Shaping of Technology.* Philadelphia: Open University Press.

Malinowski, Bronislaw
1944 *A Scientific Theory of Culture and Other Essays.* Chapel Hill: University of North Carolina Press.

Mannheim, Karl
1952 *Essays on the Sociology of Knowledge.* Oxford: Oxford University Press.

Marcus, George, and Michael Fischer
1986 *Anthropology as Cultural Critique.* Chicago: University of Chicago Press.

Martin, Brian
1996 "Sticking a Needle into Science: The Case of Polio Vaccines and the Origin of AIDS." *Social Studies of Science 26:* 245–76.

1997a "Captivity and Commitment." *Social Studies of Science.* In press.

1997b *Suppression Stories.* Wollongong, Australia: Fund for Intellectual Dissent.

Martin, Brian, C. M. Ann Baker, Clyde Manwell, and Cedric Pugh (eds.)
1986 *Intellectual Suppression.* London: Angus and Robertson.

Martin, Brian, and Pam Scott
1992 "Automatic Vehicle Identification: A Test of Theories of Technology." *Science, Technology, and Values 17 (4):* 485–505.

Martin, Emily
1987 *The Woman in the Body.* Boston: Beacon Press.

1991 "The Egg and the Sperm: How Science Has Constructed a Romance Based on Stereotypical Male-Female Roles." *Signs 16 (3):* 485–501.

1994 *Flexible Bodies.* Boston: Beacon Press.

Marx, Karl
1963 *The Poverty of Philosophy.* New York: International Publishers.

Menard, Henry
1971 *Science: Growth and Change.* Cambridge: Cambridge University Press.

Merchant, Carolyn
1980 *The Death of Nature.* San Francisco: Harper and Row.

Merton, Robert
1957 "Priorities in Scientific Discovery: A Chapter in the Sociology of Science." *American Sociological Review 22 (6):* 635–59.

1970 *Science, Technology, and Society in Seventeenth-Century England.* New York: Howard Fertig.

1973 *The Sociology of Science*. Chicago: University of Chicago Press.

1976 *Sociological Ambivalence and Other Essays*. New York: Free Press.

1984 "The Fallacy of the Latest Word: The Case of 'Pietism' and Science." *American Journal of Sociology 89*: 1091–1121.

1988 "The Matthew Effect in Science, II: Cumulative Advantage and the Symbolism of Intellectual Property." *Isis 79*: 606–23.

Millman, Marcia, and Rosabeth Moss Kanter (eds.)

1975 *Another Voice: Feminist Perspectives on Social Life and Social Science*. New York: Anchor Books.

Mills, C. Wright

1959 *The Sociological Imagination*. New York: Oxford University Press.

Mitroff, I. I.

1974 "Norms and Counternorms in a Select Group of the Apollo Moon Scientists: A Case Study of the Ambivalence of Scientists." *American Sociological Review 39*: 579–95.

Mulkay, Michael

1976 "Norms and Ideology in Science." *Social Science Information 15*: 637–56.

Mulkay, Michael, Jonathan Potter, and Steven Yearley

1983 "Why an Analysis of Scientific Discourse Is Needed." In Karin Knorr-Cetina and Michael Mulkay (eds.), *Science Observed*. Beverly Hills: Sage.

Mullins, Nicholas

1972 "The Development of a Scientific Specialty: The Phage Group and the Origins of Molecular Biology." *Minerva 10 (Jan.)*: 52–82.

1973a "The Development of Specialities in Social Science: The Case of Ethnomethodology." *Social Studies of Science 3*: 245–73.

1973b *Theories and Theory Groups in Contemporary American Sociology*. New York: Harper and Row.

Mumford, Lewis

1964a "Authoritarian and Democratic Technics." *Technology and Culture 5*: 1–8.

1964b *Technics and Civilization*. New York: Harcourt, Brace, and World.

Myers, Greg

1990 *Writing Biology: Texts in the Social Construction of Scientific Knowledge*. Madison: University of Wisconsin Press.

Needham, Joseph

1974 "Science and Society in East and West." In Sal Restivo and Christopher Vanderpool (eds.), *Comparative Studies in Society and History*. Columbus: Merrill.

Nelkin, Dorothy (ed.)

1992 *Controversy: Politics of Technical Decisions*. Newbury Park, Cal.: Sage.

1994 "Scientific Controversies: The Dynamics of Public Disputes in the United States." In Sheila Jasanoff, Gerry Markle, James Peterson, and Trevor Pinch (eds.), *Handbook of Science and Technology.* Beverly Hills: Sage.

Noble, David
1984 *Forces of Production.* New York: Knopf.

1992 *A World without Women.* New York: Knopf.

Nordstrom, L. O.
1990 " 'Bradford's Law' and the Relationship between Ecology and Biogeography." *Scientometrics 18:* 193–203.

Oromaner, Mark
1977 "The Problem of Age and the Reception of Sociological Publications: A Test of the Zuckerman-Merton Hypothesis." *Social Studies of Science 7:* 381–88.

Ortner, Sherry
1974 "Is Female to Male as Nature Is to Culture?" In Michelle Rosaldo and Louise Lamphere (eds.), *Woman, Culture, and Society.* Stanford: Stanford University Press.

Pacey, Arnold
1990 *Technology in World Civilization.* Cambridge: MIT Press.

Parsons, Talcott
1966 *Societies: Evolutionary and Comparative Perspectives.* Englewood Cliffs, N.J.: Prentice-Hall.

Pearson, Willie
1978 "Race and Universalism in the Scientific Community." In Jerry Gaston (ed.), *Sociology of Science.* San Francisco: Jossey-Bass.

Penley, Constance, and Andrew Ross (eds.)
1991 *Technoculture: Cultural Politics. Vol. 3.* Minneapolis: University of Minnesota Press.

Peters, Douglas, and Stephen Ceci
1982 "Peer-Reviewed Practices of Psychological Journals: The Fate of Published Articles, Cited Again." *Behavioral and Brain Sciences 5:* 187–255.

Pfaffenberger, Brian
1992 "Technological Dramas." *Science, Technology, and Values 17 (3):* 282–312.

Pickering, Andrew
1995 "Beyond Constraint: The Temporality of Practice and the Historicity of Knowledge." In Jed Buchwald (ed.), *Scientific Practice: Theories and Stories of Doing Physics.* Chicago: University of Chicago Press.

Pickering, Andrew (ed.)
1992 *Science as Practice and Culture.* Chicago: University of Chicago Press.

Pinch, Trevor, and Wiebe Bijker
1987 "The Social Construction of Facts and Artifacts: Or How the Sociology of Science and the Sociology of Technology Might Benefit Each Other." In Wiebe Bijker, Thomas Hughes, and Trevor Pinch (eds.), *The Social Construction of Technological Systems.* Cambridge: MIT Press.

Planck, Max
1949 *Scientific Autobiography and Other Papers.* New York: Philosophical Library.

Popper, Karl
1959 *The Logic of Scientific Discovery.* New York: Basic Books.

1963 *Conjectures and Refutations.* London: Routledge.

Porter, Theodore (ed.)
1992 "Symposium: Social History of Objectivity." *Social Studies of Science 22:* 595–652.

Price, Derek de Solla
1963 *Little Science, Big Science.* New York: Columbia University Press.

1965 "The Scientific Foundations of Science Policy." *Nature 206 (April 17):* 233–38.

1986 *Little Science, Big Science . . . and Beyond.* New York: Columbia University Press.

Proctor, Robert
1995 *Cancer Wars.* Cambridge: Harvard University Press.

Pursell, Robert
1993 "The Rise and Fall of the Appropriate Technology Movement in the United States, 1965–85." *Technology and Culture 34 (3):* 629–37.

Quine, W. V.
1980 "Two Dogmas of Empiricism." In Harold Morick (ed.), *Challenges to Empiricism.* Cambridge: Hackett.

Rabinow, Paul
1992 "Artificiality and Enlightenment: From Sociobiology to Biosociality." In Jonathan Crary and Sanford Kwinter (eds.), *Zone 6: Incorporations.* New York: Zone Books.

Radcliffe-Brown, Alfred
1952 *Structure and Function in Primitive Society.* London: Cohen and West.

Rapp, Rayna
1988 "The Power of 'Positive' Diagnosis: Medical and Maternal Discourses on Amniocentesis." In Karen L. Michaelson (ed.), *Childbirth in America: Anthropological Perspectives.* South Hadley, Mass.: Bergin and Garvey.

1990 "Constructing Amniocentesis: Maternal and Medical Discourses." In Faye Ginsburg and Anna Lowenhaupt Tsing (eds.), *Uncertain Terms: Negotiating Gender in American Culture.* Boston: Beacon Press.

1991 "Moral Pioneers: Women, Men, and Fetuses on a Frontier of Reproductive Technology." In Micaela di Leonardo (ed.), *Gender at the Crossroads of Knowledge*. Berkeley: University of California Press.

Redner, Harry
1986 *The Ends of Philosophy*. London: Croom Helm.

Reichenbach, Hans
1938 *Experience and Prediction*. Chicago: University of Chicago Press.

Reskin, Barbara
1976 "Sex Differences in Status Attainment in Science: The Case of Postdoctoral Fellowships." *American Sociological Review 41*: 597–612.

1977 "Scientific Productivity and the Reward Structure of Science." *American Sociological Review 42*: 491–504.

1978a "Scientific Productivity, Sex, and Location in the Institution of Science." *American Journal of Sociology 83 (5)*: 1235–43.

1978b "Sex Differentiation and the Social Organization of Science." In Jerry Gaston (ed.), *Sociology of Science*. San Francisco: Jossey-Bass.

Restivo, Sal
1979 "Joseph Needham and the Comparative Sociology of Chinese and Modern Science." In Robert Jones (ed.), *Research in Sociology of Knowledge, Sciences, and Art. Vol. 3* (continued as *Knowledge and Society*). Greenwich, Conn.: JAI Press.

1983 "The Myth of the Kuhnian Revolution." In Randall Collins (ed.), *Sociology Theory*. San Francisco: Jossey-Bass.

1988 "Modern Science as Social Problem." *Social Problems 35(3)*: 206–25.

1994a *Science, Society and Values*. Bethlehem, Pa.: Lehigh University Press

1994b "The Theory Landscape in Science Studies." In Sheila Jasanoff, Gerry Markle, James Peterson, and Trevor Pinch (eds.), *Handbook of Science and Technology*. Beverly Hills: Sage.

Restivo, Sal, and Julia Loughlin
1987 "Critical Sociology of Science and Scientific Validity." *Knowledge: Creation, Diffusion, Utilization 8 (3)*: 486–503.

Rip, Arie, and J. P. Courtial
1984 "Co-Word Maps of Biotechnology: An Example of Cognitive Scientometrics." *Scientometrics 6*: 381–400.

Rose, Hilary
1987 "Hand, Brain, and Heart: A Feminist Epistemology for the Natural Sciences." In Sandra Harding and J. F. O'Barr (eds.), *Sex and Scientific Inquiry*. Chicago: University of Chicago Press.

1994 *Love, Power, and Knowledge: Towards a Feminist Transformation of the Sciences*. Cambridge: Polity.

Rossiter, Margaret W.

1982 *Women Scientists in America.* Baltimore: Johns Hopkins University Press.

1987 "Sexual Segregation in the Sciences: Some Data and a Model." In Sandra Harding and J. F. O'Barr (eds.), *Sex and Scientific Inquiry.* Chicago: University of Chicago Press.

1993 "The ~~Matthew~~ Matilda Effect in Science." *Social Studies of Science 23:* 325–41.

Rouse, Joseph

1991 "What Are Cultural Studies of Scientific Knowledge?" *Configurations 1 (1):* 1–22.

1995 *Engaging Science: How to Understand Its Practices Philosophically.* Ithaca: Cornell University Press.

1996 "New Philosophies of Science in North America—Twenty Years Later: A Selective Survey." *Zeitschrift für allgemeine Wissenschaftstheorie.*

Sahlins, Marshall

1976 *Culture and Practical Reason.* Chicago: University of Chicago Press.

Salmon, Wesley

1989 *Four Decades of Scientific Explanation.* Minneapolis: University of Minnesota Press.

Saussure, Ferdinand de

1966 *Course in General Linguistics.* New York: McGraw-Hill.

Schäfer, Wolf

1983 *Finalization in Science: The Social Orientation of Scientific Progress.* Dordrecht: Reidel.

Schiebinger, Londa

1989 *The Mind Has No Sex?* Cambridge: Harvard University Press.

Schmaus, Warren, Ullica Segestrale, and Douglas Jesseph

1992 "A Manifesto." *Social Epistemology 6 (3):* 243–65.

Schumacher, E. F.

1973 *Small Is Beautiful: Economics as if People Mattered.* New York: Harper and Row.

Schutz, Alfred

1956 *Phenomenology of the Social World.* London: Heinemann.

Sclove, Richard

1994 "Written Testimony Submitted to the Subcommittee on Science of the House Committee on Science, Space, and Technology of the United States Congress." Amherst, Mass.: Loka Institute and Austin, Tex.: 21st Century Project.

1995a *Democracy and Technology.* New York: Guilford.

1995b "Research for Communities: Let's Do It." *Loka Alert 2:* 5, http://www.am-herst.edu/~loka. Amherst, Mass.: Loka Institute.

1995c "Putting Science to Work in Communities." *Chronicle of Higher Education* 41 (29), March 31, pp. B1–B3.

1996 "Democratizing Science Advisory Panels?" *Loka Alert 3:* 3, http://www.am- herst.edu/~loka. Amherst, Mass.: Loka Institute.

Scott, Pam, Evelleen Richards, and Brian Martin
1990 "Captives of Controversy: The Myth of the Neutral Social Researcher in Contemporary Scientific Controversies." *Science, Technology, and Values* 15 (4): 474–94.

Shadish, William, and Steve Fuller (eds.)
1994 *The Social Psychology of Science.* New York: Guilford.

Shadish, William, and Robert Neimeyer
1994 "Contributions of Psychology to an Integrative Science Studies: The Shape of Things to Come." In William Shadish and Steve Fuller (eds.), *The Social Psychology of Science.* New York: Guilford.

Shapin, Steve
1988 "Understanding the Merton Thesis." *Isis 79:* 594–605.

Shapin, Steve, and Simon Schaffer
1985 *Leviathan and the Air Pump.* Princeton: Princeton University Press.

Sharp, Lauriston
1952 "Steel Axes for Stone Age Australians." *Organization* 11 (2): 17–22.

Shiva, Vandana
1989 *Staying Alive: Women, Ecology, and Development in India.* London: Zed Books.

Simonton, Dean
1984 "Is the Marginality Effect All That Marginal?" *Social Studies of Science* 14: 621–22.

Small, Henry, and Belver Griffith
1974 "The Structure of Scientific Literatures I: Identifying and Grouping Special- ties." *Science Studies 4:* 17–40.

Snow, C. P.
1959 *The Cultures and the Scientific Revolution.* New York: Cambridge University Press.

Solomon, Shana, and Edward Hackett
1996 "Setting Boundaries between Science and Law: Lessons from Daubert v. Merrell Dow Pharmaceuticals, Inc." *Science, Technology, and Values* 21 (2): 131–56.

Stankiewicz, Rikard
1979 "The Size and Age of Swedish Academic Research Groups and Their Scien- tific Performance." In Frank Andrews (ed.), *Scientific Productivity.* New York: Cambridge University Press.

Star, Susan Leigh
1985 "Work and Uncertainty." *Social Studies of Science* 15: 391–427.

Star, Susan Leigh (ed.)

1995 *Ecologies of Knowledge: Work and Politics in Science and Technology.* Albany: State University of New York Press.

Star, Susan Leigh, and James Griesemer

1989 "Institutional Ecology, 'Translations,' and Boundary Objects." *Social Studies of Science 19:* 387–420.

Stephan, Paula, and Sharon Levin

1992 *Striking the Mother Lode in Science: The Importance of Age, Place, and Time.* New York: Oxford University Press.

Strathern, Marilyn

1992 *Reproducing the Future: Anthropology, Kinship, and the New Reproductive Technologies.* New York: Routledge.

Taylor, Charles

1996 *Defining Science: A Rhetoric of Demarcation.* Madison: University of Wisconsin Press.

Toumey, Christopher

1996 *Conjuring Science: Scientific Symbols and Cultural Meanings in American Life.* New Brunswick: Rutgers University Press.

Travis, C. D. L., and Harry Collins

1991 "New Light on Old Boys: Cognitive and Institutional Particularism in the Peer Review System." *Science, Technology, and Values 16 (3):* 322–41.

Traweek, Sharon

1988 *Beamtimes and Lifetimes.* Cambridge: Harvard University Press.

1992 "Border Crossings: Narrative Strategies in Science Studies and among Physicists in Tsukuba Science City, Japan." In Andrew Pickering (ed.), *Science as Practice and Culture.* Chicago: University of Chicago Press.

1993 "An Introduction to Cultural and Social Studies of Sciences and Technologies." *Culture, Medicine, and Psychiatry 17:* 3–25.

Treichler, Paula

1991 "How to Have Theory in an Epidemic: The Evolution of AIDS Treatment Activism." In Constance Penley and Andrew Ross (eds.), *Technoculture: Cultural Politics. Vol. 3.* Minneapolis: University of Minnesota Press.

Tuana, Nancy (ed.)

1989 *Feminism and Science.* Bloomington: Indiana University Press.

Turner, Graeme

1992 *British Cultural Studies: An Introduction.* New York: Routledge.

Van Fraasen, Bas

1980 *The Scientific Image.* New York: Oxford University Press.

Wallis, Roy

1985 "Science and Pseudo-Science." *Social Science Information 24 (3):* 585–601.

Watson-Verran, Helen
1988 "Language and Mathematics Education for Aboriginal Australian Children."
Language and Education 2: 255–73.

Weber, Max
1958 *The Protestant Ethic and the Spirit of Capitalism.* New York: Scribner's.

Webster, Andrew
1991 *Science, Technology, and Society.* New Brunswick: Rutgers University Press.

Westrum, Ron, Keith Simonton, and Edward Constant
1979 "The Notion of Independent Scientific Discovery." *Social Studies of Science 9:*
509–10.

Whitley, Richard
1972 "Black Boxism and the Sociology of Science: A Discussion of the Major
Developments in the Field." *Sociological Review Monograph: The Sociology of Science
18:* 61–92. Keele: University of Keele.

Winner, Langdon
1977 *Autonomous Technology.* Cambridge: MIT Press.

1986 *The Whale and the Reactor.* Chicago: University of Chicago Press.

1993 "Upon Opening the Black Box and Finding It Empty: Social Constructivism
and the Philosophy of Technology." *Science, Technology, and Values 18 (3):* 362–78.

1996 "The Gloves Come Off: Shattered Alliances in Science and Technology
Studies." *Social Text 46–47:* 81–93.

Woolgar, Steve
1981a "Critique and Criticism: Two Readings of Ethnomethodology." *Social Studies
of Science 11:* 504–14.

1981b "Interests and Explanation in the Social Study of Science." *Social Studies of
Science 11:* 365–94.

1988 *Science: The Very Idea.* London: Tavistock.

1992 "Some Remarks about Positionism: A Reply to Collins and Yearley." In
Andrew Pickering (ed.), *Science as Practice and Culture.* Chicago: University of
Chicago Press.

1996 "Evaluation Culture: Technology and Accountability in the Age of Users and
Beneficiaries." Guest lecture, Science and Technology Studies Department,
Rensselaer Polytechnic Institute, April 10.

Woolgar, Steve (ed.)
1988 *Knowledge and Reflexivity.* Beverly Hills: Sage.

Wynne, Brian
1994 "Public Understanding of Science." In Sheila Jasanoff, Gerald Markle, James
Peterson, and Trevor Pinch (eds.), *Handbook of Science and Technology Studies.*
Beverly Hills: Sage.

1996 "Misunderstood Misunderstandings: Social Identities and Public Uptake of Science." In Alan Irwin and Brian Wynne (eds.), *Misunderstanding Science? The Public Reconstruction of Science and Technology*. Cambridge: Cambridge University Press.

Yates, Frances

1972 *The Rosicrucian Enlightenment*. London: Routledge.

Yearley, Steven

1982 "The Relationship between Epistemological and Sociological Cognitive Interests: Some Ambiguities Underlying the Use of Interest Theory in the Study of Scientific Knowledge." *Studies in the History and Philosophy of Science 13 (4):* 353–88.

1995 "On Deciding Which Scientific Testimony to Admit in Court: A View from the Sociology of Science in the 'Daubert' Case." Paper presented at Rensselaer Polytechnic Institute, Science and Technology Studies Department, April 12.

1996 "Nature's Advocates: Putting Science to Work in Environmental Organizations." In Allan Irwin and Brian Wynne (eds.), *Misunderstanding Science? The Public Reconstruction of Science and Technology*. Cambridge: Cambridge University Press.

Yeo, Richard

1993 *Defining Science*. Cambridge: Cambridge University Press.

Zuckerman, Harriet

1977 "Deviant Behavior and Social Control in Science." In E. Sagarin (ed.), *Deviance and Social Change*. Beverly Hills: Sage.

1989 "The Other Merton Thesis." *Science in Context 3 (1):* 239–67.

Zuckerman, Harriet, and Jonathan Cole

1975 "Women in American Science." *Minerva 13:* 82–102.

Zuckerman, Harriet, and Joshua Lederberg

1986 "Postmature Scientific Discovery?" *Nature 324 (Dec. 18–25):* 629–31.

Index

Actor-network theory, 79, 92, 95, 105–11
Age effects, 59, 62–63, 67, 71. *See also* Cumulative advantage theory
Allison, Paul, 53, 57, 61, 157
Anthropology, 32, 134–40, 142–44
Autonomy, 57–58, 79, 85, 94, 117, 133, 149, 154; and technology, 107, 124

Barnes, Barry, 84, 86, 90–93
Bath school, 94–100
Ben-David, Joseph, 56, 71, 74
Bijker, Wiebe, 70–71, 87, 95, 158
Bloor, David, 84, 86, 87
Boundary-work, 58
Bourdieu, Pierre, 59, 118–19, 136, 166 n. 9
Bradford's law, 72
Braverman, Harry, 79, 126

Callon, Michel, 79, 92, 107–9, 121, 165 n. 9
Carnap, Rudolf, 9, 11, 13–14, 19–20, 23, 25, 27–28, 31
Causality, 33–34, 86–87
Citation studies, 75–80
Clarke, Adele, 104–6
Cole, Stephen, 41–42, 53, 59, 61, 65, 157
Collins, Harry, 39, 84, 93–99, 106
Collins, Randall, 53, 74, 85–86
Conflict theory, 85
Constructivism: analysis of content, 52–53, 64, 79, 81, 95, 108; construction of facts, 77, 101–3; postconstructivism, 152–56; and reconstruction, 139, 141, 144; typology for philosophy, 34–39, 82, 127; typology for social studies, 82–84, 129. *See also* Relativism; Sociology
Controversies, 24–26, 75, 87–100, 141–42, 152–53
Conventionalism, 18–19, 23
Crane, Diana, 60, 64, 73

Critical science studies, 113–26, 158
Cultural studies: additional sources, 158; defined, 6, 112–13; key concepts, 114–23; structuralism and poststructuralism, 137–41
Culture, 24, 29, 104, 106, 136; cultural constructivism, 83, 93; and history, 127, 131; two cultures, 16
Cumulative advantage theory, 59–64

Deconstruction, 89, 139–40
Demarcation problem, 21–22
Discourse analysis, 103
Doomsday thesis, 30
Duhem, Pierre, 18–19, 27, 39
Dumont, Louis, 116, 140
Durkheim, Émile, 37, 54

Edinburgh school, 90–92
Ellul, Jacques, 123–24
Empirical program of relativism (EPOR), 39, 94–100, 135
Ethnography, 134–35
Ethnomethodology, 92, 100, 103
Evolutionary theory, 7–8, 32, 36–37, 54, 131, 134, 139
Experimenter's regress, 20, 96
Explanation, 15–16, 33

Falsificationism, 19–22, 24, 27. *See also* Popper, Karl
Feminism: and anthropology, 138; and cultural studies, 88–89, 119–22, 140, 159; and history of science, 130; and philosophy, 45–51; and sociology of science, 60–69; and technology studies, 126; two cultures, 16. *See also* Gender
Feyerabend, Paul, 18, 23, 25, 132
Fleck, Ludwik, 23, 84

About the Author

David J. Hess is an anthropologist and tenured professor in the Science and Technology Studies Department at Rensselaer Polytechnic Institute. He is the author of various books in anthropology and science studies, including *Spirits and Scientists: Ideology, Spiritism, and Brazilian Culture; Samba in the Night: Spiritism in Brazil; Science in the New Age: The Paranormal, Its Defenders and Debunkers, and American Culture; Science and Technology in a Multicultural World: The Cultural Politics of Facts and Artifacts;* and the volume coedited with Linda Layne, *The Anthropology of Science and Technology (Knowledge and Society Vol. 9).* He is the recipient of various grants and awards, including two Fulbrights and a National Science Foundation grant in the public understanding of science, and he is the chair of the Committee of the Anthropology of Science, Technology, and Computing of the American Anthropological Association. His current research is on science, the public, and alternative cancer therapies. The first book in that series, which is a companion volume to *Science Studies,* is *Can Bacteria Cause Cancer? Alternative Medicine Confronts Big Science* (New York University Press, 1997).